This book is presented to you

Compliments of the

Minnesota World Trade
Center Corporation
and the
Minnesota Trade Office.

MINNESOTA

LAND OF LAKES AND INNOVATION

© Bob Firth/Firth Photobank

MINNESOTA

LAND OF LAKES AND INNOVATION

BY NOOD WHARTON REYNOLDS

CHERBO PUBLISHING GROUP, INC.
ENCINO, CALIFORNIA

© Bob Firth/Firth Photobank

CHERBO
PUBLISHING
GROUP, INC.

PRESIDENT **Jack C. Cherbo**

EXECUTIVE VICE PRESIDENT **Elaine Hoffman**

EDITORIAL DIRECTOR **Christina M. Beausang**

SENIOR EDITOR **Gina K. Thornburg**

PROFILES EDITOR **J. Kelley Younger**

ESSAY EDITOR **Tina G. Rubin**

SENIOR DESIGNER **Mika Toyoura**

CONTRIBUTING DESIGNER **Mary Cameron**

PHOTO EDITOR **Catherine A. Vandenberg**

SALES ADMINISTRATOR **Joan K. Baker**

PRODUCTION SERVICES MANAGER **Ellen T. Kettenbeil**

ADMINISTRATIVE COORDINATOR **Rejyna Douglass-Whitman**

REGIONAL DEVELOPMENT MANAGER **Merle Gratton**

PUBLISHER'S REPRESENTATIVES **Tim Burke, Dick Fry, Carl L. Heinrich, Patricia A. Stai**

Cherbo Publishing Group, Inc., Encino, Calif. 91316

© 1998 by Cherbo Publishing Group, Inc.

All rights reserved. Published 1998

Printed in the United States of America

Visit CPG's Web site at www.cherbo-publishing.com

Library of Congress Cataloging-in-Publication Data

Reynolds, Nood Wharton

A pictorial guide highlighting 20th-century Minnesota lifestyle and economic history. 1. Minnesota. 2. Economic history—Minnesota. 3. Lifestyle—Minnesota.

98-071769

ISBN 1-882933-21-4

DEDICATION

To my father, Dr. William P. Wharton,

the reason I came to Minnesota,

and my husband, Randy, and sons,

Drew and Reed, the reasons why this

transplanted Southerner remained.

© Greg Ryan-Sally Beyer

CONTENTS

© Greg Ryan-Sally Beyer

CONTRIBUTORS

THE FOLLOWING INDIVIDUALS HAVE MADE VALUABLE CONTRIBUTIONS TO THIS PUBLICATION BY WRITING ESSAYS ON THEIR PARTICULAR SECTORS OF BUSINESS IN MINNESOTA. CHERBO PUBLISHING GROUP GRATEFULLY ACKNOWLEDGES THEIR PARTICIPATION IN *MINNESOTA: LAND OF LAKES AND INNOVATION.*

ACKNOWLEDGMENT

I WOULD LIKE TO THANK MY EDITOR,

GINA K. THORNBURG, FOR HER ADVICE AND

ENCOURAGEMENT THROUGHOUT THIS PROJECT.

© Bob Firth/Firth Photobank

INTRODUCTION

Minnesota is striding into the twenty-first century with the energy of its past and current successes spurring it purposefully toward future achievements. A traditional dependence on natural resources blends with a strong focus on high technology, manufacturing, trade, and health care to give the state its financial strength. An educated, industrious workforce contributes to one of the most diverse and stable economies in the country.

The North Star State has made the transition from its early days as an agricultural center to a present-day world leader in technology and manufacturing, not in spite of its roots, but because of them. Meanwhile, the state known for that intangible asset called "Minnesota Nice" has preserved a small-town quality of life that has earned it countless distinctions in various national livability polls. Case in point is the southeastern city of Waseca, home of Farmamerica, the state's agricultural interpretive center, which re-creates the story of Minnesota farming from pioneer days to the present. Waseca's two leading employers are Brown Printing, one of the country's leading printers, and electronics giant E.F. Johnson. The presence of these homegrown companies that now command an international market may surprise a visitor to this town of just over eight thousand residents, but natives know better. They know it to be just one example of the balance of resourcefulness and ingenuity that will lead their state into the next millennium.

A calm lake provides a lovely setting for a home near McGregor, a hamlet in the north-central region of the state.
© Bob Firth/Firth Photobank

THE STAR OF THE NORTH

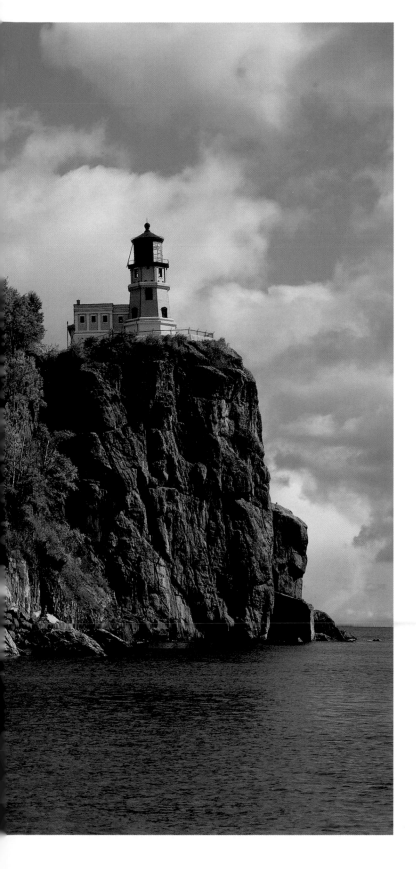

PART ONE

LIFE IN MINNESOTA. IT'S EASY—THE PLACE WHERE MORE PEOPLE THAN ANY OTHER IN THE NATION CAN BE FOUND DANGLING A WORM FROM THE END OF A HOOK OR GETTING IN A ROUND OF GOLF ON A PERFECT SUMMER DAY. IT'S ENRICHING. THE METROPOLITAN AREA OF MINNEAPOLIS AND ST. PAUL IS SECOND ONLY TO NEW YORK IN ARTS ACTIVITIES PER CAPITA. IT'S FAMILIAL, BOASTING GENERATIONS OF FAMILIES WORKING TOGETHER TO GROW CROPS AND RAISE LIVESTOCK ON THE SAME FERTILE SOIL AS THEIR ANCESTORS BEFORE THEM. IT SPARKLES WITH THE WATERS OF THE MORE THAN TWENTY THOUSAND LAKES THAT GAVE THE STATE ITS NAME, AND IT GLISTENS IN WINTER WITH ICE CASTLES AND SNOWMEN, GLEAMING SKATES, WAXED SKIS, AND SLEEK SNOWMOBILES. IT BUSTLES WITH COMMERCIAL ACTIVITY GENERATED BY ENOUGH HOMEGROWN FORTUNE 500 COMPANIES TO RANK IT SEVENTH IN THE COUNTRY IN THAT CATEGORY AND AN ENTREPRENEURIAL SPIRIT THAT OUTPACES THE NATION IN THE START-UP OF SMALL BUSINESSES. IT RANKS HIGH ON HEALTH, EDUCATION, AND THE ENVIRONMENT, AND LOW ON CRIME, UNEMPLOYMENT, AND DAILY COMMUTE TIME. THE OFFICIAL MOTTO APTLY DEEMS THE STATE THE STAR OF THE NORTH, AND THOSE WHO CALL MINNESOTA HOME KNOW IT TO BE A STELLAR PLACE IN WHICH TO LIVE, WORK, AND PLAY.

Overlooking Lake Superior on Minnesota's North Shore, Split Rock Lighthouse was built after storms in 1905 killed more than 200 sailors. Metallic deposits in the rocky coastline had deflected compass needles, making navigation perilous. Now a historic site, the decommissioned lighthouse is a favorite stop for visitors, who may tour the light tower, the fog-signal building, and a history center. © Terry Donnelly

ONE STATE, MANY IMAGES

CHAPTER ONE

THE DAY'S DRIVE FROM MINNESOTA'S NORTHERNMOST BORDER TO ITS SOUTHERNMOST IS LIKE A TIME-TRAVEL JOURNEY ACROSS SEVERAL STATES AND SEASONS THROUGH DIVERSE LANDSCAPES, COMMUNITIES, AND CLIMATES. THIS WEALTH OF GEOGRAPHIC AND CULTURAL VARIETY GIVES NATIVES AND VISITORS ALIKE PLENTY OF REASON TO LIVE OR SPEND A VACATION IN MINNESOTA, WHOSE TOURISM INDUSTRY PLACES IT 8 PERCENT ABOVE THE NATIONAL AVERAGE IN TOURISM BUSINESS RECEIPTS PER CAPITA.

A tour through rugged and pristine Northern Minnesota may reveal timber wolves, bear, moose, loons, and bald eagles, all indigenous to the area. Sparsely populated, save for the bustling port city of Duluth along Lake Superior, this region is clothed in coniferous forests, scenic waterways, and rich iron-ore deposits, which add an amber hue to local waters. The rest of the state fondly calls this area "Up North," and people flock here year-round to enjoy its open space, beauty, and soul-refreshing solitude.

Passing through central Minnesota in the winter, a traveler will see ice-fishing houses clustered on frozen lakes, transient towns that are whisked away in spring before the waters resume their flow. Along the Red River, which forms the state's western border, farmers measure the seasons of planting and harvest on some of the best farmland in the nation. The grains, soybeans, and sugar beets grown in this area are exported across the country and around the world.

In the Twin Cities of Minneapolis and St. Paul, beautiful pathways and green expanses around area lakes beckon residents to walk, run, bike, in-line skate, and cross-country ski, according to the season. A pleasure drive along scenic Highway 61 entices restless souls to watch the barges and pleasure boats churn up and down the Mississippi River.

A FLOWING HISTORY

The Dakota Indians were the first to appreciate the beauty of the place, naming their home *minisota*, meaning "sky-tinted waters." These waters have indeed carved Minnesota's

Opposite: Palisade Head State Park overlooks Lake Superior, which forms the northeastern border of Minnesota. Rocky lakeside cliffs are typical of the rugged and heavily forested Arrowhead region, whose gateway is the important and busy port city of Duluth. © Terry Donnelly. Above: A young girl proudly displays her catch of northern pike. When the lakes are firmly frozen, thousands of Minnesotans drag their ice-fishing houses onto the glimmering surfaces to engage in a traditional winter pastime. Minnesota's lakes yield walleye, northern pike, cisco, whitefish, blue catfish, crappie, bass, rainbow trout, and many other types of fish. © Bob Firth/Firth Photobank

Minnesota's waters first brought curious French-Canadian canoemen downriver to trap and trade their pelts with the Dakota, Sioux, and Chippewa nations. Soon thereafter, undaunted missionaries traveled upriver from the Illinois Territory. Later, steamboats, paddle wheelers, and barges replaced birch-bark canoes but continued to bring settlers to Minnesota's shores. Altogether, Minnesota's waters form some ninety thousand miles of shoreline, more than California, Florida, and Hawaii combined, and they flow outward in three directions: north to Canada, east to the Atlantic Ocean, and south to the Gulf of Mexico.

FULL OF RESOURCE

Once the early settlers arrived, they found that the land would support them in many ways. Fur-bearing animals inhabiting northern forests attracted a bustling fur trade in the mid-1600s. The discovery of fertile soils in the western and southern parts of the state brought a deluge of farmers from the colonies in the east and Europe. Soon thereafter, the checkerboard fields of grain gave rise to numerous flour mills and the establishment of Minneapolis as the country's largest producer of flour. In the northeast, the discovery of rich deposits of iron ore prompted another migration of workers from various states and countries in the late 1800s. An expansive lumber and logging industry

history, and the state's identity flows from them. When the glaciers that once covered this area melted, they left behind wondrous blue vistas, among them Lake Superior, the largest freshwater lake in the world; Lake Itasca, the crystal-clear source of the Mississippi River, which trickles out of the lake as a mere stream; the million-acre Boundary Waters Canoe Area, the country's only canoe-oriented wilderness preserve; and Voyageurs National Park, 218,000 primitive acres of water and a smattering of landscape disturbed by less than eight total miles of paved roads.

Opposite: Biking, skating, and walking are some favorite lakeside activities. © Bob Firth/Firth Photobank. Right: The Garrison–Mille Lacs Indian Museum portrays Ojibwa life. © John Elk III

Near New Prague, a tractor busily cuts corn, one of the principal agricultural products in the state. Minnesota also produces high yields of wheat, rye, alfalfa, and sugar beets. © Superstock

also established itself as paramount to Minnesota's development as a state. Belonging at various times to the Spanish, French, and British, Minnesota became a territory in 1849 and entered the Union as the thirty-second state in 1858.

THE STUFF OF LEGENDS

The state's uniqueness may be attributable to the telltale signs of receding glaciers and the spirit of early settlers, but a Minnesotan kindergartner today will insist it was Paul Bunyan and his trusted companion, Babe the Blue Ox, who carved the state's geographic features and breathed life into its earliest industries. According to legend, the giant

These raccoons are among abundant Minnesota wildlife that includes white-tailed deer, black bears, moose, beavers, and timber wolves. © Bob Firth/Firth Photobank

lumberjack created the lakes with his footsteps, save for Lake Superior, which he dug out by hand to provide drinking water for Babe. He cleared trees so his cooks could grow enough food to quell his insatiable appetite, and he had Big Ole, the blacksmith, dig a mine to secure enough ore for making Babe's shoes. Bunyan and Babe's deeds are still celebrated in northern Minnesota towns, where many an image of the lumberjack in his red flannel

shirt with his mighty ax and his faithful blue steed tower over cityscapes.

Other notable American icons, both imaginary and real, also call Minnesota home. The Pillsbury Dough Boy and Betty Crocker hail from the Twin Cities, and the Jolly Green Giant comes from the southwest part of the state. Mary Richards from *The Mary Tyler Moore Show* has moved on, but her Minneapolis home and the Crystal Court restaurant in which she dined are still here. Judy Garland's trip to Oz began here in Grand Rapids, and a teenaged, guitar-toting Robert Zimmerman left his home in Hibbing on his way to international fame as Bob Dylan. And in Little Falls, a youngster named Charles Lindbergh dreamed of nothing but flight after watching early aviators fly over his childhood home.

Right: Commemorating Longfellow's famous poem about the Indians of the Great Lakes is Norwegian-born sculptor Jacob Fjeld's Hiawatha and Minnehaha *above Minnehaha Falls. © John Elk III. Below: The lumber industry has been inextricably tied to Minnesota's economy since before statehood was achieved. © Jeffrey P. Grosscup*

Opposite: Fireworks illuminate the state capitol in St. Paul on Independence Day. © Greg Ryan-Sally Beyer. Above: Late winter snow laces the edge of a farm pond while the signs of spring's thaw dawn all around. © Bob Firth/Firth Photobank. Below: Under development in 1998, Glendalough State Park in northwestern Minnesota will offer an excellent aquatics studies site and self-guiding nature trail among its pristine lakes and wooded acres. © Bob Firth/Firth Photobank

THE ROOTS OF SUCCESS

CHAPTER TWO

TODAY, DESCRIBING A TYPICAL MINNESOTAN IS A DAUNTING TASK. YA SURE, MORE PEOPLE HERE CLAIM NORWEGIAN ANCESTRY THAN IN ANY OTHER STATE, AND A HIGH PERCENTAGE ARE ALSO OF FINNISH AND SWEDISH EXTRACTION, BUT THE LARGEST HMONG POPULATION IN THE COUNTRY ALSO RESIDES HERE. PERHAPS SUCH DIVERSITY IS A TESTIMONY TO THE STATE'S REPUTATION AS "MINNESOTA NICE." AFTER ALL, NEARLY HALF OF THE RESIDENTS CLAIM MULTIPLE ANCESTRY, MORE THAN ANYWHERE ELSE IN THE NATION.

Diverse ethnic heritages are celebrated everywhere and in every season among the state's 4.5 million residents. The hamlet of Berne, nestled in the southeast near an old stagecoach stop, commemorates its heritage by recreating a Swiss village every August, where guest dignitaries and artisans from Switzerland mingle with costumed locals. St. Paul's Irish community throws a frolicking parade on St. Patrick's Day. German tradition lives on in the town of New Ulm in the southwest, whose summertime Heritagefest and fall Oktoberfest are two of the most popular festivals in the Midwest.

Caring is the common thread that stitches Minnesota's cultural fabric together. Whatever their heritage, Minnesotans care about their state and their fellow Minnesotans. Recycling efforts in solid waste–reduction and yard-waste composting top the national charts, and Minnesota volunteer groups clean up the most miles of shoreline. Minnesota's foundations give more to the arts and cultural and humanitarian organizations than do those of any state except New York, and the citizens' per capita donations to philanthropic causes are the benchmark for the rest of the country.

LEADERS IN HEALTH CARE, AFFORDABLE LIFESTYLE, AND EDUCATION

Twentieth-century Minnesotans are healthy, financially well off, well educated, and hard working. An unwavering focus on high-quality health care earned the state the distinction of being among the nation's healthiest and a

Opposite: Parade participants in New Ulm keep the town's German roots thriving in the annual German Heritagefest. New Ulm was the site of fierce fighting during the Dakota War of 1862, after which Germans settled the region in large numbers. Above: Cowhorn sounds punctuate the Swedish Festival in the town of Lindstrom, named after a Swedish pioneer. Both photos © Greg Ryan-Sally Beyer

continual spot at the top of the annual Northwestern National Life Insurance Company's rankings. Home to the world-renowned Mayo Clinic, the state led the way in the health-care reform movement. The 1992 enactment of the state health-care reform law, MinnesotaCare, provided subsidized health coverage for the uninsured and emphasized preventive care for children. Today, the percentage of children without medical benefits is the nation's lowest. A low crime rate and comparatively clean

Opposite: Drummers at the University of Minnesota have every reason to be proud of their state, which, among Midwestern states, has the second-highest percentage of residents over twenty-five with a bachelor's degree or higher and the third-highest percentage over twenty-five with a high school degree. © Bob Firth/Firth Photobank. Below: "Prairie Einwanderin" wooden-masked folks join in the celebration at New Ulm's annual German Heritagefest. © Greg Ryan-Sally Beyer

environment add to the overall healthy lifestyle enjoyed by Minnesotans.

Residents' per capita income exceeds the national average, and the cost of living is relatively low. Affordable housing has made huge gains in the past five years. U.S. Census statistics rated Minnesota twenty-ninth for home ownership in 1992, fifteenth in 1994, and first in 1995 and thereafter.

An excellent educational system is something in which Minnesotans take a great deal of pride. High-quality offerings abound for preschoolers through adults. Always among the top contenders, Minnesota's high school graduation rate most recently placed second in the nation. Nearly 87 percent of all students who begin high school in the state go on to graduate, compared to a national average that is almost 20 percent lower. Ten Minnesota school districts were named among the top forty-four in the nation in *Expansion Management* magazine's 1995 fifth

annual school district review. Minnesota eighth-graders have the third-highest math skills in the nation, and college entrance exam scores are traditionally well above the national average.

ECONOMICALLY STRONG AND DIVERSE

Thanks to a balanced mix of industries, Minnesota's economy is at the national forefront in terms of strength and diversity. Bolstered by the highest workforce participation rate in the country, the state's solid performance is also due to a sturdy base of corporate headquarters and an energetic emphasis on research and development. High-technology industries, including computers and related components manufacturing; medical instruments, supplies, and products; and printing and publishing, are especially robust. Natural resources and agricultural commodities support vibrant industries in forest products, taconite production, and food processing. Manufacturing occupies the highest portion of the gross state product, and Minnesota is a national leader in service-oriented industries. Exports and tourism further contribute to the state's economic strength.

This page: These friendly faces belong to members of the Grace Community Church gospel choir performing in a summer concert and reflect the meaning of "Minnesota Nice." © Greg Ryan-Sally Beyer. Opposite: Fair-goers watch as a mouse tries to keep its balance at a game at the Bend of the River Festival in Mankato, a south-central town situated on the Minnesota River. © Joe Miller Photography

RECREATE, SPECTATE, AND CELEBRATE

CHAPTER THREE

WHEN IT'S TIME TO PLAY, MINNESOTANS ENJOY MYRIAD WAYS TO HAVE FUN OUTDOORS, USUALLY IN OR VERY NEAR A BODY OF WATER. A SHORT DRIVE FROM ANYWHERE IN THE STATE PLACES HIKERS, BIKERS, FISHERS, HORSE-BACK RIDERS, CANOEISTS, KAYAKERS, AND CAMPERS IN ONE OF MINNESOTA'S SPECTACULAR PARKS OR FORESTS. VOYAGEURS NATIONAL PARK, THE STATE'S ONLY NATIONAL PARK, CONTAINS THIRTY MAJOR LAKES AND IS A FAVORITE GETAWAY FOR CANOEISTS, BOATERS, AND WILDLIFE ENTHUSIASTS. OF THE STATE'S SIXTY-SIX STATE PARKS, SIXTY HAVE CAMPING FACILITIES AND ALL

are rich in beauty and history. Fort Snelling State Park, just south of St. Paul, preserves the fort built in 1819 at the junction of the Mississippi and Minnesota Rivers, a critical stopover for explorers, fur traders, and settlers.

Familiarity with water is a way of life in Minnesota. One in six residents owns some type of boat, and the state holds the record in the number of fishing licenses issued. However, the state's famed lakes may soon have competition from its ten thousand golf holes. Minnesota consistently places at or near the top of the nation in golf participation rates and ranked eleventh at last count in the number of golf courses, placing behind ten more populous states.

Perhaps it has something to do with being home to International Falls, the city that claims to be the "icebox of the nation," but Minnesotans like to keep moving. Rollerblades were invented here, as were water skis. One in twenty Minnesotans drives a snowmobile, more than anywhere else in the country. Residents truly know how to keep moving in and on snow and ice, skimming along on skis, skates, snowboards, snowshoes, and dogsleds. Cross-country skiing is always a delight on thousands of miles of world-class groomed trails, and the highest downhill ski area of the Midwest is situated in the Lutsen Mountains, one thousand feet above Lake Superior. In warmer weather, two major marathons, Grandma's in Duluth and the Twin Cities Marathon, draw large numbers of participants, who display their stamina for perpetual motion.

Opposite: The glittering ice castle of the St. Paul Winter Carnival draws visitors from hundreds of miles away. The carnival was begun in 1886 and includes speed-skating, ski-jumping, and ice-sculpting contests. A parade adds to the merriment. Above: This speed skater demonstrates that lakes are enjoyable no matter the season. Both photos © Bob Firth/Firth Photobank

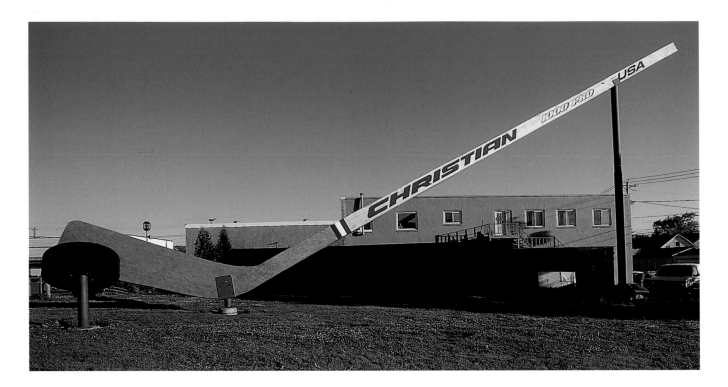

All year long, Minnesotans find a reason to celebrate. Nearly every community has an annual festival, honoring everything from SPAM (yep, it was invented here, too) to, of course, Paul Bunyan. The Minnesota State Fair bows only to that of Texas in attendance. And don't think for a minute that the merrymaking stops when the temperatures dip below freezing. Residents take a weeklong break from the ski hills, hockey rinks, snowmobile trails, and ice-fishing houses to attend the St. Paul Winter Carnival, a true fête of the season, culminated by the construction of an enchanting ice castle.

THE GREAT INDOORS

For those in the mood to stay inside, an equally vast array of arts, sports, and shopping vies for people's attention. The Twin Cities area is second only to New York in dramatic arts and in the number of symphony concert presentations. The Tyrone Guthrie Theater, with its 1,309 seats, is the largest regional theater in the country and has received several of the prestigious Tony Awards. Minnesota Public Radio has the largest membership base of public radio systems in the country. In 1974, MPR launched *A Prairie Home Companion,* which was hosted by Garrison Keillor and soon became the most popular American radio program of its time.

The sports scene has much to offer Minnesota fans. From a strong emphasis on youth and high school sports to collegiate, minor league, and professional offerings, fans never lack for a sporting event to attend. Professional

Above: The world's largest hockey stick stands guard on the lawn of the U.S. Hockey Hall of Fame (not pictured), in Eveleth. © John Elk III. Left: Humorist Garrison Keillor delivers some of his home-spun wit for A Prairie Home Companion, *broadcast from St. Paul. © Fredric Petters/Courtesy of* A Prairie Home Companion

teams include the Minnesota Vikings, Twins, and Timberwolves. Although Canada is known as the official birthplace of hockey, the town of Eveleth, Minnesota, site of the United States Hockey Hall of Fame, proclaims itself the "hockey capital" of the country. Minnesota has hosted such national contests as the NCAA basketball finals, the Super Bowl, the World Series, and the Seniors' Golf Classic.

If shopping is truly an American pastime, then Minnesota must hold at least two national titles. The country's first enclosed mall, Southdale, was built in Edina in 1956, and the largest shopping center in the United States, the Mall of America, opened in Bloomington in 1992. More people (42.5 million last year) visit the 4.2-million-square-foot shopping city on an annual basis than they do Disney World, the Grand Canyon, and the Statue of Liberty combined. On a

Pulling a golf bag at the Theodore Wirth Golf Course is not a bad idea on a stunning autumn day in Minneapolis. Minnesota golfers number more than 700,000, or almost 15 percent of the state's population. That's more golfers per capita than any other state in the country. © Greg Ryan-Sally Beyer

smaller scale, Minnesotans love to frequent the craft sales, flea markets, auctions, and antique shops that abound from border to border.

GREATEST ASSET IS NICE INDEED

With all it has to offer, Minnesota is, in the end, much more than the sum total of its lakes, golf courses, parks, theaters, and shopping malls. Although newcomers to the state will be pleased to find a thriving business climate in a setting of affordable living, excellent education systems, advanced health care, and abundant natural resources, eventually they will discover that Minnesota's greatest asset is an intangible commodity known as "Minnesota Nice." In a state where the weather can just as easily be daunting as dazzling, Minnesotans consistently display a can-do spirit of genuine friendliness and optimism. They work harder than most, play more often than others, and give of their time, talents, and resources more frequently than just about anyone else. It is "Minnesota Nice," practiced daily by Minnesotans in all walks of life, that ultimately shapes the families, neighborhoods, communities, and enterprises that make Minnesota, the Star of the North, shine so brightly.

Opposite: A whir of colorful lights adds to the excitement of the Minnesota State Fair. Held in St. Paul every August, the fair draws more than one million people. © Bob Firth/Firth Photobank. Above: Kayaking is one of many water-related activities Minnesotans enjoy. Ninety-five percent of residents live within five miles of recreational water. With almost 22,000 lakes and more than 25,000 miles of rivers and streams, it's easy to see why Minnesota leads the country in the number per capita of resident fishing licenses and recreational watercraft. © SuperStock. Below: The joy of fishing is passed on through the generations. © Bob Firth/Firth Photobank

Above: A woman and her canine companion glide along in a canoe, enjoying another favorite Minnesota diversion. © Bob Firth/Firth Photobank. Below: Lively banners and sculptures capture the spirit of Minnesota Twins games at the Hubert H. Humphrey Metrodome in downtown Minneapolis. The Twins won the World Series in 1987 and 1991. © Greg Ryan-Sally Beyer

Above: Dayton's anchors the first two-level shopping center in the country, Southdale in Edina, on the outskirts of Minneapolis. © Greg Ryan-Sally Beyer. Below: Thousands turn out every year for the Twin Cities Marathon, hailed by some as the "most beautiful urban marathon in the country." © Bob Firth/Firth Photobank

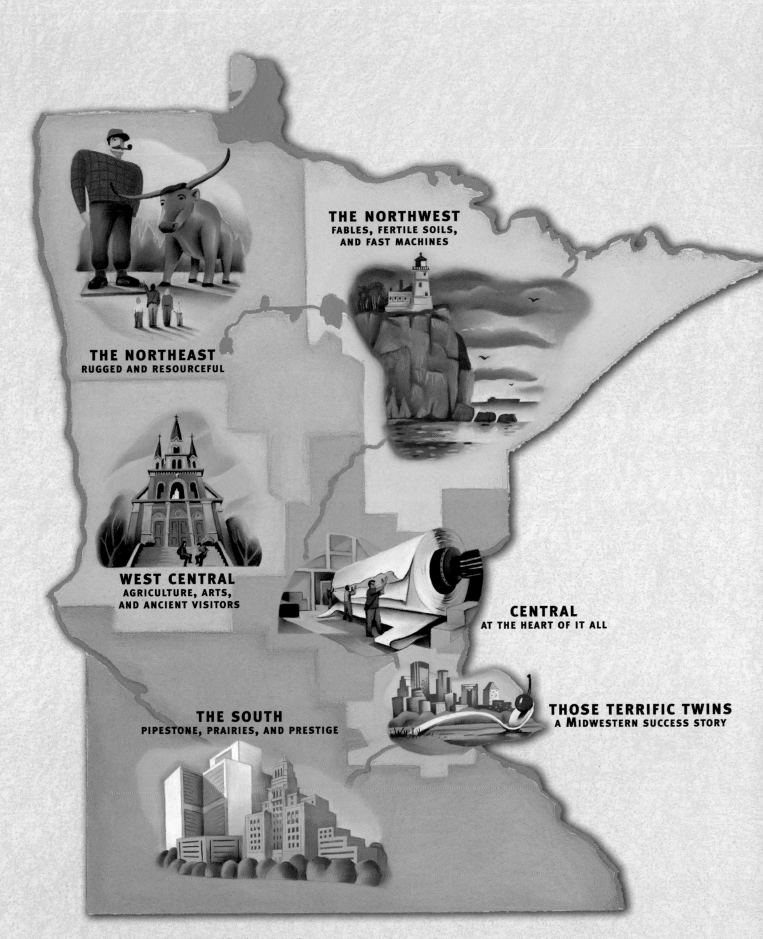

THE NORTHWEST
FABLES, FERTILE SOILS,
AND FAST MACHINES

THE NORTHEAST
RUGGED AND RESOURCEFUL

WEST CENTRAL
AGRICULTURE, ARTS,
AND ANCIENT VISITORS

CENTRAL
AT THE HEART OF IT ALL

THE SOUTH
PIPESTONE, PRAIRIES, AND PRESTIGE

THOSE TERRIFIC TWINS
A MIDWESTERN SUCCESS STORY

PART TWO
MINNESOTA: REGIONAL MOSAIC

IN MINNESOTA, YOU CAN HAVE IT ALL OR LEAVE IT ALL BEHIND. MORE CULTURAL ACTIVITIES ARE OFFERED HERE THAN ANYWHERE OUTSIDE OF NEW YORK, FOR INSTANCE, YET THE CAMPSITES IN ITS BOUNDARY WATERS CANOE AREA, A PLACE SO REMOTE THAT ALL MOTORIZED FORMS OF TRANSPORTATION ARE BANNED, ARE EQUALLY IN DEMAND. THE STATE'S BUSINESS PROFILE IS DIVERSE, WITH FORTUNE 500 CORPORATIONS, HIGH-TECH SMALL ENTERPRISES, CUTTING-EDGE MEDICAL VENTURES, AND TIME-HONORED ARTS SUCH AS GUNSMITHING AND TAXIDERMY ALL FOUND AMONG THE REGIONS. MINNESOTANS ALL OVER THE STATE STAY TRUE TO THEIR UNPARALLELED WORK ETHIC, YET THEY ALSO GOLF, FISH, AND RIDE SNOWMOBILES MORE OFTEN THAN MOST OTHER AMERICANS. MINNESOTA, ALTHOUGH VARIED IN GEOGRAPHY AND INDUSTRY, IS UNITED IN SPIRIT AND PRIDE.

CHAPTER FOUR
THE NORTHEAST
RUGGED AND RESOURCEFUL

Northeastern Minnesota is a rugged land with a complex history. Ojibwa Indians and French-Canadian voyageurs arrived first, followed by lumbermen, miners, and lighthouse keepers. In this beautiful and serene region today, moose, bear, wolves, eagles, and loons flourish, while some 317,000 people dwell in the area's principal city of Duluth.

SPLIT ROCK LIGHTHOUSE

German Celebration in Biwabik, and an Irish concert in Grand Marais maintain the area's rich cultural traditions.

Lumber camps once dominated the region's forests. Now, timber is transformed into paper and reconstituted wood products, such as particleboard and waferboard, driving the area's economy. Blandin Paper, based in Grand Rapids, is one of North America's largest producers of lightweight coated magazine paper.

Today, northeastern Minnesota's economy centers on four *T*'s, taconite, timber, transportation, and tourism, and is strengthened by health care, retail, and service industries.

It's said that Minnesota iron ore built the nation. Around the turn of the century, thousands of immigrant miners descended on the Mesabi Range and developed towns like Hibbing and Eveleth, colorful blends of European and Scandinavian languages and customs. Today, seven taconite producers ship forty-five million tons of ore out of the region on an annual basis. That translates to 70 percent of the national output and puts the iron ore industry on top of northeastern Minnesota's economic charts. Local museums preserve the importance of this industry, and ethnic festivals such as the Finnish-American Christmas Festival in Embarrass, Santa Lucia Swedish Fest in Two Harbors, Weihnachtsfest

Add the world's largest freshwater port at Duluth to the mix of mining and manufacturing and it's easy to see why transportation is the region's third *T*. Each year some 1,100 domestic and foreign ships enter the port from the Atlantic Ocean via the St. Lawrence Seaway and depart with tons of iron ore and grain. The ore arrives at the port via the Duluth, Missabe, and Iron Range Railway, a railroad with such high tonnage and revenues that it maintained a Class One ranking until recently, despite

The Aerial Lift Bridge in Duluth moves up and down to allow vessels to pass through. The great port of Duluth, on Lake Superior, began receiving ocean traffic in 1959 with the opening of the St. Lawrence Seaway. © Conrad Bloomquist/Scenic Photo!

Above left: Lichen-decorated rocks display one of nature's stunning patterns in the Grand Marais area on the North Shore. © Bob Firth/Firth Photobank. Top right: The charm and coziness of small-town Minnesota are reflected on Main Street in Eveleth. © John Elk III. Bottom right: A William A. Irvin ore boat participates in the traffic of taconite, the nation's principal source of iron ore. © John Elk III

having only a few hundred miles of track. Four regional airports also serve northeastern Minnesota.

A NATURAL PLAYGROUND

The sheer beauty of this land makes it a favorite destination for tourists. Hundreds of lodges, resorts, and campgrounds await those seeking adventure, sport, recreation, or solitude. Great downhill skiing is offered at Lutsen, the Midwest's largest ski resort. Cross-country skiers can strike out on their own or ski the lodge-to-lodge trails, stopping at each one to enjoy hot cider by a roaring fire. Each January, some one hundred mushers from around the world descend on Duluth to compete in the John Beargrease Sled Dog Marathon, second only to the famed Alaskan Iditarod in length and difficulty.

Come summer, charter fishing, sailing, hiking, rafting, and canoeing top the list of recreational pursuits. Vacationers and sightseers preferring tamer adventures can visit dozens of historical sites and museums, including Judy Garland's birthplace in Grand Rapids, Split Rock Lighthouse in Two Harbors, or the International Wolf Center in Ely. With tourism flourishing, the service and trade industries anticipate adding the most new jobs to this region in the immediate future.

Above: Sled dogs add to the many forms of travel for dauntless Minnesotans. Every January, up to one hundred mushers converge on Duluth for the John Beargrease Sled Dog Marathon, the largest sled dog race outside of the Iditarod. © Bob Firth/Firth Photobank. Below left: An eerily beautiful ice bridge on Lake Superior stands witness to the bitter cold. © Bob Firth/Firth Photobank. Below right: Canoes are stacked and ready for action in Ely, a gateway to the Superior National Forest and the Boundary Waters Canoe Area. © John Elk III. Opposite: Dad and son enjoy the peace of lake and forest while paddling on Lake One. © Greg Ryan-Sally Beyer

CHAPTER FIVE

THE NORTHWEST

FABLES, FERTILE SOILS, AND FAST MACHINES

In Minnesota's great northwest, dense forests and mammoth lakes yield to fertile farmland, vacation lakes, and rolling woods. This area of folklore is said to be formed by the fabled lumberman Paul Bunyan and his ox, Babe. It is a place of turbulent history, where warring Sioux and Chippewa nations struggled for dominance. Thanks to an early surveyor's error, it is also home to the Northwest Angle peninsula, the northernmost part of the continental United States, separated from the rest of the state by both water and Canadian soil. Today, farmers continue to till the soils of some of the richest farmland in the world, and the northwest's lakes and resorts still call to explorers. Many Native Americans have remained here, comprising about 13 percent of the population, with reservations at Red Lake, White Earth, and Leech Lake.

In the northwest, the first machine to traverse the ice and snow was manufactured in 1953. Today, nowhere are snowmobiles more a way of life. One in twenty Minnesotans owns one, and the world's leading manufacturers, Arctic Cat and Polaris, produce the crafts in Roseau and Thief River Falls, respectively. This is also hockey country. Many a

PAUL BUNYAN AND BABE, THE BLUE OX

regional high school team sports a trophy case full of state championship hardware, and professional hockey has benefited from numerous players who first laced up skates in this area.

A FAVORITE DESTINATION

Bemidji, whose name is Chippewa for "lake with river flowing through," is the local retail center and tourism headquarters. Not far away is Lake Itasca, the source of the Mississippi, where visitors from all corners of the globe come to inch their way across the stepping-stones spanning the trickling, narrow headwaters. In addition to tourism, the growth of small, diverse businesses, the presence of a four-year university, and the state's fourth busiest airport add to Bemidji's economic success.

Gaming is important to the area, driven by the Shooting Star Casino and Resort in Mahnomen on the White Earth Reservation. Fishing is also big business, especially at Lake of the Woods and Red Lake, the state's largest bodies of water.

This pair carve their tracks on some of the 14,400 miles of snowmobile trails in Minnesota, the first state to form a snowmobile safety training program. © Bob Firth/Firth Photobank

FARMS, FORESTS, AND THE FUTURE

Along the region's western border lies the Red River and some of the most productive farmland in the world. Most of the nation's sugar beets are grown here, and the region is well known for its wheat, cattle, and dairy production. The food-processing industry is understandably important here. American Crystal Sugar, an innovative and diverse grower-owned cooperative with a dominant place in the sugar market, has its headquarters and three factories in the area. Forested lands have long maintained a major presence in the region's economy. After the native pines were logged off, resourceful lumbermen replanted more-quickly growing aspens and the oriented strand board industry was pioneered as an alternative to the more expensive plywood. Marvin Windows, one of the top three wood window and door manufacturers in the world, has maintained headquarters in Warroad since 1904.

High technology has a home here as well. Computer component manufacturers and the medical and pharmaceutical industries are thriving. The University of Minnesota, Crookston, once primarily an agricultural college and in danger of closing, invested heavily in technological upgrades and now provides each of its one thousand students with a laptop computer.

Right: Patriotic sentiment warms the chilly surroundings of this ice-fishing house. Below: Dairy cows feed on a private farm. Both photos © Bob Firth/Firth Photobank

Water, water everywhere, and myriad ways to enjoy it. Opposite: Wegman Cabin near Lake Itasca. © John Elk III. Top: Lake Itasca, the source of the Mississippi, is a lovely place for an outing in a canoe. © John Elk III. Above: A common loon, the state bird, stretches its wings. © Bob Firth/Firth Photobank. Right: Tourists get a kick out of claiming to have traversed the mighty Mississippi on foot, as they can do here at the river's headwaters in Itasca State Park. © Conrad Bloomquist/Scenic Photo!

CHAPTER SIX
WEST CENTRAL
AGRICULTURE, ARTS, AND ANCIENT VISITORS

UNIVERSITY OF MINNESOTA

Although large with its 8,615 square miles, the mostly agricultural west-central region has only two cities of populations over ten thousand: Moorhead and Fergus Falls. Wild rice is cultivated from lakes in the Tamarac National Wildlife Refuge in Becker County, and turkeys are raised and processed in Perham. The west-central region is home to thriving small businesses, a bevy of the arts, bustling tourism, and the famed Kensington Runestone, proof, local Scandinavian descendants proudly claim, that the Vikings were indeed the first to visit the New World. The stone is housed in the Runestone Museum, in Alexandria. The community of eight thousand is nestled among several fine recreational lakes and is a retail and medical center for the area and its thousands of year-round tourists.

In the west-central region, good things do indeed come in small packages. For instance, New York Mills, population one thousand, has a regional cultural center heralded as a national prototype for rural arts programming. *USA Today Weekend Magazine* named the community in its Top Five Culturally Cool Towns rankings.

Once nearly deserted, Wheaton is now enjoying such an economic resurgence that there's talk of opening a recreational center and adding on to the two-doctor hospital. Thanks to the efforts of the town's economic/development director Harold Bruce—a native son who found success in California, tired of the pace, and headed home—four manufacturers opened shop and building permits rose substantially. The town's phenomenal turnaround, in fact, was the subject of a feature in the *Wall Street Journal.* The area also enjoys substantial opportunities to further one's education, with three four-year colleges (the University of Minnesota, Morris, Moorhead State University, and private Concordia College in Moorhead) and four other community and technical colleges.

Wide-open sky and prairie nurture dozens of crops and animals in the sparsely populated west-central region. Fields of wheat, soybeans, corn, and flax flourish here. © Conrad Bloomquist/Scenic Photo!

Above: The rice harvest keeps this farmer busy. © Bob Firth/Firth Photobank. Right: This replica of Hjemkomst, a Viking ship that sailed from Duluth to Bergen, Norway, in 1982, is on view at the Heritage-Hjemkomst Interpretative Center in Moorhead. © John Elk III. Below: A western Minnesota farmer pours wheat into storage. © Greg Ryan-Sally Beyer

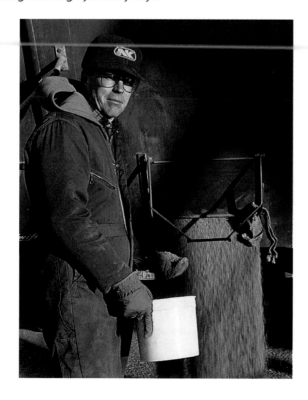

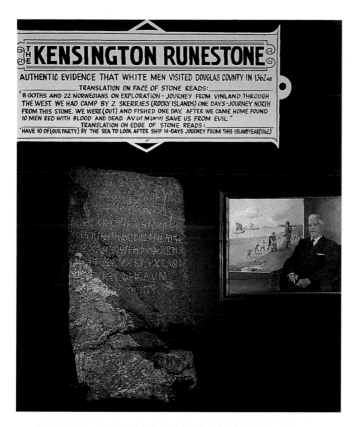

Opposite: Water rushes down Redwood Falls in Alexander Ramsey Park. © Greg Ryan-Sally Beyer. This page, clockwise from top left: The Kensington Runestone, believed to be left by Vikings in 1362, was overturned by a farmer near Kensington in 1898. It is on display at the Kensington Runestone Museum in Alexandria. © Greg Ryan-Sally Beyer. A farmer pushes through a rice paddy. © Bob Firth/Firth Photobank. Grain is loaded onto a barge at Red Wing, on the Mississippi. © Greg Ryan-Sally Beyer. Minnesota is the second-largest grower of turkeys in the country. © Greg Ryan-Sally Beyer

CHAPTER SEVEN

CENTRAL

AT THE HEART OF IT ALL

Over a half-million people live, work, and recreate in the diverse central region of Minnesota. Its northern counties comprise the Central Lakes area and some of the state's largest resorts. Tourism thrives in this part of the state, especially in and around Brainerd, the local educational, medical, and retail hub.

PAPER PRODUCTS MANUFACTURING

route to their ultimate destination, while others hold mayoral elections after the temporary city has been erected. Nearby, the Mille Lacs Indian Reservation runs several large casinos, increasing opportunities for fun and employment.

From the heavily forested regions come paper products. Major employers here are Potlach Paper in Brainerd and Hart Press in Long Prairie. Another major employer is Hennepin Paper Company, a construction paper manufacturer in the town of Little Falls, where famed American aviator Charles Lindbergh first glimpsed men in their flying machines above his boyhood home. Heavily agricultural, the northern central counties feature sizable dairy operations and agriculturally based small industries, such as Tyson Food's Motley plant, which produces imitation crabmeat.

To the south lies Lake Mille Lacs, one of the state's largest lakes. The site of great summer angling, Lake Mille Lacs is transformed into its own community in winter when hundreds of ice houses take to the hard-frozen real estate. Many communities flamboyantly celebrate this seasonal migration, parading ice houses through the streets en

BEACONS OF PAST AND FUTURE

The lands in the eastern part of the central region are more than 40 percent forested, and local communities have uniquely combined preserving their heritage with meeting present and future societal needs. The technical college in Pine City offers coursework in gunsmithing and taxidermy, while the emerging plastics industry has founded plastic-molding injection plants in Princeton, Rush City, and Mora. Crystal Cabinet Works in Princeton, a custom cabinet maker, is a major employer, as is the renowned Hazelden Foundation, a substance abuse treatment center in Center City. The central region also contains several state and federal correctional facilities.

Walleye fishing guide Don Bentley displays his catch at Eddy's Resort on Lake Mille Lacs, known for its bountiful supply of the fighting game fish. In winter, the vigorous walleye entice thousands of fishermen to the frozen lake. © Greg Ryan-Sally Beyer

Each January, the three thousand residents of Mora remember their Swedish heritage by welcoming visitors from their sister city of Mora, Sweden. They are joined by international visitors who come to participate in the annual Vasaloppet, a cross-country ski race.

A DELIGHTFUL PLACE FOR FAMILIES

The heart of the central region is St. Cloud, a thriving metropolitan area of about 160,000 people seventy-five miles from the Twin Cities. Area residents have access to four colleges, an outstanding health-care system, major retailers, and a strong and diverse economic base of education, government, services, and manufacturing. These amenities, complemented by a variety of cultural venues, help create the eleventh best area in the nation in which to raise a family, according to *Reader's Digest*. Steady employment boosts a family's sense of security, and the area offers a wide range of work opportunities. Fingerhut

Right: The St. Croix River, a major tributary of the Mississippi, flows along Minnesota's east-central border. © Bob Firth/Firth Photobank. Below: This marina on Lake Mille Lacs never lacks for boats. © Greg Ryan-Sally Beyer

Corporation, a leading mail-order house, is the principal local employer, closely followed by Frigidaire Company. Just down the road is the town of Cold Spring, home to the Cold Spring Granite Company, the largest producer of granite in the world.

A strong spirit of entrepreneurship has already garnered the area a spot of national ranking with *Entrepreneur* magazine in recent years, and the growth of high-tech industries, products, and services in the area will no doubt bring continued attention to this, the fastest-growing metropolitan area in the Midwest.

Opposite: At the edge of Lake Mille Lacs, Kathio State Park is ablaze with the colors of fall. In addition to the recreational opportunities the lake offers, it is also important for its National Wildlife Refuge. © Greg Ryan-Sally Beyer. Above: Tidy lawns, clean air, and friendly neighbors are all part of life in central Minnesota. © Bob Firth/Firth Photobank. Below: The main street of Marine on St. Croix, a hamlet of about 600 residents northeast of St. Paul, offers a charming version of life in the Midwest. © Greg Ryan-Sally Beyer

CHAPTER EIGHT
THOSE TERRIFIC TWINS
A MIDWESTERN SUCCESS STORY

The seven-county metropolitan area of the dynamic Twin Cities of Minneapolis and St. Paul claims more than one-half of the state's population. From skyscrapers to architectural classics, lakes and parks to the most active theater scene between the coasts, the Twin Cities truly have it all. *Fortune* magazine consistently ranks the Twin Cities among the nation's ten best places to do business. The area is a technological leader, home to many Fortune 500 giants, including 3M, Honeywell, Cray Research, and Medtronic.

Once known as the Mill City, Minneapolis still possesses many food-processing giants, such as General Mills, Pillsbury, International Multifoods, Cargill, and Land O'Lakes. Printing and publishing are major industries, with employers like Deluxe Checks, Lifetouch, and West Publishing, and retail is huge business, with Dayton Hudson Corporation leading the way. The Twin Cities are the nation's seventh-largest money management center, employing more than 140,000 Minnesotans, and are led by U.S. Bank and Norwest Corporation, which merged with Wells Fargo this year to form the seventh-largest bank in the United States.

The metropolitan area's economic stability and high

quality of life are enhanced by its vast educational and health resources and its efficient transportation network. Minneapolis and St. Paul top the list of the nation's twenty-five largest metropolitan areas for their percentage of high school graduates. The University of Minnesota and eight area private colleges attract students from all over the world. The Minnesota Hospital system combines with more than 7,500 medical providers, manufacturers, insurers, wholesalers, and retailers to give an area of the state, the heart of which is the Twin Cities, the nickname Medical Alley. The state's health-care employment figures are 30 percent higher than the national average.

AROUND, OUT, AND ABOUT

Traveling through the Twin Cities is never a problem. The average commute time is comparable to that of a much smaller city thanks to the excellent system of roadways. The Minneapolis–St. Paul International Airport is home to Northwest

SPOONBRIDGE AND CHERRY

Known as "the birthplace of Minnesota," historic Stillwater, on the St. Croix River near St. Paul, was the site of the convention that organized Minnesota as a territory. Industries now include lumber and related products. © Greg Ryan-Sally Beyer

Airlines, one of the nation's largest carriers, and the rail system is the country's seventh largest. St. Paul is also a major Mississippi River port.

Even with the excellent transportation system, it's hard to imagine ever wanting to leave. The area boasts one of the most extensive park networks in the country. There are more than nine hundred area lakes, two major rivers, excellent golf courses, and plenty of places to skate, ski, sled, and stay warm in the winter. Spectators can cheer on their favorite professional or college team or take in a play, concert, or exhibit. Shoppers delight in all the Twin Cities has to offer, from the charm of restored shops along St. Paul's Grand Avenue to the abundance of stores at the Mall of America, the nation's largest shopping center. Minneapolis's Aquatennial Celebration in the summer and St. Paul's Winter Carnival are great favorites of both communities.

Right: The entrance to the Mall of America reflects the grandiosity of the 4.2 million-square-foot shopping mecca. © Greg Ryan-Sally Beyer. Below: The shops, eateries, museums, and galleries of the Nicollet Mall, as seen from Twelfth Street, are connected by enclosed skyways. © Conrad Bloomquist/Scenic Photo!

Above left: The Weisman Art Museum at the University of Minnesota was designed by California architect Frank Gehry. © Bob Firth/Firth Photobank. Above right: Geometry and color construct a captivating angle on the historic courthouse in Stillwater. © Greg Ryan-Sally Beyer. Below: Torus Orbicularis Major *by John Newman graces the grounds of General Mills in Minneapolis. © Greg Ryan-Sally Beyer. Opposite: A cafe keeps busy in the Milling District of Minneapolis, once called the Mill City for its concentration of flour mills. Flour milling spurred the state economy more than any other industry in the late nineteenth century. © Bob Firth/Firth Photobank*

CHAPTER NINE
THE SOUTH
PIPESTONE, PRAIRIES, AND PRESTIGE

Intriguing history and geography endow southern Minnesota with its distinctive character. Bluffs tower above the Mississippi River in the east, and prairies and farmlands blanket the west. The area is pastoral and peaceful, filled with small fishing lakes and trout streams; winding, canoeable rivers; and abandoned railroad beds that have been converted into hiking and biking trails.

THE MAYO CLINIC

Southeastern Minnesota is the second most populous region of the state, with approximately 669,000 inhabitants. The city of Rochester is a medical hub, home to the world-renowned Mayo Clinic, and plays host to more than 1.5 million annual visitors. For several years, *Money* magazine has deemed Rochester one of the top three places to live.

Food processing is important to the region, led by Hormel Foods, an international producer/marketer of value-added food products, in Austin. Regional manufacturing outpaces state and national averages. IBM's AS/400, the world's most popular multiuser computer, has its manufacturing/research and development site in Rochester. Winona lays claim to the highest concentration of composite manufacturing firms in the country, and commercial printing's share of total employment here is four times the national average.

The towns in southeastern Minnesota are noted for their historic architecture, scenic charm, and ethnic and cultural preservation. The Root River Trail winds through a number of picturesque towns, like Lanesboro, which is rapidly becoming a Midwest artists' colony, and Harmony, home to a colony of Amish. The tourism industry is booming, and a room in a quaint inn or sleepy bed-and-breakfast is hard to come by, especially during fall when the trails are ablaze in color. Waterskiing was invented in Lake City, and each summer residents celebrate their love of the sport with a festival. When autumn rolls in, they pay tribute to the surrounding apple orchards with Johnny Appleseed Days. Nowhere is German

Pigs sniff the evening air in a farmyard near Hastings, a Mississippi River town near the juncture with the St. Croix River. Hastings' natural setting provides plenty of recreational opportunities, both on water and land, including canoeing, hiking, cross-country skiing, and golfing. © Greg Ryan-Sally Beyer

ancestry more strongly remembered than in New Ulm, and to the west, Mankato and Albert Lea celebrate their Native American heritage with pow-wows and rendezvous.

The southwestern region's mostly agricultural base has been fortified by diversification into manufacturing in the last decade. Companies like Hutchinson Technology in Hutchinson and Innovex in Montevideo have carved a high-tech niche out of the grainfields of the surrounding countryside and supply electronic components worldwide. Strong agricultural businesses include those that manufacture farm machinery and others that process food products. Farm-machinery and lawnmower manufacturer Toro has its headquarters, for example, in Windom. Schwan's Sales Enterprises, in Marshall, began as a family dairy/delivery service and evolved into the ice cream–frozen foods giant it is today. Jennie-O, a leading turkey processor, is found in Willmar.

DIVERSE PEOPLE, RICH RESOURCES

The south is steeped in cultural diversity and history. Long before the first fur trappers arrived in the north, Native Americans came to this region in search of its sacred quarries of soft, red pipestone needed to make

Right: A farmer prepares for late-spring planting of soybeans. © Greg Ryan-Sally Beyer. Below: Wind-generation towers dot Buffalo Ridge. © Joe Miller Photography

ceremonial pipes. They marked the landscape with their rock carvings and burial mounds, and now a national monument in Pipestone and a few local museums recount their story. The southwestern corner of the state was immortalized by peripatetic *Little House on the Prairie* author Laura Ingalls Wilder, who spent much of her childhood in the tiny community of Walnut Grove. Today, the town maintains a museum dedicated to its most famous resident. Droves of European immigrants,

especially Germans and Poles, put down roots in southwestern Minnesota, whereas thousands of Latinos and Southeast Asians are among the area's newest arrivals.

Like the rest of Minnesota, the area takes advantage of its natural resources, both for fun and business. Two national bass-fishing tournaments are hosted each year at Big Stone Lake, for example, and the winds that blow along Buffalo Ridge near Marshall have been harnessed by 75 wind generators. Another 325 are being planned, potentially enough to supply power to the entire state.

Among the communities in this sparsely populated region are two towns, both with populations of twelve thousand residents, considered among the hottest small places in the country. An hour's drive from the Twin Cities, Hutchinson boasts a 3M plant, solid health care, a variety of retailers, and a strong school system. Marshall, close to the South Dakota border, enjoys a strong industrial base, led by Schwan's, and the presence of Southwest State University. Both towns offer an irresistible blend of new-millennium technology and ideas and down-home comforts.

ALL IN ALL

From the Northwest Passage to the Iowa border, Minnesota exemplifies beauty, resourcefulness, hard work, innovation, and diversity. It's a place of preservation, celebration, imagination, and appreciation. Minnesota has no trouble demonstrating the myriad ways it effortlessly combines cornfields and computers, mines and medical institutions, printers and prairies, and tradition and tomorrow.

Below: The southeastern community of Lanesboro offers a small-town appeal. © Bob Firth/Firth Photobank. Bottom: The well-preserved mounds at Indian Mounds Park in St. Paul remind visitors of an ancient culture that thrived around 500 B.C. © John Elk III. Opposite: Each fall, Dakota dancers celebrate their heritage at the Mankato Powwow, which draws thousands of non–Native Americans, too. © Joe Miller Photography

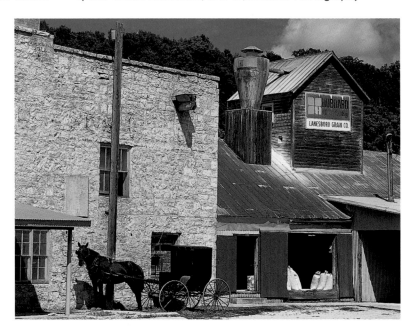

Opposite: On Red Rock Ridge near Jeffers are some two thousand petroglyphs of animals, people, and symbols, evidence of an ancient civilization in the southwestern part of the state. © Greg Ryan-Sally Beyer. Above left: Also in the southwest are beautiful quartzite rock formations, left by glaciers long ago, at Blue Mounds State Park. © Greg Ryan-Sally Beyer. Above right: A sculpture frames part of the Methodist Hospital in Rochester. © Bob Firth/Firth Photobank. Below: An Amish driver holds on to his hat. © Bob Firth/Firth Photobank

A CENTURY OF INNOVATION

PART THREE

In the beginning, Minnesota's wealth stemmed from the land. From a thriving fur trade to lumbering to the growth of farming, early Minnesotans harnessed their state's abundant natural resources to create their livelihoods. Products from beneath the surface of the earth, especially, built and sustained Minnesota's economy. Rich iron-ore veins, later supplanted by taconite, in the northern region still supply the nation more than one hundred years after their discovery, while breathing life into dozens of Minnesota communities. And the important building-stone minerals granite, limestone, and sandstone gave rise to robust industries in quarrying and stonecutting.

Today, Minnesota's diverse industries are best characterized in one of two ways: either those that evolved from the state's natural resources or those that simply developed from the resourcefulness of Minnesotans. Agriculture, mining, quarrying, and forestry are still a way of life for residents but have also engendered a host of related industries. Paper and wood-fiber products manufacturing, for example, as well as printing and publishing, are significant industries. Food processing, likewise, has a key presence in the state.

In the last half of this century, Minnesota spread its pastoral roots and took its place among the nation's leading suppliers of high technology. The strength of the state's high-tech industry arose out of a dominant presence in industrial machinery and the rapid growth of the electronic components and instrument manufacturing industries, in particular. The concentration of more than five hundred companies and institutions in the health-care industry, encompassing product and medical-device manufacturing, biotech companies, and health-care delivery organizations, is so commanding in a 350-mile radius in southern Minnesota that the area has been dubbed "Medical Alley," paralleling California's "Silicon Valley" in scope and understanding.

The creative energy, work ethic, and innovative spirit that spurred Minnesotans to grow their economy to the healthy status it enjoys today will undoubtedly carry them through many more decades of expansion as the state enters the twenty-first century.

The Minneapolis skyline rises above a colorful autumn display along the Mississippi River. The mighty Mississippi forms the southern border of St. Paul before it turns northwestward to form the dividing line between the Twin Cities. This second-largest river in the United States flows 2,340 miles from its Minnesota headwaters to its mouth in the Gulf of Mexico. © Greg Ryan-Sally Beyer

© Conrad Bloomquist Scenic Photo!

TRADE AND
ECONOMIC DEVELOPMENT

MINNESOTA WORLD TRADE CENTER CORPORATION

THE MINNESOTA

WORLD TRADE

CENTER

CORPORATION

HELPS BUSINESSES

TO VENTURE

INTO THE

GLOBAL MARKET

OR TO EXPAND

THEIR PRESENT

INTERNATIONAL REACH

The Minnesota World Trade Center Corporation is a membership organization that links Minnesota businesses to international markets. It promotes global partnerships, fosters increased participation in world trade, encourages foreign investment, and facilitates mutual assistance and cooperation among members. Member companies have access to more than 500,000 businesses worldwide.

The World Trade Center Corporation is managed and operated in cooperation with the Trade Office of the Minnesota Department of Trade and Economic Development.

The corporation currently has 200 members. Members have immediate access to a range of international trade and investment services including networking with international business experts, market research, trade leads, and a computerized communications system. In addition to the World Trade Center Corporation's own on-site services, members also receive a range of services through the World Trade Centers Association, which is a network of 300 World Trade Centers in ninety countries.

The corporation's conference center offers Minnesota businesses a world-class facility with a theater, meeting hall, board-meeting room, and classroom space. The 110-seat theater offers front- and rear-screen projection and a state-of-the-art sound system. The meeting hall is arranged to encourage an exchange of ideas. The elegantly designed executive board room includes high-tech

The Minnesota World Trade Center Corporation, housed in the towering Minnesota World Trade Center building, above, is conveniently located in the heart of downtown St. Paul.

presentation capabilities. The classroom space accommodates up to 200 people and provides advanced presentation facilities. The center's staff offers comprehensive conference planning and management services.

The center allows Minnesota businesses to conduct national or international meetings on site using a fiber-optic network. Videoconference rooms are connected to locations throughout Minnesota. The system receives communications via MNSat (Minnesota Satellite Technology), fiber-optic telecommunications systems, and the MEANS digital interactive video system.

Breakfast briefings at the center feature international dignitaries and business experts. Training sessions also are held, which address topics such as sales prospecting, obtaining financing, and technology updates. These sessions are taught by economic development and industry professionals, and can be videoconferenced statewide.

Membership in the Minnesota World Trade Center Corporation is a cost-effective way for businesses to enter international markets or expand their global activity.

Nitya Pibulsonggram (center), Thailand's ambassador to the United States, is briefed before a trade meeting.

THE TRADE OFFICE OF THE MINNESOTA DEPARTMENT OF TRADE AND ECONOMIC DEVELOPMENT

THE TRADE OFFICE

OF THE MINNESOTA

DEPARTMENT OF

TRADE AND

ECONOMIC

DEVELOPMENT

FACILITATES

CONTINUED GROWTH

FOR THE STATE'S

BUSINESS ECONOMY,

TOURISM, AND GLOBAL

TRADE ACTIVITY

By opening the doors of foreign trade to the state's businesses, the Minnesota Trade Office plays an important role in achieving the economic mission of the Minnesota Department of Trade and Economic Development. Created by the Minnesota legislature in 1983, the Minnesota Trade Office is the state's lead organization in developing international trade activities within the realm of Minnesota's economic development strategy. The Minnesota Trade Office also co-operates with, supports, and has operating responsibility for the Minnesota World Trade Center Corporation.

The Minnesota Trade Office provides a wide range of services to Minnesota companies including export counseling, education, finance, marketing, an international library, and a program to facilitate foreign direct investment. The trade office's comprehensive export education programs are presented statewide by experts in international banking, law, shipping, finance, and the markets of specific countries. The trade office also organizes participation in twenty international trade shows annually to foster overseas business relationships.

As part of the trade office, the Minnesota Export Finance Authority (MEFA) was formed to support exports by offering financial services. "MEFA helps Minnesota businesses overcome financial hurdles to exports through counseling, training, technical assistance, loan guarantees, and access to federal programs such as the Export-Import Bank of the United States, the U.S. Small Business Administration, the U.S. Trade Development Agency, and the Overseas Private Investment Corporation," says

The Minnesota Trade Office represented fourteen medical companies at the MEDICA 1997 trade show in Dusseldorf, Germany. Trade shows are an effective way for companies to locate overseas sales distributors, original equipment manufacturer contacts, and joint venture partners.

M. Noor Doja, executive director of the Minnesota Trade Office.

In addition to the trade office, the Minnesota Department of Trade and Economic Development includes three other divisions. The Business and Community Development Division provides business and community economic development planning, program development, and financial assistance to businesses, local units of government, and educational institutions. The Information and Analysis Division collects and analyzes statistical and economic data about the state, which is published every two years in *Compare Minnesota: An Economic and Statistical Fact Book*. With tourism an integral part of Minnesota's economy, the Office of Tourism implements strategic plans to increase tourism revenues.

"The size and growth of industry in Minnesota are a reflection of our status as a national and global leader. We have a vibrant and growing economy, and our mission is to facilitate its continued economic growth," says Minnesota Department of Trade and Economic Development Commissioner Jay Novak.

Foreign delegations often visit Minnesota for research, business development, and exchange of ideas. Assembled at the state capitol building, this delegation from Akita, Japan, is part of the Japan External Trade Organization's Local-to-Local Initiative Program, which matches Japanese businesses with foreign companies for mutual industrial development.

A LAND OF MANY RICHES

CHAPTER TEN

RICHES OF THE LAND WERE THE SOURCE OF WEALTH FOR THE MAJORITY OF MINNESOTANS DURING ITS FIRST ONE HUNDRED YEARS OF STATEHOOD. WHILE THE STATE HAS A REPUTATION FOR BEING LARGELY AGRICULTURAL, AND CROPS AND LIVESTOCK DEFINITELY BOLSTERED THE STATE'S EMERGING ECONOMY, IT WAS THE SPECTACULARLY COLORFUL INDUSTRIES OF LUMBERING AND MINING THAT MONOPOLIZED THE STATE'S ECONOMY IN THE BEGINNING.

For several decades, hard-working, hard-living lumberjacks considered Minnesota to be much to their liking. Jobs were plentiful, wages were high, and the climate, ill-suited for some industries, actually made logging easier. Forestry quickly became the state's first major industry. The white pine, harvested by those pioneer lumberjacks, supplied not only Minnesota's booming building trade but also those of states to the south and east. By the turn of the century, Germans, Scandinavians, Russians, and Finns had settled in the lumber camps, adding a lively blend of language and culture to the northern landscape. By day, the forests were filled with the sounds of axes and cries of "Timber!," while at night, tales of the legendary lumberman Paul Bunyan were born over the clanging of glasses and the roar of laughter.

The legend of valuable resources lying beneath the earth near Lake Superior was passed down from the Chippewa Nation to the early explorers to all subsequent arrivals to the area. But when iron was first unearthed in 1865, the discovery generated little interest, as Minnesota prospectors, like all others of that era, were convinced that gold was the only treasure worth pursuing. Eventually, the ancient legend was substantiated. The land held the largest concentration of iron ore that the world had ever seen, so large that Minnesota mines would supply more than one-half of the nation's and one-third of the world's ore for more than seventy years. Minnesota mining communities, flooded with immigrants from Scandinavia, Germany, Poland, and Czechoslovakia, flourished. By the 1940s, however, it was apparent that

Opposite: The Thunderbird open pit mine in Eveleth reveals some of the abundant deposits in the Mesabi Iron Range, one of three principal iron-rich regions in Minnesota that have made the state the nation's leading provider of iron ore for more than one hundred years. In 1993, Minnesota, with nine of the country's sixteen iron-ore mines, produced more than three-quarters of the iron ore in the United States. Above: Tourists don hard hats for a one-of-a-kind ride through the Soudan Underground Mine in Soudan Underground Mine State Park, near Vermilion Lake. Iron, a heavy metal, is the most-used metal on earth. Both photos © John Elk III

FEW FOOD PRODUCTS HAVE WITHSTOOD THE TEST OF TIME AS STRONGLY AS SPAM LUNCHEON MEAT, DEVELOPED IN AUSTIN, MINNESOTA, BY HORMEL FOODS IN 1937. OVER FIVE BILLION CANS HAVE SINCE BEEN PRODUCED. THE LUNCHEON MEAT, MADE OF 100 PERCENT PURE PORK AND HAM FLAVORED WITH SALT, WATER, SUGAR, AND A PRESERVATIVE, WAS NAMED SPAM, AN ACRONYM FOR "SPICED HAM," BY KENNETH DAIGNEAU, A BROTHER OF A HORMEL FOODS VICE PRESIDENT, IN RESPONSE TO A CONTEST HELD BY HORMEL FOODS MANAGEMENT.

the vast deposits were nearing depletion—but the rich earth was revealed to be holding one more treasure. Taconite, a substance containing iron ore, which when processed produces pellets used in blast furnaces, was found in the region, and just in time. By 1957, less than 10 percent of Minnesota's iron ore output was in taconite; by 1972, that figure had climbed to 70 percent and continued to rise. While many of the mining communities dwindled, the discovery of taconite brought new life to northern Minnesota and made a substantial contribution to the state's economy. Today, Minnesota is home to nine of the nation's sixteen ore mines and continues to produce more than 70 percent of the nation's ore.

Minerals fulfill another important segment of industrial activity in the state: quarrying. Granite deposits in central Minnesota are of unusually high quality, and limestone and sandstone are abundant in the south. Quarrying and stonecutting, in fact, rank second only to mining as Minnesota's principal mineral industries. The area is still considered to be a world leader in granite production, and quarried stone from Minnesota can be found adorning buildings across the globe.

A taconite ship loads up in Duluth Harbor. In the 1950s, when Minnesota began to run out of high-grade iron ore, engineers devised a way to make taconite, a low-grade iron ore, usable in blast furnaces, revitalizing the mining industry. © John Elk III

Although rice is not one of Minnesota's principal agricultural products, it is among the corn, oats, barley, and wheat crops that give the state its fourth-place ranking in the harvesting of grains nationwide. © Bob Firth/Firth Photobank

wasn't long before other grains—corn, oats, and barley among them—were being grown as both cash and feed crops. With the increase in feed crops, livestock production increased and soon the nation looked to Minnesota as the leading dairy and meat producer.

Food processing has understandably grown to be one of Minnesota's strongest industries, particularly in the state's southeastern region. Since 1985, employment in the food and kindred products industries has risen at a pace three times that of the national average. The mills that once led the nation in flour production have evolved into industry giants Pillsbury, General Mills, and International Multifoods. Today, value-added and convenience products have replaced milling as these companies' mainstays, but these businesses have remained among Minnesota's largest employers. And Cargill, a grain-trading business started in 1865 by the family bearing its name, has become America's largest privately held corporation, with more than seventy thousand employees and fifty separate lines of business.

THE BREAD AND BUTTER STATE

The development of agriculture as a principal industry followed the westward movement of the railroad across the state. Prior to that, farmers concentrated their efforts in the state's wooded valleys, along the Mississippi, St. Croix, and Minnesota Rivers, fearful of land where trees did not grow and water had to be excavated from deep wells. Once the fertile soils in the western regions of the state were revealed, the farmers were quick to shed their mistaken beliefs. Railroads promoted the concept of large-scale wheat farming, and at one time, raising grain seemed to be the sole occupation of Minnesota farmers. "Bonanza" farms produced enough wheat to feed the nation, quickly earning the state the nickname the "nation's breadbasket." Together, the great mills in Minneapolis soon led the country in flour production. It

© PhotoDisc, Inc.

THE UNIVERSITY OF MINNESOTA'S HORTICULTURE RESEARCH CENTER HAS DEVELOPED MORE THAN TWENTY VARIETIES OF APPLES DURING THIS CENTURY, INCLUDING THE POPULAR HARALSON, WEALTHY, AND CORTLAND. MINNESOTA WAS ALSO RESPONSIBLE FOR INTRODUCING THE CARAMEL APPLE TO THE REST OF THE WORLD. A FOOD VENDOR AT THE 1916 MINNESOTA STATE FAIR WAS THE FIRST TO CONCOCT THE DELICIOUS COMBINATION OF FRUIT AND CARAMEL.

MINNESOTA HAD EIGHTY-FIVE THOUSAND FARMS IN 1994, TWO THOUSAND FEWER THAN IT HAD THE PREVIOUS YEAR. THOSE FARMS MADE UP 4.7 PERCENT OF THE NATION'S TOTAL. THE 29.7 MILLION ACRES OF MINNESOTA LAND DEDICATED TO FARMING CONSTITUTES 2.5 PERCENT OF THE COUNTRY'S FARM-LAND. MINNESOTA CONTINUES TO RANK AMONG THE TOP FIVE PRODUCERS OF DAIRY PRODUCTS, SOYBEANS, HOGS, CORN, TURKEYS, SUGAR BEETS, BARLEY, HAY, SWEET CORN, OATS, GREEN PEAS, AND SUNFLOWERS.

Though its roots are still in domestic and international grain trading, Cargill's operations have expanded to include animal feeds, chemical products, and other commodities. This homegrown company now has more than three hundred plants and offices in over three dozen countries and owns a fleet of ships and barges.

While grains continue to rank among Minnesota's top-producing crops, vegetables, especially sweet corn,

Opposite: Sunrise warms a farm near Afton, on the Lower St. Croix River. © Greg Ryan-Sally Beyer. Right: An 1870s grain elevator in Albert Lea bespoke lower-tech times. Courtesy, Cargill, Inc. Below: A potato field in Sherburne County gets its regular dousing by an irrigator. © Joe Miller Photography

are important crops, too, and support numerous canneries and quick-freezing facilities in southern Minnesota. Also in southern Minnesota is Hormel, the largest independent meat and food processor in America. Regional employment in manufactured dairy products, grain mill products, farm product raw materials, meat products, preserved fruits, and processed vegetables is five to eight

© PhotoDisc, Inc.

resources. Marvin Windows and Doors, the third-largest manufacturer in the United States, with a growing international market, and the Andersen Corporation, considered to be the most recognized brand name in the window and patio door industry, are both Minnesota companies.

Industries based on Minnesota's abundant natural resources and agricultural commodities will long have

Below: These floating logs show how Minnesota's rivers contributed to the establishment and success of the state's timber industry. © Bob Firth/Firth Photobank. Opposite: A tugboat and gravel barges move through Lock and Dam No. 1 on the Mississippi River in Minneapolis. © Greg Ryan-Sally Beyer

times that of the national average. Industry analysts speculate that the future of this industry will revolve around natural and organic processing, low-calorie and low-fat foods, food-service productions for restaurants, and specialty items. The primary processors' proximity to the growers, the state's central location and strong transportation system, and the increase of custom food-packaging firms in the area should help the region maintain its niche in this highly competitive market.

THE PAPER TRAIL

Today, forestry, mining, and agriculture still maintain a presence in the state but have diversified and given rise to related industries. The majority of the lumber harvest is now soft pulpwood, which is made into paper and wood-fiber products. Indeed, wood-products manufacturing is one of the state's key industries. Numerous paper manufacturers call Minnesota home, among them Blandin Paper, a leading North American producer of publication papers for magazines and catalogs. The company has been the major employer in Grand Rapids for more than seventy years. The manufacture of fine wood windows and doors is also a by-product of the state's plentiful lumber

Courtesy, Land O'Lakes

MINNTAC PLANT, IN MOUNTAIN IRON, MINNESOTA, IS THE LARGEST IRON-ORE PELLET PLANT IN THE COUNTRY, WITH AN ANNUAL TACONITE CAPACITY OF 14 MILLION TONS. THE WORLD'S LARGEST OPEN-PIT IRON-ORE MINE IS THE HULL RUST MAHONING MINE IN HIBBING. SPREAD OVER 1,600 ACRES, THE MINE IS THREE MILES LONG, UP TO A MILE WIDE, AND 535 FEET DEEP. THE SOUDAN UNDERGROUND MINE STATE PARK IS THE ONLY PLACE IN THE WORLD THAT CONDUCTS A TOUR OF AN UNDERGROUND IRON MINE.

a presence in the state's richly diverse economy. However, in the next century, Minnesota's wealth will most probably be generated more from its developmental resources than its natural ones. Its labor, financial, infrastructural, and amenity resources, identified as the best in the country by the most recent Corporation for Enterprise Development study, will combine to grow new and existing businesses from International Falls to the Iowa border.

Minnesota is the nation's third-largest producer of hogs and pigs. The hogs on this central-Minnesota farm are among the state's 5.4 million swine, which comprise more than 9 percent of the annual U.S. total. © SuperStock

Above: The Rockleau open pit mine near Virginia, Minnesota, is situated between the Mesabi and Vermilion Iron Ranges. © John Elk III.
Below: A solitary combine brings in the soybean harvest near North Mankato. With 6.7 million acres devoted to raising soybeans, Minnesota accounts for 9.59 percent of the U.S. total, ranking the state third in soybean production. © Joe Miller Photography

AGRICULTURE, FORESTRY, MINING, AND FOOD PROCESSING

HARVEST LAND COOPERATIVE

Harvest Land Cooperative's sparkling new two-story headquarters building is located on a tree-lined street in Morgan, Minnesota.

A neighborly attitude prevails on the Minnesota prairie. Harvest Land Cooperative, in Morgan, Minnesota, embodies the best of that spirit. Since its inception in 1904 as Morgan Farmer's Elevator, the company has connected top suppliers with hungry consumers. Today Harvest Land Cooperative is recognized as a model of entrepreneurship by its stockholders and business partners.

In the company's early stages, Morgan Farmer's Elevator grew cautiously and independently as opportunities came to south-central Minnesota. Through mechanization, rural electrification, and declining population, it prospered, capitalizing on technological leaps.

The Elevator acquired Scenic City Oil Company in 1974, bought Morton Grain three years later, and in 1978 added Springfield's Southern Seven Terminal to its family of businesses. In 1984 the time was right for significant expansion. Morgan Farmer's Elevator merged with Springfield Farmer's Elevator, which also had begun in 1904, to form Harvest Land Cooperative.

Harvest Land prides itself on delivering products to its patron members on time, anywhere they need them.

Highly profitable, the taxable producer cooperative is owned by 1,250 stockholders, who elect a nine-member board of directors to oversee the business. Eighty-five full-time and twenty part-time employees staff the various company divisions: grain, crop production, feed, petroleum, turkey production, and administration. The cooperative also includes Harvest Land Inc., a wholly owned subsidiary corporation, and the Harvest Land Financial division with its leasing company, Northland Capital, LLC.

The cooperative's nominal territory is sixty miles north to south and thirty miles east to west, and includes towns such as Comfrey, Springfield, Wabasso, Morgan, and Morton. Even though the company has plenty of room to grow, Harvest Land Cooperative's main goal is to serve its present customers efficiently.

In 1997 almost 2,500 individuals did business with Harvest Land, whose core business is grain handling, storage, and marketing. However, the company performs many additional functions, including feed milling, bulk fuels sales, crop consultation, custom seeding, crop tillage, development and management services, and financing of crop input and equipment. Soil-analysis work led Harvest Land into the production and custom application of fertilizer and chemicals. The company also performs nutrition analysis, manufactures and delivers feed, and makes bulk sales of and delivers oil and propane. In addition, Harvest Land Cooperative operates a Card-trol fuel station in Morgan and produces turkeys.

Mike Weelborg, Harvest Land's general manager since 1965, is proud of the cooperative's dedication to serving its customers' needs in a timely manner. "If necessary, we mill and deliver products around the clock," says Weelborg.

Company executives include Gordy Jensen, assistant general manager; Ernie Kalkhoff, office manager and controller; and Dave Stuk, vice president of finance. Only Kalkhoff is a native of Morgan, a fact that reflects the area's declining population. Morgan's 1,000 residents believe it is a better place to work than the Twin Cities, with comparable benefits. Yet, with no unemployment in town, Harvest Land still needs to recruit employees from other areas.

Morgan may be a conservative agricultural community, but Harvest Land tries to be innovative, initiating procedures and letting the rest of the industry follow. "We need to be first," says Weelborg, whose underlying philosophy is to be "a facilitator of change." He used to draw up annual and five-year business plans, but he discovered his best opportunities were unpredictable. Now, Weelborg arrives at work with a fresh slate and looks for one opportunity he can seize each day. To do that, he knows he needs to be flexible and creative.

For example, Harvest Land was the first to "put grain on the ground" in 1961, and by the 1986–1987 season, it had 5 million bushels in temporary bunkers. Harvest Land facilitated live turkey production in the 1980s, hogs in the 1990s, and added a finance division in 1992; in 1993 the company purchased the Cargill Elevator and a grain-storage and -drying facility in Comfrey.

In few other industries is success so obvious, or failure so quick and unpredictable, as in agriculture. Continuous technical analysis and the skill to understand global finance are critical to the well-being of Harvest Land's members. Balance is important; consumer customers will not be promoted at the expense of producer customers. "Ideally, every one of our customers will be a success," says Gordy Jensen.

Capital improvements, such as the new microingredient hog-feed system and grain dryer at the Springfield terminal,

Harvest Land Cooperative, located in some of the most productive agricultural areas in America, specializes in grain handling, storage, and marketing.

show determination to succeed. In the past decade Harvest Land's sales leaped from $22 million to $100 million as it entered new business avenues. Construction of a new feed mill boosted grind-and-mix revenue from $56,000 to $2.5 million.

In 1997 Harvest Land produced and sold 250,000 tons of poultry and hog feed, and grain sales hit a record 14.3 million bushels. Fertilizer sales topped 30,000 tons, while chemical sales rose 20 percent from 1996 to $5.3 million—both records for the company. Spreading and spraying income jumped 25 percent. Feed sales were up 32 percent, and 4.5 million bushels of corn and 50 thousand tons of soybean meal were used for livestock and poultry feed. The Petroleum Division increased fuel sales 14 percent. Currently in its seventh year, the Turkey Production Division has generated $1.5 million in income.

"All this," stresses Weelborg, "was done with almost no point-of-sale advertising and no sales force. We are one of the largest feed manufacturers, yet we do not have a feed salesman. With Harvest Land's unparalleled service, name recognition and word-of-mouth are enough to bring in new customers."

In the future, Harvest Land hopes to create strategic alliances with private and cooperative businesses, opening up many new avenues. Committed to customer service and always a step ahead of the competition, Harvest Land Cooperative has earned its position as one of Minnesota's premier agricultural partners.

CHRISTENSEN FAMILY FARMS

CHRISTENSEN FAMILY

FARMS USES

STATE-OF-THE-ART

LABORATORY

AND BREEDING

TECHNIQUES TO

CONTINUE ACHIEVING

ITS GOAL—TO BE

THE BEST IN THE

HIGH-QUALITY,

LOW-COST

PRODUCTION OF PORK

Twenty-five years ago, three brothers from Sleepy Eye, Minnesota, received a pair of bred gilt pigs from a neighbor who wanted to encourage their entrepreneurial interest in livestock. His business advice still guides them: Practice restraint when everyone else in the industry is going full bore, and surge ahead when the industry slows down. The Christensen brothers—Bob, Glen, and Lynn—had turned the two gilts into a 140-sow operation by the time they were in high school. By using barn space rented from neighbors and applying a high-labor, low-capital approach, they were able

The Christensen Family home farm, a century farm—in operation for more than 100 years—in Sleepy Eye, Minnesota, is a leader in hog production.

to realize steady profits and eventually build their own barns.

Today that entrepreneurial enterprise is Christensen Family Farms (CFF), the largest family-owned and -managed swine business in Minnesota and one of the top dozen pork producers in the United States. From its modest beginnings, Christensen Family Farms now has emerged as one of the nation's "pork power-houses," according to *Successful Farming* magazine, and holds a position of leadership in a state that ranks third in hog production in the country. The company has expanded at an impressive rate—50 to 60 percent growth in the 1980s and early 1990s and 25 to 30 percent in recent years— without losing its rural roots. Sleepy Eye still remains home to the business, which now employs 300 people at its headquarters and thirty company-owned sites. The company has operations in three midwestern states.

CFF credits its success to working hard and being efficient without sacrificing quality.

CFF's new state-of-the-art company-owned feed mill provides rations for all phases of production.

Producing pork in a low-cost, high-quality manner is necessitated by today's market. To compete in the increasingly demanding global pork industry, CFF uses advanced technology and sophisticated management practices in farrow-to-finish (birth-to-market) pork production. The result is a healthy, lean, food product.

The CFF production system starts with genetically superior breeding stock. The company was among the first in the industry to use breeding stock based on a selection system of measured performance. Pork Storks, the company's boar facility, houses a state-of-the-art breeding laboratory and nearly 400 elite boars. CFF does most of its breeding via artificial insemination, which provides increased control over the quality of pigs produced for market. The semen from CFF boars is considered world-class porcine genetic material and is marketed to other swine producers, as well as being used in the company's own breeding program.

CFF uses a three-phase site-separation approach to production. Isolating pigs in breeding, nursery, and grow-finish stages maximizes the health and growth of the animals. Breeding of sows and farrowing occur at the company's many sow farms. CFF pioneered separate-site sow farming, having built the first turnkey sow farm in the Midwest. Piglets are transferred to

CFF works with more than ninety independent farm families who supplement their farming operations by doing the grow-finish phase of production. One of these facilities, engineered by Lester Building Systems, is shown here.

nurseries after weaning and remain there until they reach approximately fifty pounds in weight, which is when they are considered feeder pigs. Feeder pigs then enter the grow-finish phase of production, which takes them up to 260 pounds.

Christensen Family Farms prides itself on having a sixteen-year history of helping to keep farming viable for independent farmers in the Midwest. CFF works with more than ninety independent farm families in southern Minnesota and northern Iowa who supplement their farming operations by doing the grow-finish phase of production with the company. CFF provides the farm families with pigs, feed, training, medical products and services, record-keeping, and pig transportation. The farm families provide the facilities, land, and labor necessary to deliver high-quality hogs to market.

A superior technical service program is key to ensuring the production success of CFF's company-owned farms and its network of independent farm family producers. CFF service personnel experienced in all phases of

A CFF production service manager demonstrates a Ventium controller to an independent contract farmer. The controller is used for monitoring and adjusting temperature and ventilation settings in each of the finishing barns.

hog production visit sites on a regular basis to provide management assistance in the production of high-quality, low-cost pork.

A new state-of-the-art company-owned feed mill near Sleepy Eye provides rations for all phases of production. By purchasing 8 million bushels of corn and 5,500 tons of soy meal as feed ingredients each year from area crop farmers, CFF plays a significant role in strengthening the corn and soybean markets in the upper Midwest. Processed feed is delivered and pigs are transported throughout the countryside by a fleet of company-owned bright red-and-white vehicles—a familiar sight at facilitites owned by Christensen Family Farms and those owned by independent farm families. By handling its own transportation, CFF maximizes efficiency and sanitary conditions. Being able to control all aspects of production, including feed and transportation, enables the company to gain measurable advantages in cost and quality control.

Research and development play an important part in keeping the company at the forefront of quality and efficiency. CFF owns and operates two grow-finish facilities for measuring the effects of various feed rations on pigs. Research and development efforts also include studying the impact of

People with an interest in working with livestock production greatly benefit from strong businesses such as Christensen Family Farms.

feed configurations at the feed mill and semen combinations at Pork Storks.

Two other Christensen family-owned and -operated companies provide additional services to CFF, independent farm families, and other individuals and entities in hog production. Christensen Construction builds hog production facilities engineered by Lester Building Systems (a division of Butler Manufacturing Company). Christensen Construction, with annual revenues of $22 million, is the largest dealer of Lester buildings in the Midwest. Another Christensen company, CompuPig, provides computerized farm production record-keeping locally, regionally, and across the United States.

Christensen Family Farms is a major part of the $4 billion pork production industry in Minnesota, an industry with far-reaching benefits. People with an interest in working in livestock production, crop farmers, independent farm families, area merchants, landowners, construction contractors, and the meat packing industry all benefit from and are kept viable by the success of the company that began with two pregnant pigs.

Company president and founding brother Bob Christensen says, "Our success reflects the strong Midwest work ethic and the commitment of the many employees and farm families involved in our production operation. Our family remains at the heart of the organization, and we have assembled a knowledgeable, experienced, and dedicated team that helps us to continue to achieve our goal: To be the best in the high-quality, low-cost production of pork."

CFF company-owned trucks such as this one deliver feed throughout the countryside.

WASECA FOODS, L.P.

The corporate headquarters of Waseca Foods is located in Waseca, Minnesota.

In a state whose reputation is that of a breadbasket provider to the nation, Waseca Foods, L.P., stands out as a company that honors that tradition. Since 1979 Waseca Foods has enjoyed the enthusiastic support of its employees as it evolved into a highly successful member of the food industry, and became a premier supplier of industrial-food ingredients. Waseca Foods employees are proud of their company's success. In all of its operations, quality is mandatory and nothing less is expected—by any employee.

Waseca Foods is a contract manufacturer of specialty and custom food ingredients, including bakery blends, dairy solids, mold inhibitors, meat extenders, dough developers, cheese starter media, and flow agents for shredded cheese. These products eventually find their way to all parts of the country and beyond, in bakery products; cheese products; mixed snack foods; frozen desserts; breadings and batters; confectionery fillings and toppings; and an assortment of dietary formulations.

Among the processing capabilities at Waseca Foods are dry blending; liquid processing; and specialty services including coloring,

A technician monitors quality control of the newest automated packaging equipment at Waseca Foods.

agglomerating, plating, lecithinating, flavor enhancement, and thermal reaction. Facilities and equipment are designed to meet stringent USDA and Grade A Dairy quality standards. Kosher certification also is available.

The company has 60,000 square feet of manufacturing, warehousing, and office space at its seven-and-one-half acre Waseca, Minnesota, site. Within that space there are five separate production process areas and three warehouses.

Waseca Foods has a research and development facility on site to assist customers with the formulation of new products. All raw ingredients and finished products are analyzed in its quality-control laboratory, ensuring consistent product quality. An in-house logistics service directs domestic and international deliveries via truck, railroad, and ship. Additional value for customers is provided by a full-service procurement department that passes along the cost savings of Waseca Foods's centralized, high-volume purchasing.

Continuous effort to provide the best in quality and service has earned Waseca Foods a reputation as a trusted supplier of industrial food ingredients. The company believes customers deserve the highest level of service, and it provides the equipment, facilities, and knowledge necessary to take products from "concept to marketplace."

DAVISCO FOODS INTERNATIONAL, INC.

FAMILY-OWNED

DAVISCO FOODS

INTERNATIONAL, INC.,

OPERATES ITS

STATE-OF-THE-ART

DAIRY BUSINESS

FOLLOWING A

THREE-GENERATION

TRADITION OF HIGH

QUALITY, TECHNICAL

INNOVATION, AND

CUSTOMER

SATISFACTION

Most people don't think of the dairy industry as being high-tech. However, the whey protein products made by Davisco Foods International, Inc., not only are used in many foods, they also have many potential high-tech health-care applications.

Davisco Foods International is a $350 million, third generation family-owned milk processing and ingredients company that is a leader in whey protein research technology and production.

Whey fractionated protein, a by-product of Davisco's cheese-making operations, is a versatile ingredient used in such food products as infant formula, baked goods, sports drinks, and health foods.

With the introduction of ion-exchange technology developed by Davisco, the company is able to produce concentrated whey protein that is high in protein and nutritional value. The technology developed by Davisco was the first ever used in the dairy industry for large-scale whey protein production. Today Davisco produces more than ten million pounds of whey protein annually.

The Le Sueur Cheese Company and the Jerome Cheese Company are owned and operated by parent company Davisco Foods International. Davisco produces more than 500,000 pounds of cheese daily, and is one of the largest suppliers of cheese to Kraft Foods. Substantial amounts of Davisco's whey ingredient are sold for export, with approximately 60 percent going to Mexico and the Far East.

Davisco produces millions of pounds of cheese each year, yielding a whey protein stream high in both volume and consistency. The ability to produce a consistent whey stream differentiates Davisco from cheese makers whose cheeses yield varying whey characteristics.

The demand for innovative whey protein components keeps increasing as Davisco works with its customers to develop new

Davisco corporate officers (from left): Mark Davis, Jon Davis, Stanley Davis (Davisco founder), Mitch Davis, and Martin Davis.

applications. Customers seek Davisco to develop their new food products because of the company's functional, unique, and tailored ingredients. Davisco's experienced cheese makers and state-of-the-art computerized equipment create products of outstanding consistency.

"We respond to customers' needs and take pride in making their product goals a reality," says Davisco president, Mark Davis. "Our mission is simple—top performance, top quality, and emphatically satisfied customers. We believe strongly in maintaining a close working relationship with our customers to achieve our mutual goals."

Davisco produces several specialized whey products. *Versa*PRO is used for nutritional fortification, emulsification, and as a buttermilk replacement in many products, including meat and sausage, processed cheese, baked goods, and salad dressing. *Bi*PRO is a unique, natural, pure dairy whey protein isolate composed of beta-lactoglobulin and alpha-lactalbumin. It is used for beverages, meat, frozen desserts, ice cream, sports supplements, and salad dressings. *Bi*PRO also is used for therapeutic nutritional supplements and to produce lactose-free reduced calorie mixes. *Hi*PRO is an all-natural protein made from sweet

Davisco's products are made with pure whey protein derived from fresh milk.

dairy whey. It offers a well-balanced essential amino acid profile, meeting the high nutritional standards required for infant formulas and hospital foods. It also is used in baked goods, processed meats, and dairy products.

Davisco's research staff includes some of the top whey protein scientists in the world. Davisco has developed and patented twenty new ingredients. The latest high-tech applications for its products are in health care. Doctors and researchers worldwide are conducting studies to use Davisco's whey products in areas that range from boosting the immune systems of cancer and AIDs patients to promoting healthy skin. Several clinical trials for such products are in progress.

Founded in 1943 by Stanley Davis, Davisco Foods International is a privately held business with an aggressive, entrepreneurial vision. The spirit of entrepreneurship is evident in the aggressive management style of the Davis family, who constantly seek ways to improve the business operation and its products. Much of Davisco's tremendous growth during the 1990s can be attributed to an increase in Davisco's cheese business and the company's transition from processing milk to making ingredients. In addition to the stewardship of Davisco, Marty Davis, one of the president's sons, plays an active role on the National Dairy Council, making sure the industry's voice is heard in Washington, D.C. Brothers Mitch and Jon both participate as active members of the International Dairy Federation Association, and fourth son, Matt, provides his expertise industrywide in quality control activities. Like the close-knit family members who operate the business, Davisco's many employees and managers are a major part of its success.

There are five separate operations under the Davisco Foods International umbrella, including Le Sueur Cheese Company, Jerome Cheese Company, Le Sueur Food Ingredient Company, Nicollet Food Ingredient Company, and Lake Norden Food Ingredient Company. The facilities for these operations, located in Minnesota, Idaho, and South Dakota, have had a positive impact on local independent dairy farming.

Food Engineering magazine selected Jerome Cheese (based in Jerome, Idaho) as its 1994 "New Plant Of The Year" based

Davisco's cheeses are sought after by the world's leading cheese processors.

on its contribution to corporate strategy, manufacturing flexibility, applications of new technology, and degree of automation. The expansion of this whey protein isolation fractionation plant, the most technologically advanced whey-isolation factory in the world, was a critical step in making Davisco the world's largest producer of whey protein fractions.

Davisco achieves unsurpassed quality through rigorous internal standards and attention to detail. The carefully constructed systems in each of its five dairy processing plants ensure shipment of only the highest quality products. Davisco work teams achieve quality every step of the way; from the placement of the sales order through production, testing, storage, and shipping.

"Our strong commitment to service is built on a belief in excellence," says Mark Davis. "We maintain the highest quality standards. Our philosophy is that every customer is a preferred customer. Our family and employees are dedicated in working together to achieve the goals of Davisco."

Davisco has five manufacturing facilities, three in Minnesota, one in South Dakota, and one in Idaho.

WATKINS INCORPORATED

The mission of Watkins Incorporated is "to enhance lives one person at a time." Watkins is a network marketing company that offers gourmet food, health and nutrition products, personal care, and home care items, all geared toward healthier living. Watkins currently markets products in the United States, Canada, Puerto Rico, and New Zealand. The Winona, Minnesota, company was founded in 1868 by a young man named J. R. Watkins.

When J. R. Watkins sold his first bottle of liniment to a neighbor in rural Minnesota and then enlisted others to do the same, he founded "network marketing." Today Watkins Incorporated remains a leader in the network marketing industry.

The first Watkins product, called "Red Liniment," was a natural pain reliever, made with capsicum from the red pepper plant and camphor from the camphor tree, an Asian

Watkins Independent Associates Jim and Marge Grande, shown here with their son, Nathan, are a prime example of a successful Watkins family. The Grandes have been featured in many magazines, including a cover story in Success magazine.

The Watkins company has been enhancing the lives of families since 1868, when "the Watkins Man" marketed Watkins Red Liniment and other health and wellness products in a horse-drawn wagon. Today there are more than 80,000 men and women who are Watkins independent marketing associates and more than 350 consumer products.

evergreen. J. R. Watkins mixed the ingredients in his own laboratory. The firm still markets Red Liniment today. By the time of his death, in 1911, J. R. Watkins had more than 2,500 independent associates marketing Watkins products. Today there are more than 80,000 Watkins independent marketing associates.

The long, rich heritage of the Watkins company is built on quality products, unrivaled customer service, and recognition by its peers as an innovative leader. It was J. R. Watkins who originated the idea of putting a customer satisfaction "trial mark" on his bottles, creating the first money-back guarantee in history. His reputation for honest dealings and exceptional products grew with his business. The Watkins company today is one of the largest network marketing firms in North America. It is infused throughout with the same entrepreneurial spirit and drive as that of young J. R. Watkins.

Watkins was a family business when it was established in 1868, and it remains so today under the comprehensive and astute guidance of the Irwin Jacobs family. In 1978 Watkins was purchased by

Jacobs, who rose from modest beginnings to the Forbes 400 list of wealthiest Americans. The Irwin Jacobs family is dedicated to helping other entrepreneurs achieve success through their independent Watkins home-based businesses.

Son Mark Jacobs is now president of the company. Father and son work together toward the Watkins vision for the future that Jacobs first conceived when he purchased the firm. Mark Jacobs has been directing his efforts toward enhancing lives by using today's technology to keep the Watkins business opportunity and products on the cutting edge.

"It is our goal to continually increase our independent marketing associate base. This is the way we move forward in our commitment 'to enhance lives one person at a time,'" Mark Jacobs says.

Mark Jacobs is guiding this work within his charter of preparing Watkins for doing business in its third century. Since Jacobs joined Watkins, the company has doubled its independent marketing associate base to its present 80,000. He has redefined the company's role as a leader in network marketing by continuing to focus on products that promote healthier living and an opportunity that allows independent marketing associates to reach their goals. He also is in charge of continuing the company's international expansion, past New Zealand to Australia and beyond.

Home-based businesses are fast becoming a bedrock of security for North American workers—and more people are making Watkins their home-based business of choice. Watkins has worked purposefully to make it easy for its independent marketing associates to start their businesses and begin making a solid income right away. Start-up cost is minimal, and independent marketing associates are not required to make minimum purchases, keep inventories, or go to meetings. The company offers incentives such as exotic travel and cash bonuses. It seeks ways to simplify independent marketing associates' work by reducing mailing

This Tiffany window graces the entryway of the Watkins Incorporated offices, depicting Winona's Sugar Loaf Mountain and the area around Lake Winona.

Watkins Incorporated is headquartered in a beautiful office building in Winona. Designed by the noted Prairie School architect George Washington Maher, and completed in 1911, the building features highly treasured Tiffany glass, Italian tile mosaics with 24-karat-gold inlay, and fine marble under its curved roof and splendid dome.

and accounting tasks, so that more time can be focused on word-of-mouth marketing.

Watkins was named one of the top-five home-based businesses for women by *Executive Female* magazine. The magazine cited the business's low start-up costs, flexible hours, and good potential for profit.

Watkins has returned to its conceptual roots of wellness, aligning its marketing with the popular themes of healthy living and environmental protection. Its catalog promotes "healthier living since 1868" on its cover and features products made from plants, spices, and herbs that are environmentally friendly. These products are designed to help people feel better, live longer, and achieve an overall healthier lifestyle.

"We promote commonsense health and wellness," Mark Jacobs says. "There is no quick pill that's going to put you on the road to health and wellness. You have to look at everything that goes into your body and everything in your environment."

SUNRICH, INC.

A PRODUCER

OF NATURAL,

ORGANICALLY GROWN

AND PROCESSED

INGREDIENTS

AND FOODS,

SUNRICH, INC.,

IS DEVOTED TO

INNOVATION, AND

TO FOSTERING

COOPERATION

BETWEEN PRODUCERS

AND PROCESSORS

SunRich, Inc., is located in south central Minnesota, at the heart of some of the world's finest farm country. The company contracts with farmers to grow a variety of specialty crops, and contracts with food processors to provide novel raw ingredients to the domestic and international food industries.

SunRich is currently one of the largest exporters of food-quality specialty grains in the United States. This is due in part to the fact that its ongoing focus is to provide "identity-preserved" (known-heritage) soybeans, which are desired by many of the world's food processors.

SunRich is constantly researching new products, revising processes, and exploring new plant genetics to meet the changing needs of a dynamic food industry. The company works closely with several universities to develop grains that will function more efficiently in various food applications. The company is continually developing unique varieties of soybeans and corn-based grains. SunRich prides itself on the utilization of the most recent technologies in grain development to bring high-quality grain products to the food markets in a timely fashion.

Emphasizing research on new and innovative grain-processing techniques and products, SunRich has developed a wide array of natural and organic food ingredients. The company produces a variety of soy-based food ingredients such as soy milk, tofu powder, and soy beverage systems, all naturally processed without the use of chemical extractions.

SunRich has also developed a process for creating sweeteners from grains such as corn and oats. In this natural process, the sweeteners have lost none of the

Many of today's popular food products are made from whole soybeans, including (left to right, from bottom): soynuts, tofu, miso, tempeh, deep-fried tofu pouches, soy milk, and full-fat flour.

nutritional components (soluble fibers, vitamins, and minerals) of the virgin grain.

SunRich offers organically processed native corn starch, and also an organic pregelatinized corn starch (a precooked starch used in the food-processing industry). SunRich also processes various vegetables and legumes to make them "instantized," which means they can be returned to their natural state simply by adding water. Sweet Beans® is the registered trademark used for SunRich's delicious green vegetable soybeans, also referred to as peeled green soybeans, or Edamame. Sweet Beans are sold by themselves and as part of frozen entrees.

SunRich works closely with the growers and food processors. This allows SunRich control over the variety of grains planted, farming practices used in growing the grains, and procedures used to process the final product. This close involvement throughout the entire process facilitates the staff in the development of new and innovative food ingredients. This mutually beneficial business relationship also helps in achieving profitable results. SunRich's driving philosophy is to serve as the direct link between the growers, processors, and food manufacturers, and to supply high-quality products with integrity and reliability.

SunRich, Inc., based in Hope, Minnesota, is a full-service supplier of high-quality soy products.

SIGCO SUN PRODUCTS, INC.

SIGCO Sun Products, Inc., headquartered on Minnesota's west central border in Breckenridge, is a worldwide supplier of confection sunflower products and nut alternatives. SIGCO was founded in 1958 and is a family-owned company. SIGCO Sun Products, Inc., is dedicated to bringing sunflower and other great tasting healthy nut alternatives to the food industry.

More than four decades ago SIGCO's founder, sunflower pioneer Bob Schuler, began contracting with Minnesota farmers to develop and grow sunflowers for market. SIGCO's position has been one of innovation and industry leadership ever since.

SIGCO conducts ongoing research on sunflower hybrids to meet the changing needs of its customers. Reflecting the entrepreneurial spirit in which its founder successfully developed and introduced alternative food products, the company creates innovative alternates to current products. Popular choices today include reduced-fat nut alternatives such as Toasted Corn™ and Pea Nutz®.

In 1958 Bob Schuler began a venture into sunflower seeds with germ plasm from Canada and the University of Minnesota, in response to the agriculture industry's need to diversify.

SIGCO's research scientists pioneered a number of food ingredients. SIGCO was one of the first companies to produce high-oleic sunflower kernels, which have a long shelf life. This process

"THE ALTERNATIVE
NUTHOUSE"
PRODUCT LINE

SUNFLOWER

- Traditional
- SL® (Long Shelf Life)
  SIGCO SL® sunflowers have significantly higher oleic levels that increase shelf life.
- Large Inshell
- Kernel
  —Natural
  —Roasted or Flavored
- Chopped
- Meal

LOW-FAT NUT
ALTERNATIVES

- Toasted Corn™
- Pea Nutz®
- Trail Mix

opened up a whole new area for the use of the kernels in food products. The shelf life of a product with high-oleic kernels is up to five times longer than that of products made with traditional kernels.

SIGCO monitors and controls all production of products from planting the seeds in the ground to supplying finished products to its customers. SIGCO's quality assurance manager and technical sales team ensure products that set industry standards worldwide. SIGCO's professionals—in food technology, marketing, and sales—understand the dynamics of the competitive food industry, and stand ready to steadfastly support their customers.

SIGCO currently supplies products to more than thirty countries worldwide. Its plants are strategically located to better serve its customers. There are four processing plants, three in the United States, in Breckenridge, Minnesota; Wahpeton, North Dakota; and Goodland, Kansas; and one in Europe, in Tata, Hungary.

SIGCO processes sunflowers at plants in the United States and Hungary, and supplies its products to more than thirty countries.

SIGCO SUN PRODUCTS Inc

WIRED FOR THE NEXT CENTURY

CHAPTER ELEVEN

IN THE YEARS SURROUNDING WORLD WAR II, MINNESOTA HAD A REPUTA-
TION AS A QUIET, MOSTLY AGRICULTURAL STATE, WITH A GROWING PRESENCE
OF MANUFACTURING AND HEALTH CARE AND A COUPLE OF RESIDENT GIANTS —
PAUL BUNYAN, THE LEGENDARY LUMBERMAN PURPORTED TO BE RESPONSI-
BLE FOR MUCH OF THE STATE'S NORTHERN GEOGRAPHY, AND THE JOLLY
GREEN GIANT, WHO WAS BUSY RAISING VEGETABLES IN THE SOUTH. BUT IN

a former troop-glider manufacturing site in the Twin Cities, a young engineer named William Norris and his fledgling company, Engineering Research Associates (ERA), were at work creating another giant, one that would forever change the world. That giant was the mainframe computer.

While Minnesota may seem an unlikely site for the birthplace of the computer age, given the dominance of California in that field today, it was in fact a key, if not premier, hub of the development of digital technology from the 1940s through the 1970s. Along with ERA, Minnesota companies Control Data and Cray Research combined to control nearly one-quarter of the nation's newly emerging computer industry.

Norris began Control Data after splitting from ERA in 1957. The company quickly established itself as the standard to which all others were compared, since its computers were among the fastest and most high-powered on the market for some twenty-five years. Many people in the industry attribute the successful growth of Control Data and the expansion of the computer industry in general to a brilliant young engineer and visionary named Seymour Cray, who left the company in 1972 to launch his own company, Cray Research. Cray's supercomputers were responsible for breaking the limitation barriers of computing capability, paving the way into a new era. His innovations are behind such now-routine tasks as weather forecasting and automotive safety testing.

Today, ERA is now Unisys, after first being bought by Remington Rand, which later became Sperry Univac. In 1986, Sperry Univac and Burroughs Corporation underwent the then-largest

Opposite: Decades before the mouse morphed from animal to indispensable computer tool, the computer industry was getting off to a thrilling start in Minnesota, where some of the most important people in the early development of digital technology were based. © Index Stock Photography. Above: Students discover what a valuable research tool the computer has become, with the instant access to reference materials, automated libraries, and the Internet it provides. © Winnebago Software Company

ACCORDING TO A RECENT RANKING BY YAHOO, THE TWIN CITIES ARE THE SIXTH MOST WIRED METROPOLITAN AREA IN THE COUNTRY, RANKING AHEAD OF NEW YORK, BOSTON, CHICAGO, DALLAS, AND DENVER. MINNEAPOLIS AND ST. PAUL HAVE THE MOST COMPUTERS PER PERSON OF ANYWHERE IN THE COUNTRY.

merger in the history of the computer industry and Unisys was formed. Currently, the firm is among the top ten high-technology firms in the state, employing more than 3,300 Minnesotans among its 35,000 employees worldwide. Responsible for four decades' worth of major contributions in the engineering and delivery of large-scale computing systems, Unisys has shifted its focus heading into the next century and is now on the cutting edge once again, this time in the area of information management.

Control Data also remains in the top ten of Minnesota high-tech companies, after splitting into two companies in 1992. Control Data Systems is a global participant in software and services. Its Rialto line of directory-enabled products and services aids large government and business institutions in the

Minnesota-born Hutchinson Technology, now with locations worldwide, is known for its suspension assemblies, which are used to position read/write heads accurately above the flying disks in rigid disk drives. © Hutchinson Technology

creation of client-server enterprise networks for a variety of applications. Its spin-off, Ceridian Corporation, an information-services company, has surpassed its parent in terms of revenue, number of employees, and ranking among Minnesota's high-tech companies.

Cray underwent a merger with Silicon Graphics in 1996 to form the world's premier scientific and technical computing company. The new company is the world's only one-stop computer shop for complete solutions, which encompass high-powered visualization workstations, the most advanced software computing applications, and the new generation of supercomputers.

As dominant as these three companies have been in the history of computers, they are by no means the only high-tech computer companies in Minnesota. IBM is the largest computer enterprise in the state, with more than six thousand employees, most of whom are employed at the facility in Rochester, home of IBM's AS/400, the

most popular multiuse computer in the world. A recipient of the prestigious Malcolm Baldridge National Quality Award, IBM Rochester also develops small-format, high-capacity hard drives and manufactures aluminum disk substrates. The company's first network computer, the IBM Network Station, was also created and developed in the Rochester laboratory.

Though the Silicon Valley area severely eclipsed Minnesota to dominate the computer industry after development of the personal computer in the 1980s, the state is showing definite signs of reemerging to its former status. After its division in 1992, Control Data tripled its value within five years. Cray Research, still based in the Twin Cities suburb of Eagan after its merger with Silicon Graphics, is developing a "high-performance computing architecture" known as scalable, shared-memory multiprocessing, or S2MP, which is expected to become nothing short of the industrial standard well into the next century.

The resurgence is not just limited to the metropolitan area or the large companies. Small towns and small companies alike are also contributing to the rebirth. Caledonia, population 2,800, in the southeastern corner of the state, is home to Winnebago Software Company,

This 1954 "Univac," or universal automatic computer, heralded the dawn of a new high-tech era. In 1960, Sperry Rand Corp. in St. Paul unveiled the Univac 1107, which processed information much faster than previous versions. © UPI/Corbis-Bettmann

the pioneer of the development of library automation software. Local school librarian Pam Griffith and her husband, Jeb, created a program for Pam's use when she lost her library assistant because of budget cuts. When word of Pam's "new assistant" spread, other librarians began requesting the program. Today, school, public, academic, and special libraries on all seven continents use the software and services.

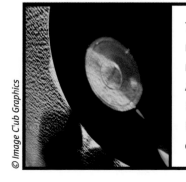

© Image Club Graphics

THE MINNESOTA SOFTWARE INDUSTRY INCLUDES 1,600 FIRMS, WITH ANNUAL GROWTH AT THE RATE OF 73 PERCENT. IN 1997, SOFTWARE WAS THE NO. 1 MAGNET FOR VENTURE-CAPITAL FUNDING IN THE STATE.

Above: A man magnifies a circuit board while performing his detail-oriented work, typical of the industry. © Chris Salvo/FPG International. Below: The colorful circuitry allows the exchange of vast amounts of data. © Telegraph Colour Library/FPG International

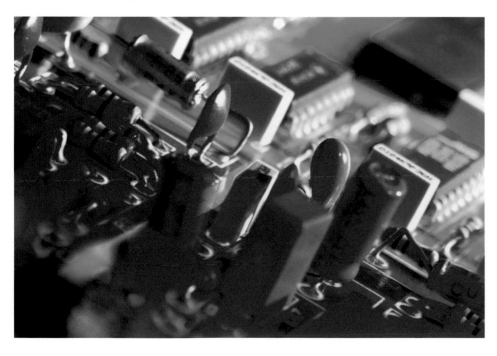

Further west, Mankato is the home of Clear With Computers (CWC), the market leader in interactive-selling software. With its strong international focus, the sales forces in more than forty global blue-chip companies consider CWC to be a crucial element in maintaining their competitive edge.

To the north is the city of Hutchinson, headquarters of Hutchinson Technology. The company was started by two enterprising young college graduates in the only place they could afford, a vacant chicken coop. Seven thousand employees and numerous worldwide locations later, Hutchinson is recognized as the world's leading supplier of suspension assemblies, which are used in a variety of disk drives.

DURING WORLD WAR II, ENGINEER WILLIAM NORRIS AND A TEAM OF ALLIED SCIENTISTS AND ENGINEERS WORKED TOGETHER TO CRACK THE CODE USED BY GERMAN U-BOATS. TO DO IT, THEY BUILT A MATHEMATICAL MACHINE THAT COULD PERFORM COMPUTATIONS AT A SPEED FAR FASTER THAN COULD HUMANS. AFTER THE WAR, NORRIS SAW THE VALUE IN BUILDING A SIMILAR MACHINE FOR USE IN BUSINESS. HIS SEARCH FOR AN INVESTOR

AND A MANUFACTURING SITE BROUGHT HIM TO MINNESOTA, WHERE THE UNIVERSITY OF MINNESOTA SUPPLIED EXCELLENTLY TRAINED ENGINEERS AND SCIENTISTS, WHO PUSHED THE ENVELOPE ON COMPUTER TECHNOLOGY.

Minnesota boasts many other technological leaders, among them National Computer Systems, the nation's largest single provider of a variety of software and services used in kindergarten through twelfth-grade education and the world's largest commercial provider of testing and assessment services. Digi International, six times named to *Forbes*'s "200 Best Small Companies in the U.S." list, provides both the hardware and software for seamless connectivity for mulituser, remote access, and LAN markets, and three-year-old UbiQ is getting serious recognition for its advancements in bringing smart-card (such as phone or grocery-store "club" cards) technology to the United States. Ontrack, in Eden Prairie, leads the international effort to protect and recover data and software, and Information Advantage is recognized throughout the industry as the innovator of the field of on-line analytical processing (OLAP) software applications and toolset. Another homegrown company, SSESCO, is the best in the world at providing scientists and engineers with visualization and analysis technological tools for use in the environmental industry.

Machines haven't fully taken over, yet. These workers are needed to monitor the process control in their computer lab. © Tom Raymond/Tony Stone Images

The burgeoning computer industry is taking a proactive stand on finding workers for itself. The University of Minnesota has created one of the country's most highly regarded "Techno MBA" programs, and the Minnesota High Technology Council recently rolled out an "Upgrade to Minnesota" recruitment campaign in the Silicon Valley in an attempt to lure experienced high-tech workers to the state.

As the technological age enters the next millennium, Minnesota may once again find itself poised on the cutting edge. Driven by the creation of the Internet, demand now calls for personal computers to have the ability to be interconnected, to network, and to function like their predecessor, the mainframe. Still a resource to Minnesota are the engineers and technicians who pioneered the mainframe industry, few of whom exited the state in the midst of widespread job loss associated with the personal-computer revolution of the 1980s. Many experts feel these former leaders are just the visionaries needed to wire the next century. After all, they've already proved they know the way.

These rows of circuit boards require highly skilled technicians to keep them running properly. © Jeff Kaufman/FPG International

Above: The CD-ROM, which stands for compact disc read-only memory, *is now a commonplace source of information and entertainment.* © Index Stock Photography. *Below left: Workers at Ontrack Data International in Eden Prairie are part of a software and data-retrieval company with more than $35 million in annual revenues.* © Ontrack. *Below right: Students search for library materials with software developed by Winnebago Software Company, which is based in Caledonia, Minnesota.* © Winnebago Software Company

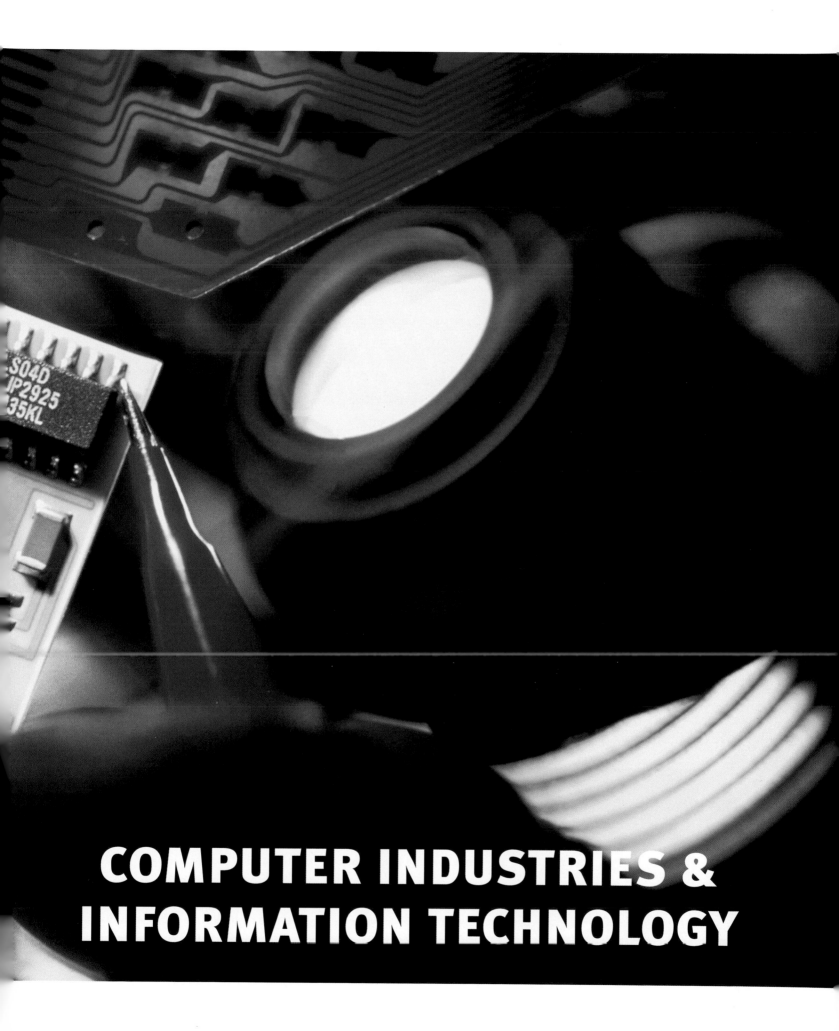

COMPUTER INDUSTRIES & INFORMATION TECHNOLOGY

COLORSPAN CORPORATION, A VIRTUALFUND.COM ENTERPRISE

The well-known and well-respected firm of ColorSpan Corporation has earned its reputation as an innovative company among graphic arts, photography, and publishing professionals worldwide, especially for such printing applications as signage, posters, banners, murals, and the reproduction of art and photography. ColorSpan is a subsidiary of VirtualFund.com, Inc. (formerly LaserMaster Technologies, Inc.) and is part of its Digital Graphics Business Unit.

The company, which is based in Eden Prairie, Minnesota, was founded as LaserMaster Corporation in 1985 as a software business, which focused on using PC-card hardware to enhance the performance of laser printers for computer-aided design (CAD) output. Through innovations such as its patented "TurboRes" resolution-enhancement software, and creative marketing, the company launched the "plain-paper typesetting" market with laser printers that could produce output from 800 dots per inch (dpi), to 1,200 dpi, and then to 1,800 dpi, bringing typesetting quality to the desktop.

Later, another development, ThermalRes, enabled publishers and print shops to do prepress jobs in-house without the usual hazardous chemicals. PressMate-FS Personal FilmSetter uses a heat-activated film to produce both positive and negative films. These films are functionally equivalent to film from chemical-based imagesetters and are used to produce plates for offset printing machines.

ColorSpan's second-generation, thirty-six-inch-wide, drum-based wide-format inkjet printers provide fast, professional high-quality eight-color printing of fine art and digital art.

In 1993 the company introduced its first wide-format, thermal inkjet printer, Display-Maker, to a chorus of "Wow!'s." At the time no market existed for reasonably priced "wide-format color" and at first people were not sure how to put this new technology to use. As a result, the company launched a marketing campaign portraying Big Color solutions that the new printers made possible. Among their many uses, ColorSpan's Big Color digital printers produce high-quality, wide-format output for:

- graphic design and advertising
- architecture and engineering plans
- art originals and fine art reproductions
- exhibition graphics
- courtroom and litigation graphics
- photography and mapping
- travel and entertainment signage
- restaurant displays
- backlighted signs
- outdoor signs

Big Color printers—at a cost lower than standard electrostatic plotters or traditional photographic processes—have revolutionized the way customers are able to create large-scale graphics. Today that market alone is expected to grow to $18 billion by the year 2000.

Today ColorSpan's core business is designing and manufacturing innovative wide-format color printing products and related aftermarket products

Eight pigmented ink colors combine with FineArt archival paper and Artist matte paper for high-quality art originals and reproductions (up to thirty-six-inches wide).

A new family of DisplayMaker HiRes 8-Color series includes forty-two-inch-, fifty-two-inch-, and sixty-two-inch-wide DisplayMaker printers. All the printers use ColorSpan multidensity inks, producing continuous-tone printing with an apparent image resolution of 1,200 dots per inch. The DisplayMaker HiRes 8-Color series includes several new tools, such as AutoJet, AutoSet, AutoInk, and AutoTune, designed to allow users to maintain consistent image quality while producing images in an unattended environment.

and services. Its goal is to become a principal supplier to both resellers and original-equipment manufacturers. To reflect this direction, the company changed its name in 1997 from LaserMaster Corporation, which focused on laser technology, to ColorSpan Corporation, which emphasizes color inkjet printers and supplies. The Internet also plays a large part in achieving these goals. Through Web sites such as Media-By-Air and Supplies-By-Air, other enterprises of VirtualFund.com, Inc., wide-format media is available as part of the company's electronic commerce initiatives.

Since 1994 the company has designed and manufactured several proprietary print engines. They include PressMate-FS Personal FilmSetter for chemical-free film separations; the DisplayMaker Express industrialized digital color printer for images up to fifty-four-inches wide; the DesignWinder and Giclée PrintMakerFA; and the DisplayMaker HiRes 8-Color series.

ColorSpan's DisplayMaker HiRes 8-Color series is available in twelve models, including the DisplayMaker 6000, the first color inkjet printer to produce eight-color images up to sixty-two-inches wide. Models vary by size of output, raster image processor (RIP) support, and other features designed for the first-time user or high-production service bureaus. Also available are forty-two-inch and fifty-two-inch models that offer a variety of features, including a "Cosmic Automation Eye," which performs many functions automatically, including printer calibration. All of these models include eight print heads for 1,200-dpi printing. Each of ColorSpan's Big Color printers can be driven by one of ColorSpan's print servers or a RIP from third-party manufacturers. Some models of the DisplayMaker HiRes 8-Color series have an embedded RIP, which makes the printers truly plug-and-play. The RIPStation, which is preconfigured for speed and reliability, will run a single DisplayMaker or DesignWinder. The ColorMark Pro print server simplifies networking and provides consistent color to many different output devices.

Publishing technology changes continually and rapidly, and the technology of even a decade ago was quite different than that of today. Still, customers have many of the same needs, regardless of the changes that occur in printing. Quality, speed, price, and improved productivity are four prevailing customer needs that ColorSpan regularly meets.

Other ColorSpan innovations are broadening the demand for its products and creating new standards by which products are measured. The patented Big Ink Delivery System, the first such system on the market, increases ink capacity tenfold. Further advances, such as improving the color gamut by adding two light and medium cyan and magenta ink cartridges to produce stunningly vibrant hues and more subtle gradations, are typical of the way ColorSpan intends to keep meeting future challenges and raising the standards for wide-format inkjet printing. Additional information about ColorSpan and its products is available at its Web site: www.colorspan.com.

ColorSpan is one of several enterprises of VirtualFund.com, Inc. For more than thirteen years, the professionals of Virtual-Fund.com have mastered the challenges of running a fast-paced technology-driven organization. Today's businesses also include:

Plain-paper typesetters, chemical-free FilmSetters, and supplies (Web site: www.lasermaster.com);

Supplies for wide-format inkjet printers (Web site: www.suppliesbyair.com);

Global information technology (IT) consulting (Web site: www.edscorp.com);

Software development for electronic commerce (Web site: www.e-comtools.com).

ANALYSTS INTERNATIONAL CORPORATION

A PIONEERING

CONSULTING FIRM,

ANALYSTS

INTERNATIONAL

CORPORATION

PROVIDES SYSTEMS

ANALYSIS, DESIGN,

PROGRAMMING, AND

MAINTENANCE—

GUIDING CLIENTS

SAFELY INTO

THE YEAR 2000

AND BEYOND

High technology is one of the nation's fastest growing economic sectors, and among high-tech companies some of the leaders in growth are in the area of Information Technology (IT) services. One of the country's largest IT consulting firms is located in the Twin Cities. With its worldwide headquarters in Edina, Analysts International Corporation (AiC) works with some of the biggest names in business today.

Frederick W. Lang, who guides AiC as its chief executive officer, founded the company in 1966 and soon was joined by Victor C. Benda, who serves as AiC's president. In the 1950s Lang made a name for himself by winning major downhill and slalom skiing championships, and his tolerance for risk on the slopes would later prove an asset in the business world. Following a successful term with the computer giant UNIVAC developing the first computerized air traffic control system, Lang launched AiC. It was a time when few companies were focusing on computer technology.

The worldwide headquarters of Analysts International Corporation is located in Edina.

Shown are Analysts International Corporation's principals: Victor C. Benda (left), president and Chief Operating Officer; and Frederick W. Lang (right), chairman and Chief Executive Officer.

As the company's name implies, AiC was started with the idea that, rather than making or reselling computer hardware and software products, it would provide the service of analyzing its customers' needs for computer technology. In the relatively new computer technology frontier of the 1960s, the notion that other businesses would require such consulting services was unique and extremely astute. Now such services are indispensable in the IT arena.

Along with consulting, AiC offered customers three basic midwestern values: excellence, integrity, and innovation. These principles were important touchstones in the way that AiC conducted business, and they still are essential ingredients in AiC's offerings to its customers.

Today AiC is one of the leading information technology consulting firms, with offices in more than forty locations in the United States, Canada, and the United Kingdom. AiC annual revenues exceed the half-billion dollar mark, and the company is growing at a rate of 20 percent to 25 percent per year. It currently employs 5,000 people. *Business Week* and *Forbes* magazines have selected AiC for inclusion in their annual lists of

"100 Best Small Companies" and "200 Best Small Companies." Robert W. Baird & Company Inc., a NYSE brokerage firm, calls AiC "a favorite of ours in the software services industry, in part because of its tremendous track record."

AiC provides its clients with a wide range of IT services, including project management, Year 2000 software compliance, systems analysis and design, programming, and software maintenance and training. The

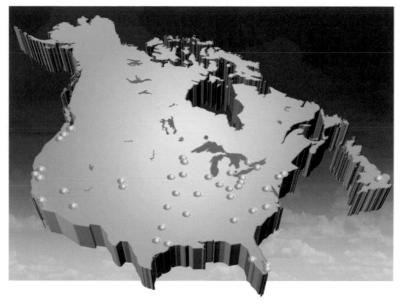

AiC has more than forty locations in the United States; Cambridge, England; and Toronto, Ontario.

excellence, integrity, and innovation remain constant. The heart of AiC's business strategy remains its commitment to total customer satisfaction.

AiC's assets are its people, and, given the demand for IT professionals, the company is perpetually in a recruitment mode, looking for consultants to meet the needs of its growing

company's customers encompass Fortune 100 firms, government agencies, and small entrepreneurial start-ups. AiC's rapid growth is due to the solid relationships formed with its customers; 90 percent of the company's business comes from existing clients, which include IBM, American Express, Boeing, 3M, and US West. While technology and software change, AiC's fundamental principles of

client base. Because of AiC's focus on helping its clients solve IT problems, the company favors consultants with diverse backgrounds such as finance or engineering. From the start, AiC has hired the best consultants available in the marketplace, and has established a reputation based on excellence. The company's credo of "hire the best people, establish a reputation for quality work, and instill everyone with an urgency for growth," has helped define AiC's character.

As the Year 2000 draws closer, AiC is experiencing new opportunities with businesses preparing their computer systems for the millennium date change. Without exception, businesses must address the Year 2000 issue to ensure that their systems continue working properly. More than 10 percent of AiC's current business comes from Year 2000 assessment, software program remediation, or the replacement of existing software. AiC estimates that Year 2000–related work will actually continue well into 2005 and beyond.

The arrival of the new millennium has taken on additional significance for AiC; soon after the year 2000, AiC will achieve its first billion dollar year in revenues. As a publicly traded company (NASDAQ: ANLY), that is an important milestone and a strong signal to both the financial markets and AiC's customers.

Changes in technology will take AiC in new directions, but the company's fundamentals will always remain the same— "provide excellence, integrity, and innovation." These principles are at the heart of this dynamic Minnesota company.

Analysts International Corporation identifies business-critical issues for its clients and helps them utilize information technology to its fullest extent.

COMPUTER NETWORK TECHNOLOGY

Computer Network Technology (CNT) is a leading provider of high-performance networking solutions for Web-to-host integration, high-speed data access, and Storage Area Networks. The company's products and services are used by organizations around the world to build and run large, business-critical networks. These products allow mainframes and open systems to share information.

CNT was founded in 1983 and became a public corporation in November 1985. It is listed on the Nasdaq National Market under the symbol CMNT.

CNT redesigns network infrastructures and reengineers Web-to-host applications for mid- to large-size organizations, in industries such as insurance, financial services, manufacturing, government, health care, utilities, and telecommunications. CNT products and solutions support many of the world's largest data centers, such as those at NationsBank, General Electric, Boeing, the U.S. Department of Defense, U.S. Bancorp, and Reliance Electric. More than half of the Fortune 100 companies are CNT customers. The company employs more than 600 people around the world.

CNT operates at the nexus of a network, connecting old with new, and local with distant, across mainframes, the Internet, and open systems, all with high performance, security, and integrity. With CNT solutions, customers gain

CNT offers world-class customer support, which maximizes the value of the customer's network.

greater connectivity and data access; increased value from stored data; Web browser access to mainframe resources; and a communication infrastructure between mainframes and open systems.

CNT has evolved along with enterprise networks. In the mid-1980s, the company's focus was on channel extension, enabling customers to place data centers and users where it made business sense, instead of being limited to locations dictated by technology. Financial services companies in New York City used CNT Channelink systems and high-speed links to move back-office operations to the suburbs, while keeping Manhattan users connected at native performance levels. In addition, data centers were proliferating, and Channelink systems were used to connect them.

In the late 1980s and early 1990s, this trend was reversed as many large companies sought to reduce costs by consolidating data centers. Channelink network processors played a key role in that pursuit as well, allowing companies to eliminate hosts while keeping peripherals where

Engineers plan future products by keeping up with industry innovations and directions, along with new technology.

they were needed. CNT today provides interfaces to more than 150 devices, connectors, and LAN/WAN protocols.

CNT's newest strategic thrust relies on its strengths in enabling Storage Area Networks (SAN). Corporate computing today is a complex mix of servers, protocols, storage devices, channels, and networks. And as more and more vital corporate information resides outside the data center, companies want assurance that their data is safe and available to all who need it. A SAN makes that possible by liberating storage devices from attachment to particular servers. Instead, storage capacity can be available directly over the SAN, shared by different servers, without impacting system performance. Companies can thus increase the protection of their information and its accessibility while reducing the costs of storage resources and storage management.

The CNT FileSpeed solution leverages CNT's expertise in channel networking by providing very high-speed data movement between mainframes and open systems, enhancing SAN performance. The new UltraNet family of networking products offers the best price/performance in the industry for applications such as archiving, backup and recovery, remote vaulting, data migration, disk mirroring, and data sharing.

Companies today are interested in creating a strong Web-to-host link to broaden into areas such as electronic commerce and customer self-service. By connecting the mainframe to a Web browser, companies gain efficient, cost-effective ways for employees to work together or with customers; lower mainframe-use costs; reduce software distribution and support costs; and allow new applications to use existing applications and data.

Manufacturing employees ensure the quality of CNT products.

The CNT Application Re-engineering Environment (CARE) solution suite provides Web-to-host integration. It allows companies to get at the applications stored on mainframes without making any changes to the applications.

"Companies must address needs such as electronic commerce, customer self-service, and company mergers and acquisitions. Web-to-host integration is a key component in meeting these needs," says Thomas G. Hudson, president and chief executive officer.

CNT's products, support, and training are sold to end users and system integrators; to Original Equipment Manufacturers (OEMs) in North America, the United Kingdom, France, Germany, Australia, Japan, and Hong Kong; and through more than thirty distributors around the world.

Computer Network Technology

Educational services help customers and employees get the most from CNT products.

PaR SYSTEMS, INC.

THE GANTRY ROBOTS

DESIGNED,

CONSTRUCTED, AND

INSTALLED BY

PaR SYSTEMS, INC.,

ARE LEADING

LARGE-SCALE,

HIGH-PRECISION

SYSTEMS USED

FOR REMOTE

MATERIAL HANDLING

IN INDUSTRIES

WORLDWIDE

PaR Systems, Inc., is a privately owned corporation located in St. Paul, Minnesota, and is a leader in the design, construction, and installation of large-scale, high-precision, gantry robotic systems for a wide variety of manufacturing industries. In its thirty-seven years of experience, PaR has provided more than 700 system installations worldwide.

The company manufactures standard PaR-brand XR® and Vector® gantry robots and various equipment for the remote handling of material in a wide range of applications. PaR also is the United States distributor of the MBR (modular-based robot) products manufactured by CIMCORP in Finland, which provide low-cost solutions to many material-handling applications.

PaR was founded as a spin-off company from General Mills. To help the World War II effort, the General Mills electromechanical division developed manipulator arms, which were used to remotely handle nuclear materials critical to the nation's Manhattan Project. After the nuclear power plant building boom ended in the 1970s, PaR shifted its expertise to robotics, introducing its first gantry robot in 1980. After a series of changes in ownership, PaR became a private corporation in 1993. Today its robotic systems are marketed to government organizations and the aerospace, marine, automotive, commercial nuclear power, research, and general manufacturing industries.

An XR® Series robot defastens an F-15 wing using vision systems and special end effectors.

PaR has successfully developed the necessary technology to make robots accurate enough to perform the high-precision operations needed in aerospace production. Since robots have a higher learning capacity and more flexibility than machine tools, the use of robots has been able to expand not only machining operations but also the complex operations necessary for the complete assembly or disassembly of large aircraft components. PaR also is a leader in adaptive robotic control, critical to these applications.

PaR has complete engineering and manufacturing capabilities for special applications. Some unique examples include building two of the largest operating robots in the world used in nondestructive inspection of fully assembled jet fighters and making large robotic systems used to remove paint from many types of aircraft.

PaR works with a customer's engineering staff from system conception through final design and installation. PaR's dedicated and experienced people, from program managers and staff engineers to assembly technicians, quality control personnel, and field service technicians, have contributed greatly to the company's well-earned reputation for systems reliability and customer satisfaction.

This PaR-built refueling platform in Sweden moves fuel bundles between the core and fuel storage areas. It can be operated manually or automatically.

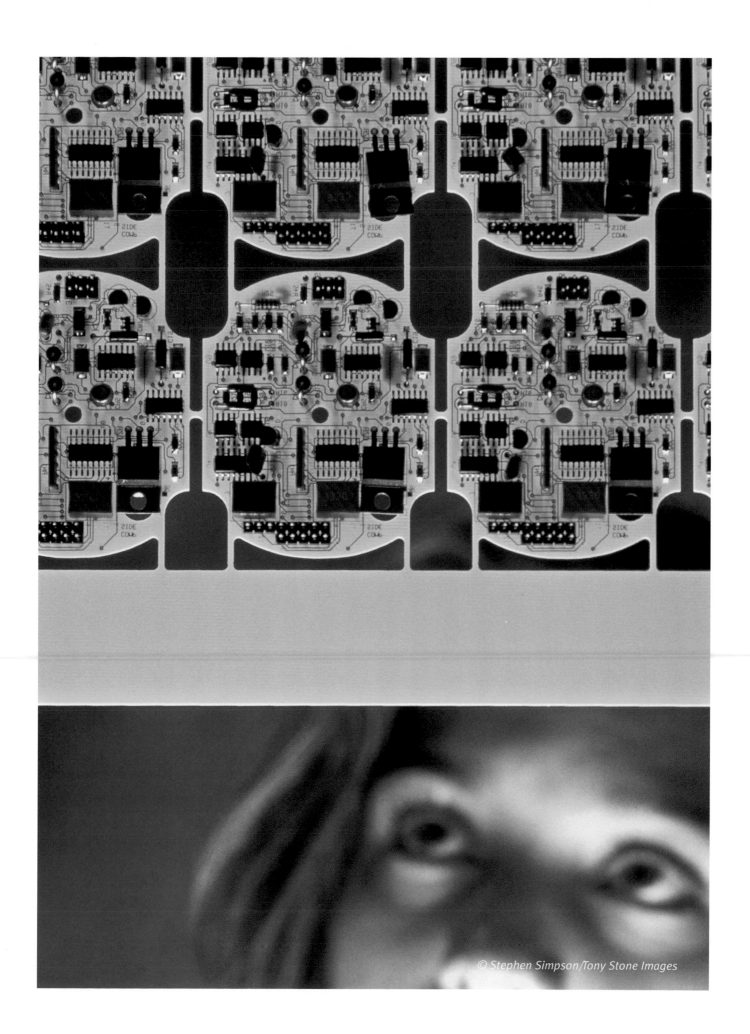

© Stephen Simpson/Tony Stone Images

BY ALL MEANS, COMMUNICATE

CHAPTER TWELVE

LACK OF COMMUNICATION MAY BE AN ISSUE AMONG TALK-SHOW GUESTS, BUT NOT AMONG MINNESOTANS. THE STATE BOASTS AWARD-WINNING TELEVISION STATIONS, THE NATION'S PREMIER PUBLIC RADIO NETWORK, A GAMUT OF NEWSPAPERS AND MAGAZINES COVERING GENERAL AND SPECIALIZED MARKETS, A FIFTEEN-THOUSAND-MILE FIBER-OPTIC BACKBONE (ONE OF THE LARGEST IN THE WORLD), AND A PRINTING AND PUBLISHING INDUSTRY THAT

is growing at a rate four times the national average.

The history of television in Minnesota dates to 1948 when Hubbard Broadcasting founded the first NBC affiliate in the nation, KSTP-TV. Situated on the boundary line of Minneapolis and St. Paul, KSTP was among the country's first television stations and was the only one between Chicago and the West Coast. Today, the Twin Cities area ranks as the eleventh-largest metropolitan market and includes all the major networks. It also

has a strong public television station, KTCA, which currently produces approximately 15 percent of its own programming, including the popular *Newton's Apple* series. Hubbard Broadcasting continues to be a pioneer in the industry. In 1993, it founded the U.S. Satellite Broadcasting Company, which launched the first high-power direct-broadcast satellite, allowing most of the country to receive more than 150 television channels.

Minnesota Public Radio (MPR) has the largest membership base, seventy thousand subscribers, of any public radio network in the country and is also the largest regional public radio system, with twenty-nine stations. The list of accomplishments does not stop there. The country's most successful and popular radio program of the latter part of the century, *A Prairie Home Companion,* was developed by MPR and the show's host, native Minnesotan and humorist Garrison Keillor.

The *Star Tribune,* formerly called the *Minneapolis Star Tribune,* is the state's largest newspaper, with a circulation approaching one-half million. Most every community in the state publishes its own hometown paper and many also print a visitors guide. Alternative newspapers such as the Minneapolis-based *City Pages* bring news with a different perspective, as do numerous specialty publications, among them *The Asian Pages* and the *Senior Times.*

Opposite: A communications tower juts into the sky above Arden Hills, a northeastern suburb of St. Paul. © Michael Burian.
Above: A man mixes sound at a sound board. © J. B. Smith/Uniphoto, Inc.

WARREN G. HARDING WAS THE FIRST AMERICAN PRESIDENT EVER TO SPEAK OVER THE RADIO. HE DID SO FROM THE MINNESOTA STATE FAIR IN SEPTEMBER 1920.

Minnesota is well known for its areas where one can truly get away from it all and enjoy acres of remote, pristine wilderness, but thanks to a progressive telecommunications industry, connecting to the outside world is possible from virtually any location. For starters, Minnesota's fully digital telecommunications web features one of the world's largest continuous fiber networks. Thanks to a cooperative effort between major communication companies US West, Sprint/United Telephone Company of Minnesota, GTE of Minnesota, and Frontier Communications, together with a group of local independent phone companies organized as Minnesota Equal Access Network Services (MEANS), every county in the state is served by a fifteen-thousand-mile fiber-optic backbone. All along the backbone, telecommunications companies have built a video-conferencing network, which links Minnesota businesses and organizations with locations across the state and around the world. High-speed network capabilities, such as integrated services digital network (ISDN), are increasingly available in locations in greater Minnesota, as is local toll-free access to the Internet. A recent MEANS study revealed that approximately 80 percent of the state can get on-line with a local, toll-free call. Communications giant AT&T, a major presence in the state, is at work creating technologically "borderless" communities.

THE WAY OF THE HIGH-TECH FUTURE

The whole state seems to be preparing for the digital future. Winona, a town of twenty-five thousand in the southeast corner of the state along the banks of the Mississippi River, once enjoyed the status associated with being a main stop for river and rail traffic

Whether sitting in a cafe, standing in line at the post office, or driving to work, consumers can keep on top of appointments and in touch with family and colleagues using the cellular telephone. © Image Club Graphics

A television crew allows homebound viewers to enjoy the ice palace at St. Paul's annual Winter Carnival—without the chill or need for mittens. © Greg Ryan-Sally Beyer

but was left stranded when Interstate 90 located across the river in LaCrosse, Wisconsin. Determined not to let the information superhighway pass them by, some local businessmen with deep roots in the community and a wealth of technical expertise formed Luminet, intending to wire the entire town and create applications in telemedicine, economic development, and distance learning. Their vision includes attracting world-class businesses and organizations who desire to conduct business with their international offices while enjoying the quality of life offered by a small town nestled among beautiful river bluffs. In the center of the state, the first community to test a new technology that combines cable television, telephone service, and the Internet is St. Cloud. There, the longtime Minnesota energy provider Northern States Power is entering the telecommunications industry through its subsidiary Seren Innovations. The subsidiary's broader-band coaxial cable will allow

subscribers to enjoy such options as virtual video stores and Internet speeds up to one hundred times faster than dial-up modems.

Recognizing the phenomenal growth and potential of the cellular communications field, forward-looking leaders in Mankato came together in 1997 to develop the nation's first curricula designed to train engineers and technicians for careers in this arena. A partnership among Mankato State University, which will offer two bachelor's degrees in engineering technology; South Central Technology College, which will train wireless communication electronics technicians; and representatives of the international communications industry, including AT&T, Lucent Technologies, and Motorola, is

ADC Telecommunications, with headquarters in Minnetonka, is the leading global supplier of transmission and networking systems for use in telecommunications, cable television, broadcast, and wireless and enterprise networks. The company was started in the Minneapolis basement of Ralph Allison in 1935.

responsible for implementing the program, known as the "Mankato Connection."

In 1996, Minnesota was designated as a United Nations Trade Point and the site of the first Secure Electronic Authentication Link (SEAL) laboratory in the world. Both efforts aim to establish a system of globally secure electronic commerce. The state also hosts the premier North American and sole U.S. gateway for secure electronic commerce with Asia, Africa, and the Pacific. Minnesota earned these distinctions in part because of its history of unique accomplishments in telecommunications, including the University of Minnesota's develop-

Right: The publications of the world-renowned addiction-recovery center Hazelden Foundation, based in Center City, have helped many thousands of people. © Hazelden Foundation. Below: These fiber-optic bundles are seemingly delicate components of one of the strongest communications networks in the world. © Jon Riley/Tony Stone Images

ment of Gopher, one of the first Internet search engines, and Minnesota E-Democracy, the world's first election-oriented Web site.

Those requiring proof that not everything in the world is going electronic need only look to the strength of the printing and publishing industry in Minnesota. It is the second-largest manufacturing sector in the state, with nearly fifty-five thousand employees, the majority of whom are employed by commercial printers. From 1985 to 1994, printing/publishing employment grew by 28.2 percent, compared to the national average of 7.8 percent, and the state's Department of Economic Security sees no sign of the trend's slowing down.

Among the 1,800 printing and publishing establishments in the state is the Taylor Corporation, the nation's largest printer of wedding and business stationery and one of the twenty largest printers in the United States. The North Mankato–based company has more than forty-five operating divisions, including Schmidt Printing in Byron, a leading printer of magazine insert cards. The town of Waseca is headquarters for Brown Printing, a leading producer of business and trade publications, special-interest consumer magazines, catalogs, and retail inserts. West Publishing in Eagan publishes some sixty million legal tomes, textbooks, and pamphlets annually and provides information additionally in paperless formats, such as CD-ROM. St. Paul–based H.M. Smyth found its niche in specialized labels and now distributes a wide variety to Fortune 500 clients.

Numerous other specialized printers and publishers do business in Minnesota as well. The Mayo Clinic is currently one of the principal entrants in the field of

Workers at Carlson Craft, a Taylor Corporation company, print wedding invitations using AB Dick presses. Taylor Corporation has more than forty-five divisions. © Carlson Craft

THE TAYLOR CORPORATION, WHICH SPECIALIZES IN PRINTING WEDDING INVITATIONS AND BUSINESS STATIONERY, WAS THE FIRST COMPANY IN THE COUNTRY TO ESTABLISH AN ON-SITE CHILD-CARE CENTER FOR EMPLOYEES' USE.

© Image Club Graphics

medical publications, and the Hazelden Foundation is the world's primary publisher of literature focused on addiction and recovery. Wild Wing Galleries and The Hadley Companies are two nationally recognized publishers of quality art prints by America's top wildlife and landscape artists. Deluxe Checks, one of the country's largest printers of commercial and personal checks, has a large facility in Minnesota, as does Lifetouch, a leading yearbook printer and photography studio. And Jostens is known nationwide to millions of people who recognize it as their high school yearbook publisher and supplier of

class rings. Jostens also creates gift products and recognition/award items. All of these companies display an inventive spirit to achieve the best in communications.

Moving into a new century, Minnesota is sure to maintain its high communications standards in print, radio, and television. By harnessing the creative drive of its brightest innovators, the state will retain its spot at the pinnacle of communications technology.

Below: A worker monitors the hot stamping of printed labels. © Lonnie Duka/Tony Stone Images. Opposite: The St. Paul Dispatch devoted twenty pages to mark the coming of a new age, when the Northwest got its first TV station. © KSTP-TV

3,000 Sets Near St. Paul; Sales Top Expectation

With nearly 3,000 television receivers now within tuning range of KSTP-TV, the Twin Cities area will set a new record for the number of receivers in operation as television broadcasting begins.

Engineers' figures reveal that in many cities less than 100 receivers were actually in use when the visual broadcasts were inaugurated. Milwaukee recently claimed a record when 240 sets were known to be in operation receiving the first programs televised there.

Stanley Hubbard, president and general manager of KSTP, said that the estimate of 3,000 sets in operation now is "fairly close," and predicted that distributors of the various makes of television receivers will place an additional 15,000 in the Twin Cities area by the end of 1948.

The distributors themselves admitted that the Twin Cities market for receivers has opened up much more rapidly than anticipated, and most companies said that sales are now outdistancing the ability of service crews to install the sets.

One Twin Cities' outlet reported that it is now averaging 30 sales daily, and is at least eight days behind in making installations.

It was also apparent that sales to householders have far exceeded the installations in taverns and other public places. Of the estimated 3,000 receivers in the area, not more than one-tenth are in the bars, television officials said.

"The growing interest of family groups in television reception at home can be explained by the fact that most manufacturers have produced comparatively low-priced models," C. H. Stevenson, executive secretary of the St. Paul and Minneapolis Appliance Dealers associations, stated.

Most companies are offering models retailing from about $170 upwards to $2,000 or more, he said. The lowest price models have a visual screen 7 by 7 inches, satisfac- [continued] tory for small family audiences.

Householders expecting to purchase the receivers should remember that the quoted price does not include installation, which should be made by a qualified technician, because a special type of antenna is necessary and its directional position must be adjusted to eliminate "ghost" images on the receiver screen. At present, installation of a receiver with a service contract for a year, costs about $55.

In the Twin Cities, where nearly all of the Minnesota sets have been installed up to the present time, persons may expect to pick up a clear, sharp image on their video screen, Hubbard said.

St. Paul retailers estimated that because of the population ratio, Minneapolis television receiver sales are probably about twice as great as St. Paul sales. It was estimated that St. Paul installations might be near 1,000 this week.

The potential Minnesota-Wisconsin market for television receivers could not be interpreted by distributors in terms of the number of sets which may ultimately be sold, but KSTP officials said there are approximately 1,750,000 people in the area reached by the KSTP-TV signal.

WTCN Will Televise This Fall

WTCN, American Broadcasting Co. outlet for the Twin Cities, has signed a contract with the ABC network for television coverage of news and special events throughout the world.

This service will rush films of outstanding importance to the WTCN-TZ transmitter by air and wirephoto.

WTCN-TZ, the television station, has been in the planning for sometime. The construction permit for the television station was granted by the Federal Communications Commission in 1946. Numerous trips to eastern television stations and equipment manufacturers have been made by F. Van Konynenburg, vice president and general manager, John M. Sherman, technical director, and Max Karl, program manager, to study operations and inspect new equipment developments.

WTCN-TZ will present the latest in ultra-modern equipment and program facilities when it takes to the air in the fall of 1948, Van Konynenburg said.

The initial operation of WTCN-TZ will be with its full transmitter power and from its final type high efficiency antenna atop the Foshay tower building in Minneapolis.

In addition to the facilities for transmitting remote and studio picture programs, the station will be equipped with the latest modern type of local film facilities so that events may be brought to the Minnesota viewing audience as fast as airplane service can transport them here. Later it is expected that network coverage programs will be broadcast to the Twin Cities and Minnesota at the same time the events happen. This will be accomplished by coaxial cables.

Programming plans are going forward in all departments of the station for early fall WTCN-TZ inaugural.

Television Starts Here Tuesday With Daily Programs On KSTP

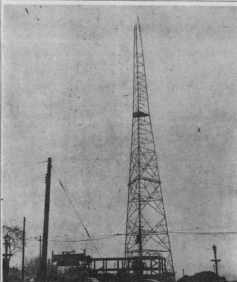

Here is the KSTP television tower at the St. Paul Minneapolis city limits just shortly before it was completed for broadcasts starting Tuesday.

Half-Million Dollars And Two Years Of Work Make Way For First Broadcast

T-Day comes to St. Paul Tuesday.

It is on that day when television passes from the experimentation stage to a commercial basis, with KSTP broadcasting the Minneapolis baseball game from Nicollet park, that city.

There have been preliminary television broadcasts such as a basketball game, but Tuesday will be the first time that an event will go over the KSTP giant 571-foot tower located at the St. Paul-Minneapolis city limits on University ave.

To show there is no favoritism, the tripod tower has one leg in St. Paul, another in Minneapolis, and the third right on the intercity boundary line.

T-Day comes to KSTP as the result of more than two years of work, after the Federal Radio commission has given its approval of the application. According to John Fricker, technical director of the station, the project will cost more than $500,000.

The tower, composed of 128 tons of steel, took two and a half months to erect and is placed on a foundation of nearly 300 tons of concrete, each footing being 37 tons. The foundation is the height of a two-story building.

The effective radiated power for pictures is 24,700 watts and 17,300 watts for sound.

Television fans within a radius of 60 miles are certain to see the pictures. Those living 20 miles further out are considered "probables."

Present plans call for 6-day, 30-hour per week television broadcasts. This does not mean that each day will have five [continued] hours devoted to TV, Fricker said. "We may broadcast six or seven hours one day and only three or four another," he said.

Special arrangements have been made with the National Broadcasting Co. Fricker said, to get films of certain acts and rebroadcast them from the Twin Cities station.

Poll Shows Many Plan To Buy Video Sets Soon

One of every five persons interviewed in a week long poll taken among people in the studio audiences of ABC's Welcome Travelers radio show expects to buy a television set in the near future. Of the 856 persons who cast ballots, slightly more than 50 per cent said they had seen a telecast.

Congratulations KSTP on your "FIRST" in Television

Your new "Tower of Sight" that stretches its steel arms into the stratosphere to grasp and bring to this community the new world of television entertainment from the airwaves, is a symbol of progress of which you may well be proud. It is another "FIRST" in a long succession of advances that are monuments to KSTP's greatness.

Television, as mighty in its aura as atomic development, is the today and tomorrow of radio. We are happy to have had a part in making possible the plaudits you have won from your fellow citizens for presenting it to St. Paul and the great Northwest.

Builders of the New KSTP Television Transmitter Building & Tower

KRAUS-ANDERSON, Inc.
General Contractors for KSTP Television Transmitter Buildings
501 So. 8th St., Mpls.   MA in 8467

ELECTRIC MAINTENANCE CORP.
Electric Contractors
2265 Wabash Ave.   NE stor 4811

ROBERT E. FOLEY
Construction Corporation
KSTP Television Tower Construction
48 Griswold Street   Binghamton, New York

PARK CONSTRUCTION CO.
Excavating & Grading
1405 11th Ave. So., Mpls.   AT lantic 6593

LIEBENBERG & KAPLAN
Architects & Engineers for KSTP
1300 LaSalle Ave., Mpls.   MA in 2404

STANDARD CONSTRUCTION CO., Inc.
General Contractors for Tower Footings
606 Hamm Bldg.   GA rfield 6584

RAINVILLE-CARLSON, Inc.
Roofing & Sheet Metal Work
2929 Lyndale Ave. So., Mpls.   RE gent 5229

SPENCER AIR CONDITIONING CO.
Air Conditioning
1315 Glenwood Ave., Mpls.   AT lantic 3221

CHARLES HARRIS PLUMBING CO.
Plumbing & Heating Contractors
474 University Ave.   EL khurst 7744

EDWIN JOHNSON & SONS
Plastering Contractors
210 Gorham Bldg., Mpls.   GE neva 2982

READY MIXED CONCRETE CO.
Ready Mixed Concrete
37-20th Ave. So., Mpls.   AT lantic 6547

© Lonnie Duka/Tony Stone Images

© Stuart Westmorland/Tony Stone Images

COMMUNICATIONS, MEDIA, PUBLISHING, AND PRINTING

ADC TELECOMMUNICATIONS, INC.

ADC Telecommunications, Inc., designs, manufactures, and markets telecommunications and networking systems to meet the needs of the global community in the twenty-first century

Founded in 1935, ADC Telecommunications, Inc., is a global telecommunications and networking systems supplier headquartered in Minneapolis, Minnesota. ADC is one of Minnesota's fastest-growing businesses. It has jumped from about $300 million in revenues in 1991 to become a $1 billion-a-year manufacturer of key elements in telecommunications networks. ADC has about 6,500 employees, including more than 2,800 in the Twin Cities.

ADC systems, products, and services perform critical functions that ensure the quality and reliability of communications networks worldwide. The company designs, manufactures, and markets transmission systems, networking systems, and broadband connectivity products for fiber-optic, copper twisted-pair, coaxial, and wireless broadband global networks. ADC also provides in-depth systems integration services to its customers, enabling them to maximize the performance of their networks. The company's products are used by telephone companies, other public network

ADC uses state-of-the-art engineering systems to design telecommunications products that are used by global service providers such as cable television operators and telephone companies.

providers (such as wireless, broadcast, and cable TV operators), and by private enterprise voice, data, and video networks.

ADC business units work in collaboration with customers to create more efficient ways of managing and transmitting information within both public and private communications networks, delivering practical solutions that range from coax and fiber-optic components to complete end-to-end broadband systems. ADC business units are located worldwide.

"The world of the twenty-first century will center around high-speed access to networks that will deliver information to our homes and businesses. In the next millennium, the division among people will be between those with access to electronic information and communication and those without. Instant access will drive everything, from consumer and business decisions to the democratic political process. To be without access to information and communications technologies will result

ADC Telecommunications, Inc., is headquartered in Minneapolis, Minnesota. The company has manufacturing, sales, or service offices in seventeen countries around the world and employs approximately 6,500 people worldwide.

in isolation from many key aspects of modern life," says William J. Cadogan, chairman and chief executive officer of ADC Telecommunications.

ADC's goal is universal high-speed access. Today the key barrier to high-speed information/communication access is the local loop bottleneck. This bottleneck strangles the flow of information to and from residential and business consumers. In the home it limits the speed at which people can access the Internet, making downloading information tedious and costly. In the workplace it limits the ability to efficiently transfer files from outside the local area network. Advanced services such as video conferencing are limited to costly equipment setups that require special transmission lines. These limitations are frustrating, but only temporary. ADC is dedicated to leading the way to universal high-speed access.

At ADC's manufacturing facilities all products are tested to assure high-quality standards are met.

"It's all about meeting customer needs. Our customers, the service providers, are being confronted today with meeting the challenges of a competitive environment. Consumers have more choices available to them and are making better-informed decisions on how they receive information/communication services. New alternate-access companies are challenging traditional telephone companies for both long distance and local telecommunications services. Direct broadcast satellite services are challenging cable television with innovative service delivery. To survive and thrive in this competitive landscape means service providers must install advanced technologies that are flexible enough to deliver today's services economically while not limiting tomorrow's capabilities," says Cadogan.

"The choice to the service provider is clear: Provide these high-demand, high-growth, high-speed services or lose the most dynamic, growing piece of the communications market. Since we view our customers as our partners, their success in this challenging environment is key to our success. We are committed to providing solutions to unlock their networks to the large opportunities available today and well into the future," Cadogan says.

ADC believes in the value of the community. The employees in Minneapolis participate in a wide variety of events and programs that strive to give back to the community in many ways. ADC's out-of-state divisions have a similar record of community involvement. ADC's employees are reliable and active volunteers. To support and encourage this commitment, ADC matches employee contributions to approved nonprofit organizations.

ADC Telecommunications is committed to serving not only the local community, but also the global community, by developing telecommunications systems that will meet the needs of the twenty-first century.

ADC's products provide innovative solutions for the transmission of data, voice, or video signals over copper, fiber-optic, and wireless networks to businesses and residences.

THE JOHN ROBERTS COMPANY

The prestige of a business organization is reflected in all the communications it produces, especially its printed materials.

To meet the needs of the business community, The John Roberts Company has developed a special concept it calls "Orchestrated Printing"—the flawless coordination of all details, no matter how small or complex the job, from prepress through shipping.

Founded in 1951, The John Roberts Company is a full-service commercial, direct-mail, and catalog printer that specializes in orchestrating the complete print production of high-quality multicolor catalogs, annual reports, brochures, flyers, inserts, statement stuffers, and custom-made specialty products.

The company uses both sheet-fed and heat-set web offset technologies in its printing operations, including a complete line of one- to six-color sheet-fed presses, as well as commercial full-size and half-size heat-set web presses. In addition to the printing operations, the company offers a complete prepress department, including electronic prepress for making printing proofs and plates.

Other prepress services range from complete desktop publishing capabilities to electronic stripping. With

Built in 1974 on a fourteen-acre parcel of land in Coon Rapids, the John Roberts facility has undergone a number of expansions through the years and today exceeds 220,000 square feet.

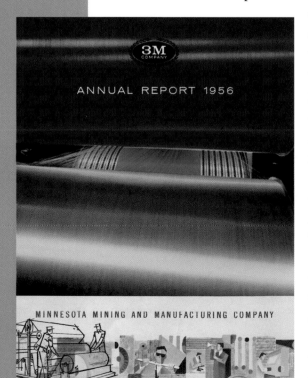

In the 1950s, as The John Roberts Company's reputation for quality printing spread throughout the industry, major companies such as 3M began to depend on this small firm to serve important printing needs.

state-of-the-art technology, prepress professionals color-correct, retouch, ghost, vignette, and silhouette images toward perfection. And to ensure quality and consistency, John Roberts assembles customer separations into composite plate-ready film.

The bindery department provides post-press finishing services, including complex die-cutting, folding, perforating, and custom imprinting, while the shipping department coordinates the coast-to-coast distribution of finished materials.

With more than 370 employees, the company is currently listed by *Graphic Arts Monthly* as the eighty-sixth largest privately held commercial printer in the nation, based upon annual sales.

"Whether printing quantities of a few thousand or larger quantities up into the millions, our dedicated staff of professionals has an absolute commitment to provide our customers with quality, service, and value for their printing dollar," says chairman Robert A. Keene, who cofounded the company with John Chelberg in the Midway district of St. Paul in the early 1950s.

Each John Roberts sales representative works with an account coordinator as a team, to ensure the flawless and on-schedule completion of every printing job. A computerized operations system is designed to keep clients informed about the progress of their projects and the shop operates twenty-four hours per day, seven days a week.

Located in Minneapolis/St. Paul, John Roberts enjoys better distribution for shipments and ready access to markets throughout North America. An extensive list of clients demonstrates the success that the company has had in producing outstanding printing for more than forty-five years. This list includes Fortune 500 companies, major manufacturers, advertising agencies, and travel-related and hospitality companies.

As a concerned corporate citizen, John Roberts has worked closely with the Environmental Protection Agency (EPA) to create its own Environmental Management System and a Mentoring Program to teach smaller printing companies about the management of environmentally sound printing. The program is designed not only to protect the environment, but also is focused on ensuring the safety and health of all employees. The company also has made a commitment to ISO-9002, and is well along the way toward certification to this standard.

"As a company, we feel our participation will provide an excellent vehicle to address many industry-specific issues, and to share knowledge with regulatory staff that can lead to greater understanding of mutual goals and increased efficiency for both the regulated printing industry and the EPA and state regulatory staff," says Keene.

As part of this effort, John Roberts participates in mentoring programs, where larger and more sophisticated companies develop models of training programs to help smaller businesses both achieve and stay in compliance with EPA requirements, while remaining competitive.

By establishing its own program, John Roberts hopes to expand the use of mentoring as a means to raise the level of awareness and knowledge of environmental issues among smaller printing companies, particularly those with fewer than twenty-five

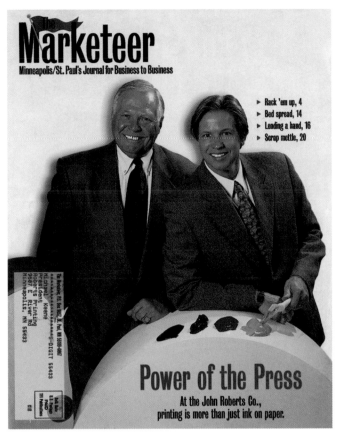

The Marketeer
Minneapolis/St. Paul's Journal for Business to Business

▶ Rack 'em up, 4
▶ Bed spread, 14
▶ Lending a hand, 16
▶ Scrap mettle, 20

Power of the Press
At the John Roberts Co.,
printing is more than just ink on paper.

Recognized for environmental leadership and the efficiency of its equipment, John Roberts ascribes much of its growth to outstanding customer service.

employees. Objectives include providing direct aid to several selected project printers, consulting face-to-face with management and key staff, and demonstrating tools that can help smaller companies meet their environmental responsibilities.

Robert A. Keene views responsibility as a basic part of industry leadership. "Our 'Corporate Brand Promise,'" he says, "is to 'passionately pursue the ultimate customer experience.'"

In keeping with this promise, it is the goal of every employee to place the customer at the heart of every decision and action. For its part, the company strives to create a fair and safe environment that is beneficial to employees and the community. This is the type of thinking that has allowed John Roberts to remain competitive in the market for more than four decades—and it provides a positive direction for the future.

To maintain high standards of quality and service, the John Roberts management team created the concept of "Orchestrated Printing."

THE STAR TRIBUNE COMPANY

The Star Tribune Company has contributed in many ways to the growth of the Twin Cities. Throughout its rich history, the company has been a trusted, dependable source of at least three of the necessary ingredients for an informed, involved community:

- comprehensive news coverage
- reliable consumer information
- independent editorial commentary

The *Star Tribune* newspaper and its predecessors have served the Minneapolis–St. Paul area and the upper Midwest for 130 years. The *Star Tribune* is the nation's seventeenth-largest daily metropolitan newspaper and the twelfth-largest Sunday paper in the United States. In addition to its newspaper, The Star Tribune Company produces a variety of print, direct-marketing, and electronic services targeted to niche markets.

The Star Tribune Company also has been one of the community's largest and most progressive employers, providing an environment that values teamwork, lifelong learning, and innovation.

When the *Tribune* first went to press, in May 1867, no one could have predicted that it would become a preferred source of news and information for the Twin Cities.

John and Gardner (Mike) Cowles were Des Moines newspapermen who in 1935 bought the *Minneapolis Star,* an evening newspaper eventually merging it with the *Tribune.* A consummate newsman, John Cowles told his organization to give the public a stronger newspaper, deliver it better, and promote

The Star Tribune Heritage Center is a state-of-the-art production facility in Minneapolis.

Today The Star Tribune Company produces a wide variety of print, digital, and direct-marketing products.

it effectively. He wanted to present the news "as honestly and fairly and intelligently as possible." In 1986 the *Star and Tribune* opened a St. Paul bureau in an attempt to gain circulation and advertising to the east of Minneapolis, and launched a St. Paul edition in 1987. "Minneapolis" was no longer part of its nameplate. *Star Tribune* was now the "Newspaper of the Twin Cities." In 1987 the company built the new Heritage Center production plant, at a cost of more than $100 million.

Today more than 75 percent of Twin Cities adults use at least one Star Tribune product or service. More than 10,000 businesses, including major retailers, use the *Star Tribune* newspaper for marketing support—from daily display advertisements to targeted advertising supplements. The Star Tribune Company offers Twin Cities consumers and marketers a major daily newspaper, multiple special-interest publications, and interactive telephone- and digital-based information services.

In June 1996 the paper launched its on-line service (www.startribune.com), which became the leading electronic news and information service for the Twin Cities region and the state of Minnesota. The startribune.com network of services updates news and information throughout the day and provides interactive discussions, searchable classified advertising, real estate information, and many other services.

As customer needs and interests have changed over the years, so, too, have Star Tribune's products. Today the company provides an array of information vehicles in a variety of formats—print, voice, digital, and direct mail—for its Twin Cities customers.

OPEN DISCUSSION = BETTER DECISIONS

Communities speed their own decision making and certainly derive numerous other benefits, tangible and intangible, from direct, open discussion of news and policy issues that effect the local community, as well as state, national, or international issues. The *Star Tribune* newspaper provides a daily forum involving its editorial pages, in which topics and issues of the day are discussed and debated. In addition to the company's own institutional views that are presented in its editorials, the newspaper also provides space daily in which others can express

Many of today's Star Tribune features also appeal to new and growing readers.

Today the Star Tribune produces a variety of products and services in addition to its core newspaper.

their views—some of which agree, and some of which disagree sharply—with those of The Star Tribune Company.

CONSUMERS AND MARKETERS VALUE STAR TRIBUNE PRODUCTS

While The Star Tribune Company builds its services around its core newspaper product, it provides far more. Marketers meet their current and future customers through products created and distributed by Star Tribune. At the same time, consumers rely on Star Tribune information about the topics important to them and their families—whether delivered in familiar green trucks, on the telephone, in the mail, or over the Internet.

Like other Twin Cities businesses, the Star Tribune's product mix and facilities have benefited from heavy investments over the last fifty years. The company and its employees make other, more personal investments, as well. For example, The Star Tribune Foundation is one of the community's most active contributors focused on programs that help its neighbors in need.

In March 1998 Cowles Media merged with McClatchy Newspapers, a company that also emphasizes journalism over marketing. Like Cowles, The McClatchy Company is a public company controlled by a community-oriented family. The McClatchy Company launched its ownership of The Star Tribune Company with the commitment to contribute at least $3 million per year throughout the Twin Cities for each of at least the next ten years.

The Star Tribune Company, like Minneapolis and St. Paul, has worked and invested and grown over the years. In doing so, it has earned the community's trust and gained its position as Minnesota's preferred source of news and information. And that legacy is the most important of all.

StarTribune
It's where you live.

MEANS TELCOM

IN A PIONEERING,

ENTREPRENEURIAL

SPIRIT, MEANS

TELCOM BUILDS

AND DELIVERS

TELECOMMUNICATIONS

SERVICES FOR

ENTERPRISES,

GOVERNMENT, AND

RESIDENCES IN

MINNESOTA, AND

CREATES A MODEL

FOR OTHER STATES

Founded in 1988, MEANS Telcom provides state-of-the-art voice, data, and video communications throughout Minnesota. The company, originally named "Minnesota Equal Access Network Services, Inc.," was formed by a group of local independent telephone companies to offer their customers a choice of long-distance service providers.

These entrepreneurial firms made a commitment to develop a "telecommunications highway" to make leading-edge telecommunications available throughout Minnesota at a time when few long-distance companies were investing in services for rural areas. The companies worked together to build a jointly owned fiber-optic network. Fiber optics and digital signaling offer customers greater clarity and reliability for data and video communications. Today MEANS Telcom has grown into a multimillion-dollar corporation providing advanced telecommunications services to both rural and urban Minnesota businesses and residences.

The resulting 2,000-mile fiber-optic network, administered by MEANS Telcom, currently serves more than 230,000 commercial and residential phone lines. It links communities throughout Minnesota, including all of the major metropolitan areas, and now carries traffic not only for long-distance telephone service, but also for

the Internet, videoconferencing, and private lines. MEANS Telcom also provides access to networks in several other states—South Dakota, Iowa, Wisconsin, and Illinois, including the Chicago area. Besides providing access to other long-distance firms, MEANS Telcom also sells long-distance service.

With such expanded capabilities in place, MEANS Telcom is able to offer its customers a wide range of service options, including interactive videoconferencing, Internet access, 800-number long-distance services, and prepaid calling cards.

"Expanding both services offered and geographic areas covered is the key to MEANS Telcom's future," says the firm's president and CEO, David H. Kelley.

INTERNET SERVICES

As part of its expansion efforts, MEANS Telcom acquired Minnesota Regional Network, the state's largest Internet service company, in November 1997 and created a wholly owned subsidiary of MEANS Telcom called "MRNet." The new MRNet merged the Internet services operations of both companies, thereby providing the vast majority of Minnesota's connections to the Internet. MRNet is one of the most experienced Internet service organizations in the nation, having provided and supported access to the Internet since 1987. MRNet customers include Fortune 500 corporations, public and private universities and colleges, public and private research foundations, and government agencies in Minnesota.

"The completion of this transaction can be considered both the end of an era and a step in the continuing evolution of the Minnesota regional network," says Dennis Fazio, chief technology officer of MRNet. "Our leadership as one of the founding organizations of the modern Internet and our efforts to establish Internet capability throughout Minnesota and

In October 1991 MEANS Telcom began its quest to provide state-of-the-art telecommunications services to greater Minnesota by laying a statewide network encompassing more than 2,000 miles of fiber-optic cable. The cable is buried underground using large trenching equipment.

among its various constituencies has sometimes required that we transform our corporate structure. Now the early academic and research era of the Internet has passed and an era of unconstrained commercial growth is upon us. We have situated ourselves to be a leader in this new era."

The merger creates a strong regional presence with unmatched capabilities for moving data, information, and commerce electronically. "Bringing together MEANS Telcom's existing strengths in telephony with MRNet's strengths in Internet technology gives us the components needed for a business striving to be competitive in the communications industry of the future," Kelley says. "I envision the newly merged corporation as a provider of a new class of Internet services for customers; a magnet for talented employees whose interests lie in emerging technologies; and a business whose vision helps reinforce Minnesota's status as a leader in high technology. This is an exciting moment in the history of MEANS Telcom, but more importantly, it marks the beginning of a new era in Minnesota's communications industry."

THE LEARNING NETWORK

Another part of MEANS Telcom's expansion was derived as a result of the work of the Learning Network of Minnesota. This program, established by the Minnesota Education Telecommunications Council (METC), seeks to give all Minnesotans access to enhanced learning opportunities and information resources through telecommunications technology. METC administered a $15.2 million Telecommunications Access Grant to link public libraries and elementary and secondary school districts to the Learning Network. MEANS Telcom was selected by more than 75 percent of the grant recipients to develop the network infrastructure and deliver the telecommunications technology needed for these links.

The Learning Network of Minnesota has opened the door to the world for thousands of Minnesota students and community members by providing access to the Internet and to international videoconferencing services. Here students perform research on the Internet in a computer lab, where they are able to take advantage of the most recent news and information available on-line.

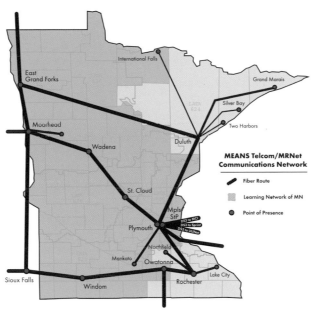

MEANS Telcom/MRNet Communications Network

— Fiber Route
▢ Learning Network of MN
● Point of Presence

Together MEANS Telcom and MRNet provide advanced telecommunications and Internet services to Minnesota and beyond. This map illustrates the combined strength of MEANS Telcom's 100 percent fiber-optic network that spans more than 2,000 miles with the reliability of MRNet's three clear-channel DS3 connections to different Internet backbone providers.

More than 470 school districts and public libraries throughout the state now have this access. Among its benefits, the Learning Network allows

• educators to share interactive video instruction with other locations around the state, nation, and even the world;
• students to access information on the Internet;
• administrators to transmit data to state agencies and officials; and
• members of communities, urban and rural alike, to communicate via electronic mail.

As to future pursuits, MEANS Telcom's vision is to help create a national version of what it has accomplished on the state level for Minnesota. As recently as June 1998, MEANS Telcom helped launch the Independent Network Consortium (INC), a limited liability corporation, whose pursuit is to build a nationwide network of independent telephone companies. The same pioneering, entrepreneurial spirit that propelled MEANS Telcom to flourish in Minnesota provides a strong foundation and a model for nationwide success.

RURAL CELLULAR CORPORATION

Rural Cellular

Corporation

succeeds and

continues to grow

through strategic

acquisitions and

partnerships, and by

providing early

availability of new

technology such as

its PCS wireless

transmission services

to rural areas

In 1990 forty independent rural telephone companies merged their cellular partnership interests and Rural Cellular Corporation (Nasdaq NMS: RCCC) was founded. The company is one of the nation's first cellular providers, urban or rural, to become profitable. It has succeeded by adding new innovative services and through strategic footprint expansion. Today, Rural Cellular Corporation operates in nine states, providing service in portions of Minnesota, North Dakota, South Dakota, and Wisconsin, as well as in the states of Maine, Vermont, New Hampshire, Massachusetts, and New York.

Rural Cellular Corporation is headquartered in Alexandria, Minnesota.

Headquartered in Alexandria, Minnesota, Rural Cellular Corporation is a full-service wireless-communication solutions provider offering cellular, paging, and emerging Personal Communication Services (PCS) to its customers. PCS, a new form of wireless digital transmission, allows communication anywhere at any time with excellent sound quality. PCS technology equipment can utilize digital and analog transmissions, voice mail, pagers, and Internet access.

The company's subsidiaries include Rural Cellular Corporation Minnesota, Wireless Alliance, LLC, Rural Cellular Corporation Maine, and Rural Cellular Corporation Atlantic. These strategic partnerships and acquisitions have afforded Rural Cellular Corporation the opportunity to expand its operational foothold.

Rural Cellular Corporation Minnesota is one of the largest providers of cellular and paging services in northern Minnesota, encompassing 600,000 people. Its 38,000-square-mile service area is adjacent to Minnesota's three largest metropolitan areas: Minneapolis/St. Paul, Duluth, and Fargo/Moorhead.

Wireless Alliance, LLC, a joint venture started in late 1996 with APT Inc., an affiliate of Aerial

Richard P. Ekstrand is founder, president, and chief executive officer of Rural Cellular Corporation.

Communications, Inc., provides PCS service in select markets of Minnesota, Wisconsin, North Dakota, and South Dakota. The Wireless Alliance service area encompasses 708,000 people.

Rural Cellular Corporation Maine, which was established through the May 1997 acquisition of Unity Cellular Systems, Inc., provides cellular service to central Maine, covering more than 500,000 people.

Rural Cellular Corporation Atlantic, headquartered near Burlington, Vermont, encompasses approximately 1.1 million people and offers cellular service in portions of the states of Vermont, New Hampshire, New York, and Massachusetts. Rural Cellular Corporation acquired this footprint in July 1998.

Rural Cellular Corporation is noted for its investment in the training and professional growth of its employees, whom it recognizes as the reason for the company's ongoing success. As a responsible corporate citizen, the company promotes employee volunteerism and contributes airtime, phone use, and monetary donations to schools and social programs throughout its service areas.

"We are proud to provide a variety of communication lifestyle solutions for our customers," says Richard P. Ekstrand, founder, president, and chief executive officer. "Rural Cellular Corporation will continue to focus on the needs of our customers, employees, shareholders, suppliers and partners, and communities in the future."

OVATION COMMUNICATIONS

From basic service to customized networks, Ovation Communications offers its customers a full range of telecommunications services at significant cost savings. Based in the Twin Cities, Ovation is a "competitive local exchange carrier" (CLEC), a term derived from the Telecommunications Act of 1996. This congressional mandate allows telecommunications companies to provide local residential and business services in competition with larger incumbent carriers, giving telephone customers the benefit of more choices.

"We expect Ovation to become a major force in the regional communications market and beyond," says Ovation Communications founder and CEO, Tim Devine. "We see ourselves as a long-term significant player."

Led by Devine, Ovation's industry-savvy management team has been able to design, package, and price its services based on its collective real-world experience. The end result is that Ovation offers customers the same services as major carriers, but with lower prices and higher levels of customer service. Whatever service customers need, from basic service to complex networks, Ovation offers a single, centralized source for local and long-distance service and billing.

As an employee-owned company, Ovation's people recognize the importance of each of their customers. "We believe our customers benefit from Ovation's local presence and primary focus on local service. Because we are more focused than major carriers, and employee-owned, our people are very service-oriented and responsive to our customers and their special requirements," says Ovation's vice president of marketing and communications, Paul Thibeau.

Like the major carriers, but unlike local companies that primarily resell local and long-distance service, Ovation is building and operating its own digital fiber-optic networks, which are interconnected to other phone companys' networks. Ovation's fiber-optic technology enhances both voice and data communications, offering customers consistent quality and reliability.

As the company gains new funding, it is investing largely in expanding its fiber-optics network into new markets. To keep pace with today's fast-changing high-tech telecommunications environment, Ovation's laboratories develop technological solutions to answer customers' needs. Ovation also provides collocation facilities, whereby its customers can locate their telecommunications equipment on-site at Ovation switch sites.

This investment in technology and in solutions to fill customers' needs is a key to Ovation's strategy for meeting the growing demand to expand the information highway during the next millennium. "We are building Ovation Communications because we have a better way," Devine says. "We believe in building partnerships with our customers—and that the elements of these partnerships will set us above and beyond our competitors."

"The key to achieving our goals is Ovation's strong team of people, all of whom are dedicated to making our company a success," says Tim Devine.

HUBBARD BROADCASTING

BROADCAST

PIONEER HUBBARD

BROADCASTING

LEADS THE WAY

WITH MEDIA

INNOVATIONS FOR

THE LISTENING AND

VIEWING AUDIENCES

OF MINNEAPOLIS–

ST. PAUL

In 1998 Hubbard Broadcasting's station KSTP-TV celebrates half a century on the air in Minnesota. From its uncertain beginnings to its role as a trusted member of the Twin Cities community, the station has played an important part in the history of television since 1948. However, KSTP-TV's legacy can be traced back to the infancy of the commercial radio industry.

Hubbard Broadcasting began in 1923 with one radio station, WAMD, "Where All Minneapolis Dances." It was the first radio station in the world to survive solely on advertising revenue. Later renamed KSTP, it became a leading commercial station in the Twin Cities.

Stanley E. Hubbard, the man who founded the station as KSTP, believed passionately in the power of commercial broadcasting and was a key innovator as broadcast technology evolved. In 1938 Hubbard Broadcasting purchased from RCA the first television camera ever sold. In 1939 KSTP-TV demonstrated this new technology at the Minnesota State Fair, giving an estimated 200,000 people their first look at television.

During the coming years persistence and imagination sparked a string of remarkable introductions and innovations. In 1948 KSTP-TV began broadcasting—the first television station in the Twin Cities. That same year KSTP-TV became the first NBC affiliate in the country not owned by a network and by 1950 it was the first to offer daily newscasts. In 1954 KSTP-TV was the first station in the area to broadcast a program in color and in 1960 it was the first station in the world to broadcast all its programs in color.

In 1981 Hubbard Broadcasting formed U.S. Satellite Broadcasting (USSB), a company dedicated to developing high-power direct-to-home satellite broadcasting using small, eighteen-inch dish antennas. Today USSB is the nation's Digital Broadcast Satellite (DBS) licensee of longest standing and provides an unparalleled line-up of premium movie services available to millions of homes through the Digital Satellite System. In 1984 Hubbard Broadcasting's Conus Communications became the first satellite news gathering cooperative in the world. It is still the largest news service of its kind.

Guided by more than seventy years of experience, Hubbard Broadcasting continues its journey on the path of innovation. With a variety of media units including prominent radio and television properties in Minnesota, New Mexico, and New York; Conus Communications; two programming production companies; and USSB, Hubbard Broadcasting is among the leaders paving the way into the twenty-first century.

1948 *50* *1998*
YEARS
KSTPTV

Hubbard Broadcasting brings news, information, and entertainment media to audiences throughout the Twin Cities.

© Image Club Graphics

ST. PAUL PIONEER PRESS

As Minnesota's

first newspaper,

the *St. Paul*

Pioneer Press

upholds its

tradition with

award-winning

journalism

and leading-edge

technology

Julie Wasmundt of St. Paul has delivered the Pioneer Press to Woodbury customers since 1996. © Carolyn Kaster

In 1849 James Madison Goodhue traveled up the Mississippi River by steamboat to the new territorial capital of St. Paul. This frontier lawyer and editor unpacked his printing equipment and published the state's first newspaper, the *Minnesota Pioneer*. That weekly paper was the forerunner of today's daily *St. Paul Pioneer Press*.

In 1927 the *Pioneer Press* and the *St. Paul Dispatch* were acquired by Ridder Publications. The papers later were merged, and today the *St. Paul Pioneer Press* serves daily and Sunday readers in the Twin Cities Metro East region and throughout western Wisconsin. It is one of thirty-one daily newspapers in the Knight Ridder family of print and on-line products.

The *Pioneer Press* prints 85 million newspapers a year at its modern press across the Mississippi River from downtown St. Paul. But the process begins at the newspaper's downtown office, on Cedar Street. There, its

Pioneer Planet *Webmaster, Eric Wolfram, contemplates the day's on-line content offerings.* © Carolyn Kaster

award-winning news staff writes, edits, and photographs the day's news. Stories and pictures, along with advertising, are composed onto pages, and sophisticated microwave and telephone transmission equipment sends the pages to press. The *Pioneer Press* uses 400 tons of ink and 300,000 miles of newsprint per year.

The *St. Paul Pioneer Press* is widely regarded for its newsroom efforts to focus on reader needs and interests, and for companywide customer service excellence. A team-based newsroom reorganization in late 1995 was designed to bring news coverage even closer to readers. The newspaper maintains news bureaus in Washington, D.C.; the state capitol (St. Paul); North Metro (Shoreview); Minneapolis; and Wisconsin (Hudson). The paper's customer initiatives include the creation in 1995 of a full-time newsroom "reader advocate" position, and the development of a companywide network of customer advocates, to improve communication and speed action on customer issues that cross department lines. A customer Info Desk gives information to the public from stories in the newspaper's electronic library.

The newspaper makes an ongoing effort to develop special news and advertising sections that appeal to its readers' interests. These include *Market Week* for stock and mutual fund listings, the *Best of the Mall* weekly Mall of America shopper, and a monthly *Homestyle* section focused on home furnishings, home improvement, and new construction.

Recent innovations include the launch of four zoned community editions geared to providing the local and neighborhood news readers want. New features "topics" pages also were introduced in mid-1998.

The *St. Paul Pioneer Press* strives to always keep pace with change in the media industry. With a test launch in December 1995 of its on-line service, *PioneerPlanet*, the *Pioneer Press* became the first Knight Ridder newspaper to package its content service with Internet access. An innovative, user-friendly redesign was introduced in July 1998. Associated on-line products include the "Just Go" arts and entertainment site, the "HomeHunter" real estate site and the "JobHunter" employment site.

Pioneer Press also prides itself on its commitment to the community. Activities it sponsors include the annual *Pioneer Press* Medallion Treasure Hunt, the Minnesota State Fair, and the annual "Once Upon a Story" children's story-writing contest.

An innovative education program, Pioneers in Education, is among the Pioneer Press's key outreach efforts. The program involves community and business partners in initiatives to bring newspapers to area classrooms.

The *St. Paul Pioneer Press* recycling program reflects its goal as an industry leader and "good corporate citizen" to act responsibly toward the environment. The *Pioneer Press* was the first newspaper in the area to switch from petroleum-based to soybean-based color inks. Recycling programs involve paper, ink, plastic, metals, and other materials.

Pioneer Press *editors huddle to discuss the day's leading news stories.* © Carolyn Kaster

The newspaper has been recognized with many awards for excellence in writing and design. In 1986 and in 1988 it received journalism's highest honor, the Pulitzer Prize, for feature writing. In 1996 the *Pioneer Press* was named one of the ten best-designed papers in the world by the Society of Newspaper Design. In 1998 the *Pioneer Press* was honored by the Religious Public Relations Council (RPRC) for publishing the nation's best religion section and was named among the top-five business sections in its circulation category. The newspaper also was named by the Associated Press (AP) among the nation's top-twenty for its Sunday sports section.

"Several ingredients contribute to the region's robust commercial climate: a diversified business base, a skilled, well-educated workforce, a lower unemployment rate than the national average, and a healthy per capita income. As Minnesota's first newspaper, we are proud to serve this region," says publisher Rick Sadowski.

The Pioneer Press's *Goss Metroliner presses use approximately 400 tons of ink and 300,000 miles of newsprint each year.* © Carolyn Kaster

BY ROAD, RIVER, RAIL, & SKY

CHAPTER THIRTEEN

TOURISTS MAY KNOW MINNESOTA FOR ITS THOUSANDS OF LAKES, BUT COMMUTERS, TRAVELERS, AND SHIPPERS KNOW THE STATE FOR ITS THOUSANDS OF MILES OF ROADWAYS AND RAILROAD TRACKS, NUMEROUS MAJOR WATERWAY PORTS, AND AN INTERNATIONAL AIRPORT, WHICH COMBINE TO GIVE MINNESOTA A TRANSPORTATION INFRASTRUCTURE THAT IS SECOND TO NONE.

Although Minnesota is the fourteenth largest state in area, its road system is the fifth-largest road system in the country, with more than 130,000 miles of roadway. Of these, 5,000 miles are part of the National Truck Network. The roadway system is a key component to the state's overall transportation infrastructure, heavily relied on by the state's agriculture, processing, manufacturing, and retail and wholesale trades. Business and pleasure vehicles travel a total of nearly forty-three billion miles on its streets and highways every year.

Minnesota's central location enables its businesses to access a large and immediate consumer market. According to the most recent U.S. Department of Commerce statistics, over forty-nine million people live within five hundred miles of Minneapolis and St. Paul. Within that same jurisdiction, there are more than one million businesses and over eighty thousand manufactur-ers. Trucking dominates as the main means of moving Minnesota freight, carrying about 80 percent of manu-facturing freight in and out of the state. Approximately 4,700 intrastate and 30,000 interstate carriers as well as numerous pri-vate fleets provide Minnesota with truck transportation services.

Those staying closer to home find getting around to be a breeze in Minnesota. Urban roadway studies found the Twin Cities metropolitan area to have the shortest average commute time of twenty large metropolitan areas studied and gave it high marks for low roadway congestion as well.

A total of twenty-seven rail-roads, including four private companies, currently operate in Minnesota. There are four major carriers that own near-ly three thousand miles of rail lines. Burlington Northern Santa Fe is the largest, with 56 percent of the rail lines under its ownership. The CP Rail System, Union Pacific

Opposite: This freeway leading into downtown Minneapolis is part of a vast and well-oiled transportation system that gives residents something to boast about—some of the shortest average commute times in the country. © Greg Ryan-Sally Beyer. Above: Chris Fiero, a pilot with Helicopter Flight, Inc., at Crystal Airport in Minneapolis, prepares for takeoff. © Greg Ryan-Sally Beyer

Courtesy, Northwest Airlines

thirteenth busiest airport in the country in landings and takeoffs and ranks eighteenth in the world in passengers accommodated. Nonstop flights from this facility send passengers to most major North American cities and several European and Asian destinations. Less than eight miles from either downtown Minneapolis or St. Paul, the airport is quickly and conveniently reached. MSP consistently ranks high among the nation's busiest airports for on-time arrivals and departures. A vital part of the Metropolitan Airports Commission are six smaller reliever airports, which provide alternative facilities for corporate and smaller aircraft that would otherwise substantially increase the traffic at MSP. These reliever airports together account for more than 2,500 daily takeoffs and landings, more than twice the number of MSP.

Railroad, and Canadian National Railways round out the list. Twenty rail-water intermodal systems operate in the state as well. Amtrak provides passenger service to only six communities in Minnesota, so in an effort to increase the use of rail to move people as well as goods, the state is currently studying the feasibility of increased use of passenger rail. The Twin Cities Commuter Rail Study and the Wisconsin-Illinois-Minnesota High Speed Rail Corridor Study will present their findings early in 1999.

The Minneapolis–St. Paul International Airport (MSP) functions as the hub for air travel in the upper Midwest. Served by sixteen air cargo companies and seventeen passenger airlines, including four Minnesota companies (Northwest Airlines, Mesaba Aviation, Sun Country Airlines, and Great Lakes Aviation, Ltd.), MSP is the

This tractor-trailer hauls goods up I-35.
© Conrad Bloomquist/Scenic Photo!

An iron ore train rolls through Taconite Harbor in northern Minnesota. © Greg Ryan-Sally Beyer

A total of 138 publicly owned airports exist throughout the state, including 15 with scheduled passenger service by regional or major carriers. According to one Department of Transportation study, nearly 90 percent of Minnesotans live within fifty-five miles of an airport with scheduled air service.

While jet airplanes and high-speed rail will no doubt be part of the future, the way of transport that was most vital to Minnesota's past, its waterways, will continue to play a vital role in the state's transportation story. Travel along the 231 miles of the Mississippi River that wend through Minnesota, once the state's main link to the world, was nearly nonexistent after the advent of first the railroads, then trucks and planes. But when Congress

IN-LINE SKATING TYPICALLY CONJURES UP IMAGES OF CALIFORNIA, BUT THE INDUSTRY ORIGINATED IN MINNESOTA. IN 1980, THE HOCKEY-PLAYING OLSON BROTHERS CAME ACROSS A FORM OF IN-LINE SKATES IN A SPORTING-GOODS STORE AND DECIDED THEY WOULD MAKE A GREAT OFF-SEASON TRAINING TOOL. THEY REFINED THE PRODUCT AND ASSEMBLED THE FIRST ROLLERBLADE IN THE BASEMENT OF THEIR PARENTS' HOME IN MINNEAPOLIS. MINNESOTA HOCKEY PLAYERS WERE THE FIRST

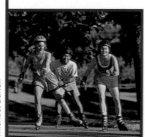

TO EMBRACE THE CREATION, THEN NORDIC AND ALPINE SKIERS AND, AFTER THE SALE OF THE COMPANY IN 1984, THE ENTIRE COUNTRY. TODAY, ROLLERBLADE IS THE WORLD LEADER IN THE IN-LINE SKATE MARKET.

authorized the deepening of the upper Mississippi in 1930 and created a system of locks and dams, traffic on the river was restored. Between 1935 and 1972, barge traffic in and out of the Twin Cities ports alone increased more than eightyfold. Today, the river system supports five port areas. The state's agricultural products, primarily corn, soybeans, and wheat, account for 7 percent of the total U.S. agricultural exports made via the Mississippi

Opposite: A barge rests in between jobs on the Mississippi. © Bob Firth/Firth Photobank. Below: A student receives some pointers from an instructor at the Flying Scotchman Flight School at Crystal Airport. © Greg Ryan-Sally Beyer

WATER SKIING WAS BORN WHEN RALPH SAMUELSON STRAPPED PINE BOARDS TO HIS FEET AND GRABBED ONTO A ROPE ATTACHED TO THE BACK OF A MOVING BOAT ON LAKE PEPIN, OFF THE SHORES OF LAKE CITY, MINNESOTA. THE YEAR WAS 1922, AND LAKE CITY STILL COMMEMORATES THE CREATION WITH AN ANNUAL CELEBRATION KNOWN AS WATER SKI DAYS.

© PhotoDisc, Inc.

In 1918, when ore was discovered underneath Hibbing, the citizens elected to do the only conceivable thing: move the town. Enterprising miner Carl Wickman and partners saw the need to transport the miners between their new location and the booming mine, so they constructed a twelve-passenger bus, the only one at the time in the United States (save for those manufactured by a private New York company for its own use). Soon, Wickman and partners operated a fleet of eighteen busses throughout northern Minnesota, spawning the birth of a nationwide bus company that would come to be known as Greyhound.

River. Coal, fertilizer, minerals, cement, steel products, petroleum, and vegetable oils are among the other products shipped out of Minnesota's river ports.

Minnesota's other great waterway is the Great Lakes–St. Lawrence Seaway. Four ports along Lake Superior generate a combined total of 80 million tons of cargo. Iron ore and taconite are the primary loads, while grain, coal, limestone, and a variety of manufactured goods are also shipped to a number of U.S. and foreign markets. The state benefits from its extensive waterway

Above: This airplane is one of the many on-time arrivals at Minneapolis–St. Paul International Airport. © Bob Firth/Firth Photobank. Below: The "Aurora3," a solar vehicle developed by University of Minnesota students, stages a 78-mile-per-hour run down Highway 212 between Chaska and Glencoe. © Charles Habermann

system because its low cost of transportation provides shippers with a substantial savings when they are shipping freight that is not time sensitive.

As with everything else Minnesotan, the transportation system reflects a balance of the old and the new, the traditional and the innovative. Cirrus Aircraft Design, with its headquarters in Duluth, recently unveiled a much-anticipated new aircraft using state-of-the-art technology, including all-composite construction made from materials developed by 3M Aerospace in St. Paul; and aviation pioneer Northwest Airlines continues to think globally, having recently joined in partnership with the Dutch KLM Airlines to expand its international market. When people board their flights at Minneapolis–St. Paul International, they will be the only passengers in the world to be guided by an innovative global positioning system,

The Minneapolis–St. Paul International Airport in Minneapolis has become an important hub for travel in the upper Midwest and between the United States and the rest of the world. © Conrad Bloomquist/Scenic Photo!

which provides their flight crews with the most accurate aircraft navigation information possible. As they climb into the skies above the metropolitan area, perhaps passing over Honeywell, the Minnesota Fortune 500 company responsible for creating the new navigational system, they may look out their windows to see a barge laboring along the Mississippi River with a cargo of Minnesota wheat and to spy small children scampering along the banks, waiving to it. It's the same scene, albeit from a different perspective, enjoyed by passengers traveling through Minnesota on stagecoaches 150 years ago.

© Greg Ryan-Sally Beyer

TRANSPORTATION

NORTHWEST AIRLINES

HEADQUARTERED IN

MINNEAPOLIS–ST. PAUL,

NORTHWEST AIRLINES

AND ITS STRATEGIC

PARTNERS PROVIDE

SEAMLESS SERVICE

TO MORE THAN

400 CITIES IN OVER

80 COUNTRIES AROUND

THE GLOBE

Northwest Airlines, the largest subsidiary of Northwest Airlines Corporation, is the world's fourth largest airline and America's oldest carrier with continuous name identification. The airline began operating on October 1, 1926, flying mail between Minneapolis–St. Paul and Chicago. Passenger service began the following year. On July 15, 1947, Northwest Airlines, which pioneered the Great Circle route, began service from the United States to Tokyo, Seoul, Shanghai, and Manila. The year 1997 marked Northwest's fiftieth anniversary of service to Japan, making it the first airline in history to mark such a milestone.

With its global travel partners, Northwest serves more than 400 cities in over 80 countries on six continents. The airline offers more than 1,700 flights every day including nonstop flights from nine U.S. cities to Japan: Anchorage, Detroit, Honolulu, Las Vegas, Los Angeles, Minneapolis–St. Paul, New York, San Francisco, and Seattle–Tacoma. The carrier's comprehensive U.S. system spans forty-eight states and the District of Columbia, with hubs in Minneapolis–St. Paul, Detroit, and Memphis.

Northwest strengthened its U.S. route system in 1986 by acquiring Republic Airlines, thus gaining its Detroit and Memphis hubs. The airline is affiliated with several regional airlines as well,

A Northwest Orient Airlines Boeing 747 flies over the Grand Hotel in Taipei, Taiwan. Northwest began service to Taipei (formerly Formosa) in 1950. The airline removed the word "Orient" from its name in 1986, when it acquired Republic Airlines.

which operate as Northwest Airlink and offer dozens of connecting flights daily.

In 1993 Northwest formed a unique alliance with KLM Royal Dutch Airlines, based in Amsterdam, to offer seamless service between the United States and cities around the world. In 1997 the two airlines signed a long-term global joint venture agreement to continue to expand their worldwide commercial cooperation.

In addition to the key players, a successful global alliance such as that of Northwest and KLM requires a number of major airlines and select regional partners to provide convenient, reliable, and seamless customer service. To this end, Northwest has built and is continually extending its network as part of its ongoing commitment to better serve passengers' travel needs.

Northwest's fleet of more than 415 aircraft includes Boeing 747s, 757s, 727s, McDonnell Douglas DC-9s and DC-10s, and Airbus A319s

The Twin Cities derive between 40 to 45 million dollars per year in economic benefit from the flight between Minneapolis–St. Paul and Tokyo alone.

and A320s. One of the world's largest cargo airlines, Northwest also operates a dedicated fleet of eight B747 freighters.

Named "Airline of the Year" with KLM by *Air Transport World* magazine in 1998, Northwest has received many accolades. In 1997 it ranked second in a *Fortune* magazine business survey of the world's most admired companies. Mesaba Airlines, part of the Northwest Airlink group, was named 1998 "Regional Airline of the Year" by *Air Transport World*.

Northwest's partnership with Minnesota is an integral part of the company's history and future—as it is of the state itself. Studies by the Minnesota Department of Trade and Economic Development show that the Twin Cities derive from 40 to 45 million dollars per year in economic benefit from the flight between Minneapolis–St. Paul and Tokyo alone. According to the 1992 USA-BIAS study, new international routes can add from $100 to $300 million annually to the local economy depending upon the number of flights per week. Northwest operates as many as 178 international flights per week depending on the time of year. Northwest's total contribution to Minnesota's economy adds up to more than $2.3 billion annually—with 20,000 employees, the airline supports the largest private payroll in the state. From Minnesotans' perspective, as hosts of a hub city they enjoy a broad choice of domestic and international flights, the convenience of more nonstop flights, and the economic activity that comes from serving as an international hub.

Northwest's mission, that "the people of Northwest Airlines will provide reliable, convenient, and consistent air transportation that meets or exceeds customer expectations and earns a

A Northwest Airlines DC-9 soars across the Minneapolis skyline. Northwest began flying airmail between the Twin Cities and Chicago in 1926, and carried its first commercial passenger the following year.

sustainable profit," is a reality. John Dasburg, the carrier's president and chief executive officer, reflects that "the airline's business strategy is the embodiment of its mission, including the critical elements of reliability, convenience, and consistency, delivered by the best people."

Northwest Airlines Corporation stock is publicly traded through NASDAQ under the symbol NWAC. The company may be accessed on the Internet at www.nwa.com.

Northwest Airlines marked its fiftieth anniversary of uninterrupted service to Asia on July 15, 1997. Northwest's WorldPlane, a Boeing 747-400 decorated with artwork by nineteen children from the United States and Asia, was the most visible symbol of this historic milestone.

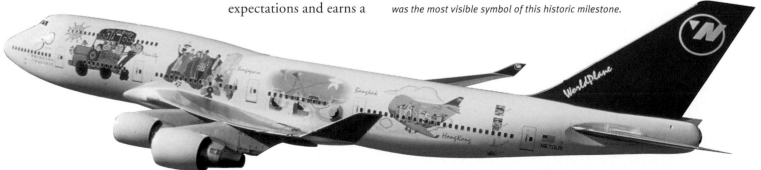

METROPOLITAN AIRPORTS COMMISSION

BALANCING

THE PROMOTION

OF AIR COMMERCE

WITH SAFETY

AND ENVIRONMENTAL

CONCERNS, MAC

BRINGS AIRLINES

THE LOWEST COST

PER PASSENGER

OF ANY MAJOR

AIRPORT IN THE

UNITED STATES

Thanks to the foresight of Governor Harold Stassen of Minnesota more than fifty years ago, the state today has one of the most important and busiest airport systems in the world. Although aviation was a new industry at that time, the benefits it offered to the growth of the Twin Cities' postwar economy did not escape Governor Stassen's understanding.

On his recommendation, the legislature created the Minneapolis–St. Paul Metropolitan Airports Commission (MAC) in 1943. The agency balances the promotion of air commerce with safety and environmental concerns. Its jurisdiction is Minneapolis and St. Paul, as well as the counties of Anoka, Carver, Dakota, Hennepin, Ramsey, Scott, and Washington, nearly all of the present Twin Cities metropolitan area.

A public corporation, MAC owns and operates seven airports: Minneapolis–St. Paul International Airport—Wold Chamberlain Field (MSP) and six reliever airports that serve business customers and general aviation. The six include Crystal and Flying Cloud in Hennepin County, Airlake in Dakota County, Anoka County/Blaine in Anoka County, Lake Elmo in Washington County, and St. Paul Downtown Airport in Ramsey County.

Air cargo constitutes an important market at MSP; the MAC is seeking to expand the number of international air cargo flights as a service to the Twin Cities business community.

The governor of Minnesota appoints a chairperson and twelve of MAC's fourteen commissioners for four-year terms. Eight commissioners represent designated metro districts, four are from smaller cities served by commercial or general aviation airports, and two seats are reserved for the mayors of St. Paul and Minneapolis, who may serve or appoint a surrogate. MAC's professional staff of 400 includes police and fire personnel, environmental specialists, and maintenance crews.

Longtime residents of the Twin Cities remember that the land upon which MSP sits was the home of a two-mile oval racetrack built in 1915 on remote farmland. The racetrack failed, and in 1920 the Aeroclub of Minneapolis made the infield its base. The site has been an airfield ever since.

A BOON TO LOCAL ECONOMY

Much of the story of the airport is a history of its oldest and largest carrier, Northwest Airlines. Then called Northwest Airways, it was formed in 1926 to carry United States mail; it began

The new six-lane roadway in front of the Lindbergh Terminal was expanded in 1996, and provides convenient access to arriving and departing passengers at MSP.

passenger service in 1929. For many years it flew from both the racetrack site and the riverside airfield in downtown St. Paul (later called Holman Field; now St. Paul Downtown Airport). Two years after World War II ended, Northwest became a scheduled carrier to the Far East, consolidating its maintenance facilities and gates at the racetrack location.

Today MSP is among the busiest airports in the world. From 64,088 takeoffs and landings in 1945, that number reached 491,273 by 1997 (only twelve airports had more), 88 percent of which were commercial, charter, or cargo flights. As for passengers, while 327,201 passengers passed through MSP in 1945, by 1997 the figure had risen to 30 million (including in-transit passengers), making MSP the world's eighteenth-busiest airport.

To calculate MSP's influence on the Twin Cities' economy, one need only look at the jobs it creates. A few years ago, 25,000 jobs were directly tied to MSP, and about half that number was related to the purchasing power of airport employees. Spending by MSP visitors created 35,200 other jobs. At least 36,000 jobs in local corporate headquarters depend upon convenient air service.

Operating revenue in 1997 was more than $100 million. The airport generates $5.5 billion in annual business revenue, which amounts to $4.2 billion in personal income to Minnesotans. It also results in $382 million in state and local taxes, and contributes $125 million to the Federal Aviation Trust Fund for airport and air traffic control improvements.

A new air traffic control tower, opened in 1996, contains state-of-the-art radar and communications equipment, and gives controllers an unrestricted view of runways and taxiways at MSP.

CHANGING TIMES BRING EXPANDED OPPORTUNITIES AND INCREASED EFFICIENCY

In the 1950s, a departing passenger could walk from the remotest parking space through check-in to the plane in minutes. Today state-of-the-art security systems and large terminals adequate for intercontinental jumbo jetliners reveal the complexities of air travel as the century comes to a close. Commissioners continually wrestle with decisions that will affect future air service. Perhaps the most significant of these was the 1996 decision to expand and improve MSP to meet travelers' needs for another twenty-five years. Runway 4/22 was extended from 8,250 feet to 11,000 feet to facilitate nonstop flights to destinations in Asia and Europe. Because departures to Osaka, Hong Kong, and Amsterdam are routine, the new International Arrivals Facility, with speedy, efficient customs and immigration processing, was opened in 1996.

Among MSP's improvements is the state-of-the-art Honeywell Differential Global Positioning System, which allows controllers to fix the position of aircraft in their range to within six feet vertically and horizontally, giving flight

Minneapolis–St. Paul International Airport currently accommodates more than thirty million passengers a year on domestic and international flights.

crews instantaneous and highly accurate navigation information. Also new are an air traffic control tower, better access roads, and a revamped ground transportation center.

MSP is a premier world airport by any definition. It is served by four regional carriers and all the major airlines with just one exception (Southwest). Thanks in part to the Northwest/KLM alliance, it provides one-stop or nonstop service to 175 destinations including twenty international cities, and has more charter flights to the southern United States, Mexico, and the Caribbean than any other airport.

The St. Paul Downtown Airport also received millions of dollars in improvements. It is a favorite for corporate aircraft because it has less traffic than MSP yet is about the same distance to downtown Minneapolis, and is only minutes from the capitol in St. Paul.

By operating its airports efficiently, MAC has established the lowest cost per passenger to airlines of any major airport in the country. This encourages domestic and international air service through MSP, sometimes at the expense of airports on either coast, and is always in line with the commission's goals of providing more service for consumers and of building America's North Coast Gateway to Canada, Europe, and Asia. MAC also is working to make its airports good community neighbors with a $400 million program to retrofit homes in airport flight paths with sound insulation.

Growth does not come entirely without cost, but MAC operates without any state or local funding. Although the commission has authority to raise funds through a tax on metropolitan properties, it has not done so since 1969. Instead, direct-use fees on landing, hangar and terminal rentals, concessions, and parking cover annual operating expenses. Major construction projects are funded through the sale of bonds and are repaid by user fees.

In addition to Northwest, MSP is now served by such international carriers as KLM Royal Dutch Airlines, Icelandair, and Air Canada; more than 230 nonstop flights are offered weekly to nine cities including London, Amsterdam, Reykjavik, Tokyo, Osaka, and Hong Kong. MSP has earned worldwide acclaim for its excellent winter operations and the ability of the field maintenance crew to keep the airport safe and operational in often-difficult weather conditions.

JETWAYS

RECOGNIZING A NEED

FOR HIGH-QUALITY,

EFFICIENT BUSINESS

TRAVEL, JETWAYS,

A BRILLIANT

INNOVATOR IN

THE CORPORATE

TRANSPORTATION

MARKET, MAKES

PRIVATE CORPORATE

JETS AVAILABLE TO

COMPANIES THROUGH

A SHARED PLAN

At the turn of the millennium, an important aviation trend is predicted to gather momentum— the idea of shared ownership of corporate aircraft. Currently, shared- or fractional-ownership programs may escape general notice. However, in Minnesota, Jetways has taken a leadership position in making these options available.

With a membership in Jetways, individuals and businesses are able to share the costs and, more importantly, the talents of professionals dedicated to the highest standards in business aviation. Members are able to fly in the fleet's variety of aircraft for an allocation of hours based on numbers of shares purchased.

The small- to medium-sized jets save time for businesses in several ways: in the custom-planning process; the boarding process; and in the actual flight experience. At Jetways, arrangements for a flight can be made with one telephone call to the certified dispatchers/schedulers. The Jetways staff schedules the aircraft, selects the proper crew, and identifies the smaller airports nearest to the destination, arranging for hotels, rental cars, and limousine services, also, at the customer's request.

The aircrafts' leather-appointed interiors are designed for comfortably conducting business or simply relaxing.

Members are able to fly in the Jetways fleet's variety of aircraft for an allocation of hours based on numbers of shares purchased.

The complexities of setting up and maintaining a fine-quality in-house flight department can be considerable. At Jetways the staff takes pride in making these complexities appear to be easy and straightforward, allowing members to focus on running their own businesses. The pilots at Jetways are full-time professionals who have the most advanced recurrent training, cockpit resource-management training, and customer-service friendliness.

Members can focus on conducting business, while enjoying a high-quality flight experience. Through this service, small- to medium-sized companies have the benefits of corporate-owned aircraft usually available to Fortune 500 companies.

"Aviation is the key to business growth. In the coming years, there is no doubt that small- to mid-size companies will avail themselves of the same service known to the giants of industry, a service which can be used as a tool for growth—business aircraft with a twist—jets that are shared with others, reducing the cost of business travel to a fraction of former levels," says Jetways president Bill Waterman.

"The future in business belongs to those who position themselves on the cusp of this trend, controlling costs, productivity, situations, and time with this personal jet transportation," Waterman says.

DART TRANSIT COMPANY

When he founded Dart Transit Company in 1934, Earl Oren may have had only one trailer, but he also had the ingredients for success: inspiration, firm principles, and desire. Today Dart Transit Company—still a family-run business—is the largest trucking firm in Minnesota and is recognized throughout the industry as an innovative provider of transportation services.

Fueled by a deep, abiding belief in the entrepreneurial spirit, Dart is dedicated to providing outstanding customer service, a business principle that has carried the company to its present leadership position in the trucking industry.

Dart offers its customers the convenience of one-stop shopping. With just one phone call, a shipper can schedule a wide variety of transportation services: door-to-door truckload service, rail/truck intermodal service, air freight, and third party outsourcing. During that same phone call, a customer can also access the company's warehouse services to take advantage of product storage with shipment on demand.

Its customer base is a veritable who's who of American industry. The list includes General Mills, Target Stores, 3M, Coca-Cola, Whirlpool, Procter & Gamble, and Reynolds Aluminum.

Dart Transit Company operates as a truckload carrier in all forty-eight contiguous states and the lower tier of Canadian provinces. Under the stewardship of the

Satellites provide instant communications links between dispatchers and Dart trucks.

company president, Donald G. Oren, Dart ranks among the twelve largest truckload carriers in the U.S.

During the 1970s and 1980s, Mr. Oren provided the leadership that led to a dramatic increase in truck productivity. His pioneering trailer designs included a number of patented features that greatly expanded the usable cargo hauling capacity of truck trailers. These advances reduced the number of trucks needed to haul freight—reducing traffic congestion and lowering shipping costs. Don Oren further led the industry by developing larger trailers, spearheading the growth of standard trailer lengths from 42 to 53 feet long and standard widths from 96 to 102 inches. Dart also operates 57-foot trailers through Fleetline Inc., its Texas-based affiliate.

Dart is especially proud of its exceptional safety and on-time performance record. On-time performance routinely exceeds 98 percent and the company's driver safety training program has become a model for the motor carrier industry.

Dart's innovative efforts are driven by the desire to become the nation's premier provider of transportation services. Even as it utilizes the newest technologies, Dart holds its focus on its core values: performance that exceeds customer expectations, and protecting the motoring public through safe operations. These are the hallmarks of a true transportation leader.

© Conrad Bloomquist/Scenic Photo!

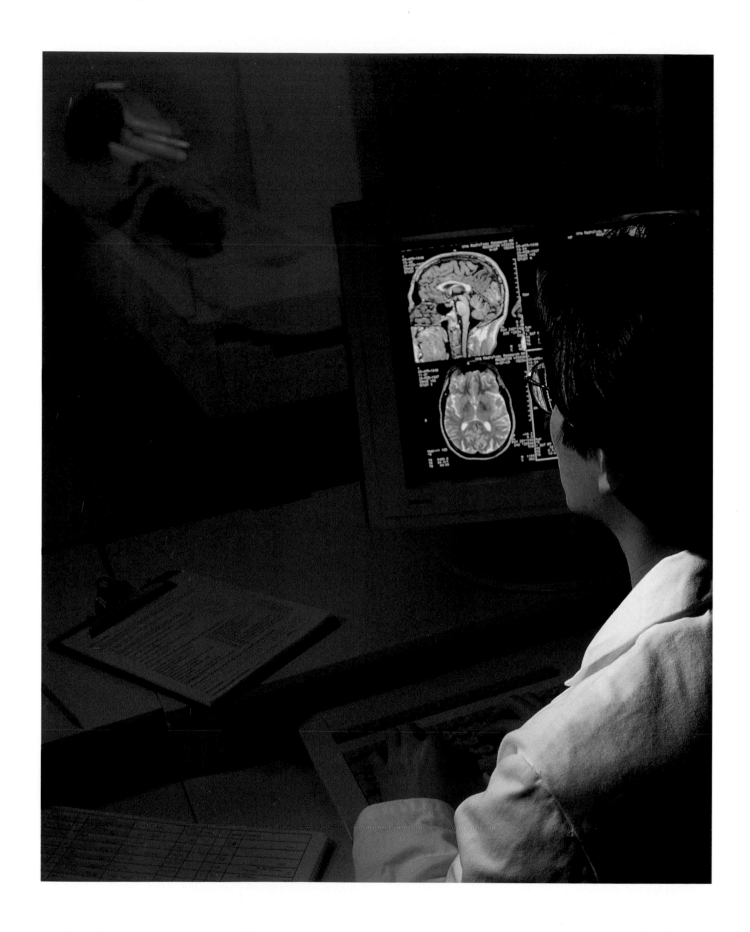

THE BEST IN HEALTH CARE

CHAPTER FOURTEEN

GOOD HEALTH. HERE IN MINNESOTA, IT IS SO ABUNDANT IT'S PRACTICALLY A NATURAL RESOURCE. THE STATE CURRENTLY RANKS AS THE HEALTHIEST IN THE NATION, ACCORDING TO THE 1996 RELIASTAR RANKINGS, A DISTINCTION IT HAS ENJOYED FOR FOUR OF THE SEVEN YEARS THE SURVEY HAS BEEN IN EXISTENCE, ECLIPSED ONLY BY UTAH ON THE THREE OTHER OCCASIONS. COMBINING TO PLACE MINNESOTA AT THE TOP ARE SEVERAL IMPRESSIVE

qualities: top rankings in low incidences of heart disease, the second-lowest rates of premature deaths and workers on disability status, and one of the lowest percentages of low-birthweight babies in the nation. Minnesota excels in access to primary health care and a high level of support for public health care.

Health-care legislation has long been a priority in Minnesota, and the state boasts a history of thoughtful health-care reforms that have served as models both for other states and for national legislation. The innovative Health-Right Act, later renamed MinnesotaCare, subsidizes health-care delivery to uninsured and underinsured low-income residents, with a particular emphasis on children and expectant mothers. Thanks to this act, funding for which comes from a provider tax and premiums paid by enrollees, more than 90 percent of children under the age of eighteen have health insurance coverage.

Under MinnesotaCare, the state's entire uninsured population has remained stable while the national trend in this category displays substantial growth. Another laudable goal of the act has been to enable small businesses to purchase insurance coverage for their employees at similar terms to those formerly only offered to larger companies.

As the laws surrounding health care changed about five years ago, so did the organization of many health-care providers throughout the state. Large metropolitan clinics began purchasing small rural practices, extending to their staff and patients a fuller spectrum of medical services and resources. Long a national leader and innovator in the area of managed care, Minnesota providers continue to find ways to lower prices while maintaining or improving the quality of care. The recent decrease in total Medicare receipts reflects the relative efficiency of the state's health-care

Opposite: State-of-the-art technologies, including this CAT scan machine, assist physicians in helping their patients in many ways. © Jackson Smith/Uniphoto, Inc. Above: High-tech equipment is also an integral part of preparing to enter the work world, as this college student in a medical research laboratory learns. © Uniphoto, Inc.

THE UNIVERSITY OF MINNESOTA HOSPITALS AND MEDICAL SCHOOL HAD A NUMBER OF MEDICAL FIRSTS, AMONG THEM: THE FIRST SUCCESSFUL OPEN-HEART SURGERY (1952); THE CREATION OF THE WORLD'S FIRST SUCCESSFUL HEART-LUNG MACHINE (1955), WHICH ENABLED CARDIAC SURGEONS TO PERFORM LONGER, MORE-EXTENSIVE OPERATIONS; THE WORLD'S FIRST SUCCESSFUL HEART-VALVE REPLACEMENT SURGERY WITH AN ARTIFICIAL VALVE (1958); THE WORLD'S FIRST PANCREAS TRANSPLANT (1966); THE WORLD'S FIRST SUCCESSFUL BONE-MARROW TRANSPLANT (1968). THEY ALSO BUILT THE FIRST TOTAL-BODY CAT SCANNER IN THE WORLD.

THE ROOTS OF QUALITY

Although Medical Alley is a relatively recent phenomenon, neither the spirit of innovation nor the setting of benchmarks for quality is new to health care in Minnesota. The world-renowned Mayo Clinic, in Rochester, began when Dr. William Worrell Mayo and his two sons, Drs. William J. and Charles H. Mayo, responded to the request of the Sisters of the Order of St. Francis to direct their new hospital, built to care for the victims of

Below: More than 85 percent of the patients who come to Mayo are outpatients. Mayo's expertise ranges over more than 100 medical and surgical specialties. © John Elk III. Opposite: In 1952, a team of surgeons at the University of Minnesota Hospitals and Medical School performed the world's first successful open-heart surgery. Courtesy, University of Minnesota. Opposite below: This computer-manipulated image shows how a Medtronic neurostimulator would be used to alleviate a tremor. Medtronic is known for its medical devices worldwide. © Medtronic

delivery system. Overall, health-care costs in Minnesota are 18 percent below that of the national average.

Throughout the state, there are nearly seven thousand health-care manufacturers, providers, insurers, retailers, and service establishments, with some 217,000 employees. Health care's share of state employment is 7 percent higher than the national average. One 350-mile corridor of southern Minnesota possesses so many medically related companies and institutions that it has been dubbed "Medical Alley," paralleling California's "Silicon Valley" and North Carolina's "Research Triangle" in significance and composition. Medical Alley has become synonymous with cutting-edge innovation and hallmark quality, which permeate all aspects of the state's health-care industries.

Case in point: Minnesota's concentration of employment in the manufacture of medical products alone is more than twice that of the national average and the second highest in the nation. So rapid is the growth in this sector that the creation of new medical-device manufacturing establishments nearly doubles the state average for manufacturers. One shining success story is SCIMED, a division of Boston Scientific Corporation. Based in the Twin Cities suburb of Maple Grove, the company is the leading manufacturer of disposable devices used in non-invasive coronary procedures such as angioplasty. Minnesota also ranks high in the production of electromedical devices, surgical appliances and supplies, and ophthalmic goods. Together, Minnesota medical-product companies generate over $3.5 billion in annual sales.

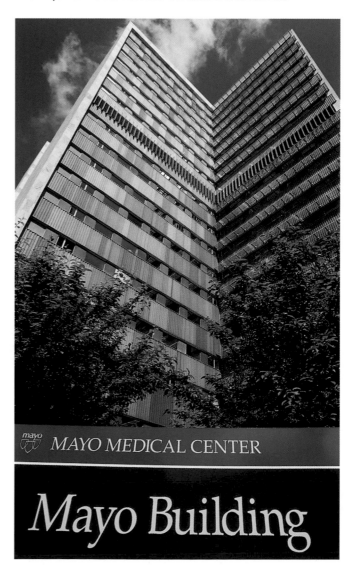

MAYO MEDICAL CENTER

Mayo Building

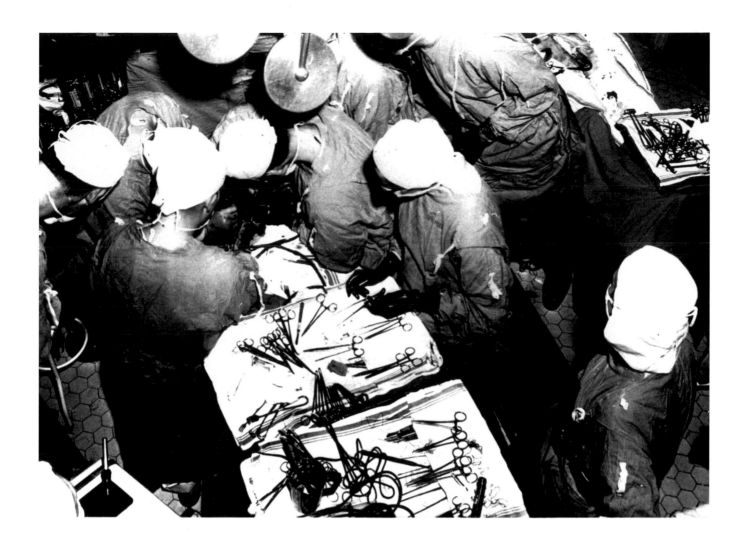

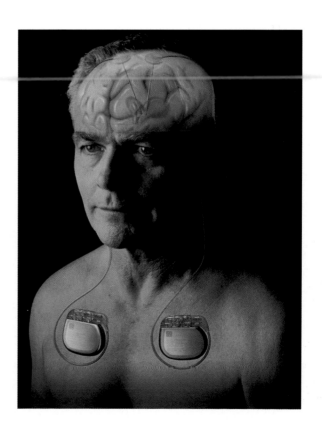

THE MAYO CLINIC HAD NUMEROUS MEDICAL FIRSTS AS WELL. THEY WERE THE FIRST TO OPEN A GRADUATE SCHOOL OF MEDICINE AND TRAIN MEDICAL SPECIALISTS. THE SCHOOL OPENED IN 1915 AND TODAY MORE THAN ELEVEN THOUSAND ALUMNI PRACTICE SPECIALIZED MEDICINE THROUGHOUT THE WORLD. MAYO'S BLOOD BANK, FOUNDED IN 1933, WAS AMONG THE NATION'S FIRST AND SERVED AS A MODEL FOR THE COLLECTION, STORAGE, AND TRANSFUSING OF BLOOD. IN 1945, WORK DONE IN CONJUNCTION WITH TREATING TUBERCULOSIS ESTABLISHED THE FIRST LABORATORY PRINCIPLES FOR EVALUATING CHEMOTHERAPY. THE FIRST HIP-REPLACEMENT SURGERY, WHICH HERALDED THE AGE OF JOINT REPLACEMENT, WAS PERFORMED AT THE MAYO CLINIC IN 1969.

a cyclone in 1883. What started as a small, family forty-bed practice evolved into the international model for the group-practice delivery of medicine adopted the world over. Today, Mayo is a system of clinics and hospitals that includes more than twenty-five thousand employees and administers to the needs of some four hundred thousand patients annually. It is the world's oldest and largest multispecialty group practice. Patients from all over the globe come to consult with specialists in virtually every medical field. Research and education are also vital components of Mayo. The clinic has a medical school and a graduate school of medicine. Mayo is a primary source for medical

Above: The University of Minnesota Hospital and Clinic enjoys a beautiful setting on the banks of the Mississippi River in Minneapolis. © Greg Ryan-Sally Beyer. Below: The latest devices in medical technology require highly trained operators to ensure their proper use and functioning. © Mayo Clinic

research and is revered as a leader in the diagnosis and treatment of disease. In addition to the staff scientists, more than one-third of the medical staff engages in regular research. The clinic's special method of medical practice and cost containment has served as the model for the state's health-care reform.

implantable and interventional medical therapies. Today, the Fridley-based company remains on the cutting edge of medical technology.

Just forty-five miles away from the busy metropolitan area lies the Hazelden Foundation, a residential and outpatient alcohol and drug treatment center recognized throughout the world as a leader and role model in the industry since 1949. Chemically dependent people from all walks of life, including numerous celebrities, have sought help to overcome their addictions in this prestigious facility. Hazelden's publishing company is also the premier publisher of information on addiction and one of the largest specialty publishers in the world.

As the baby-boomer generation prepares for its retirement years in the twenty-first century, the need

While the Mayo Clinic was making a name for itself in medical innovation during the middle part of the twentieth century, some ninety miles to the north the University of Minnesota Hospital was forging ahead with its own pioneering developments. Several university surgeons with a vision to operate inside the human heart were responsible for the development of the specialty of cardiac surgery in the early 1950s. As cardiac surgery advanced, the medical team at the university hospital designed the first clinically usable pacemaker. Its designer went on to found Medtronic, the world's leading developer-manufacturer of pacemakers and other

DR. CHRISTIAAN BARNARD, THE SOUTH AFRICAN CARDIAC SURGEON WHO PERFORMED THE WORLD'S FIRST HEART TRANSPLANT, AND DR. NORMAN SHUMWAY, WHO MADE IT A CLINICALLY USEFUL PROCEDURE, BOTH RECEIVED THEIR CARDIAC SURGERY EDUCATION AT THE UNIVERSITY OF MINNESOTA.

© John Elk III

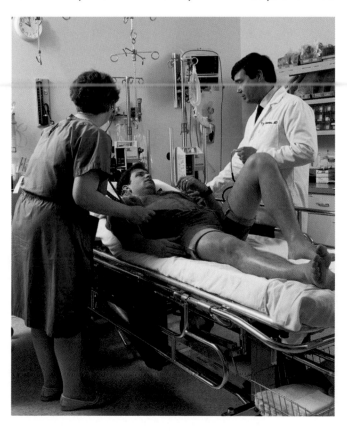

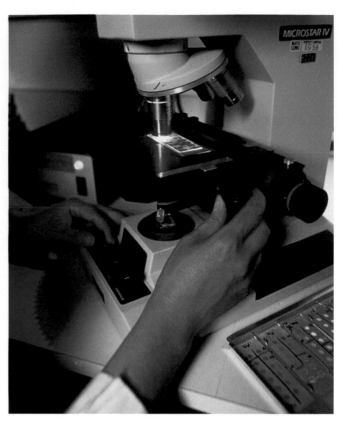

for quality health care will only increase. The demand for diagnostic and therapeutic devices and supplies will grow, as will dedication to the research, development, and manufacture of new products and delivery methods. Fortunately, the quality, innovation, and tradition associated with Minnesota's health-care industry will position it well in the domestic and international marketplaces for years to come. In turn, the growth can be counted on to produce a ripple effect throughout other areas of the state's economy as various industries will be called on to apply their services to support the demands created by the medical industry's growth.

Above left: Minnesotans enjoy a longer life expectancy than other Americans. © Uniphoto, Inc. Above: Work in medicine and medical technology calls for people with a love for detail and precision. © Mayo Clinic. Below: The best in personal care is offered by Minnesota's doctors. © Uniphoto, Inc.

THE UNIVERSITY OF MINNESOTA HAS ANOTHER WORLD-RENOWNED MEDICAL FACILITY, BUT FOR SLIGHTLY MORE UNUSUAL PATIENTS. THE UNIVERSITY'S RAPTOR CENTER IS THE LARGEST MEDICAL FACILITY IN THE WORLD FOR THE CARE AND TREATMENT OF BIRDS OF PREY AS WELL AS ENDANGERED OR RARE SPECIES OF BIRDS. THE TREATMENT TECHNIQUES PRACTICED HERE HAVE BEEN EMPLOYED BY VETERINARIANS THROUGHOUT THE WORLD.

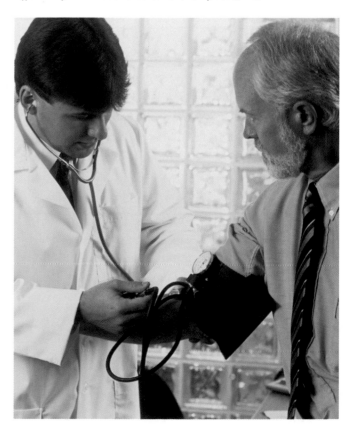

Above: Life Link III, a critical-care service at Minneapolis–St. Paul International Airport, operates two helicopters and two fully equipped aircraft to handle medical emergencies. © Greg Ryan-Sally Beyer. Below: These Minnesota workers assemble medical catheters. The state has more than five hundred registered medical-device manufacturers. © Jeffrey P. Grosscup

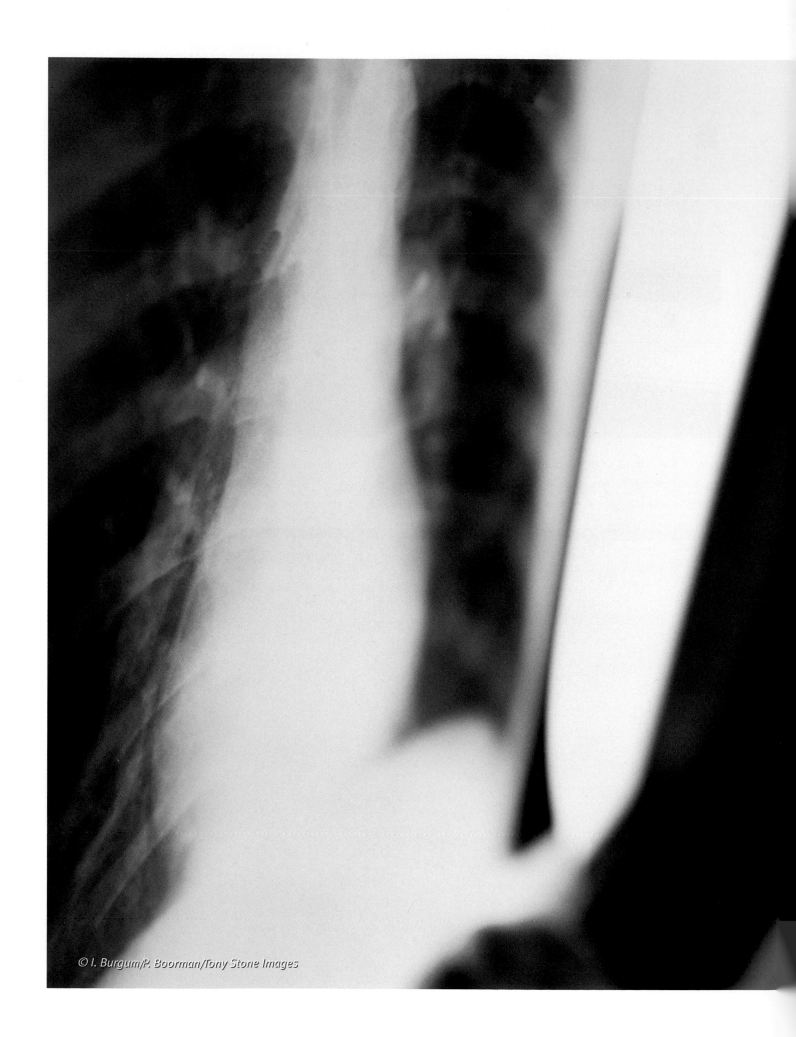

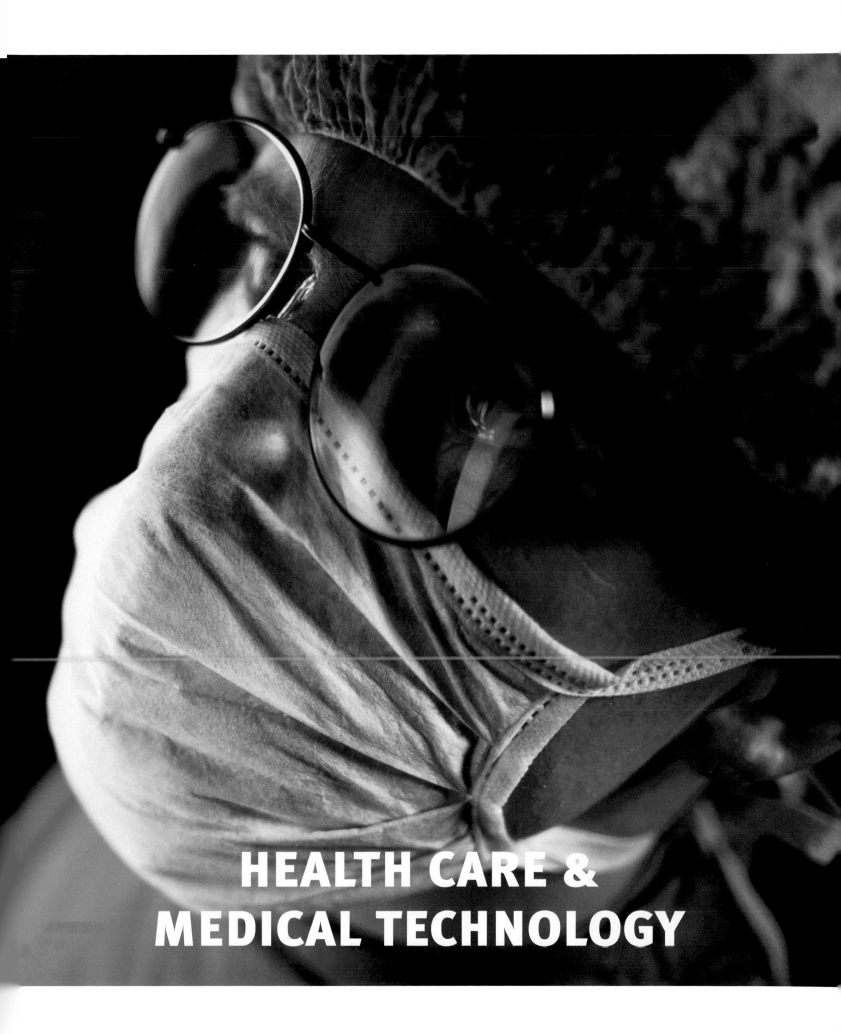

HEALTH CARE & MEDICAL TECHNOLOGY

HAZELDEN FOUNDATION

WORLD-RENOWNED

FOR ITS INNOVATIVE

TREATMENT OF

CHEMICAL

DEPENDENCY,

HAZELDEN

FOUNDATION

APPROACHES RECOVERY

THROUGH COUNSELING

AND EDUCATION,

HELPING PATIENTS

ACHIEVE BALANCE

IN THEIR LIVES

Dignity. Respect. Treatment. Education. From these four principles, Hazelden has built a solid, worldwide reputation for its ability to treat chemical dependency. Whether the difficulty is alcoholism or addiction to other kinds of drugs, Hazelden's professionals can help turn a person's life around, whether male or female, young or old, regardless of education or occupation.

When Hazelden began its nonprofit work in Center City, Minnesota, in 1949, its multidisciplinary approach to chemical dependency treatment was unknown. Today it is the core of most treatment programs.

The complexities of chemical dependency and the myriad ways it is exhibited show the importance of Hazelden's research and medical elements in the recovery process. One of Hazelden's first steps was to teach the public about chemical dependency. Contrary to popular opinion, chemical dependency is not a moral weakness, but a disease that was recognized as such by the medical community more than forty years ago. The disease is treatable and people do recover.

Hazelden's Center City campus, situated on 500 acres on South Center Lake northeast of the Twin Cities, includes primary residential units for inpatients, as well as areas for family and outpatient programs. © Jim Barbour

According to the American Medical Association, 24 million people in the United States are addicted to alcohol or other drugs. A survey by the Conference Board of New York estimates that the combined cost of substance abuse to U.S. businesses in 1996 exceeded $200 billion. Of the billions of dollars involved in American health care, at least 15 percent goes toward treating the effects of chemical dependency. Sadly, only 1 percent is used to treat the addiction itself.

Hazelden is concerned by the alarming rise of chemical abuse problems among young people. Hazelden Center for Youth and Families created a program that has helped thousands of young people begin to rebuild their lives. Because a young person's difficulties can have serious effects on parents and siblings, Hazelden makes treatment a family affair, offering a separate parents' program at HCYF.

The Twelve Steps of Alcoholics Anonymous are the basis for Hazelden's treatment method, but the interdisciplinary approach, treating all aspects of a person—including spiritual, emotional, and physical—is necessary because of the complexity of chemical dependency.

Hazelden's beautiful campus provides an extensive system of trails, giving patients and visitors a chance to enjoy the outdoors. © Jim Barbour

Hazelden has facilities in Chicago; New York City; West Palm Beach, Florida; and several areas in Minnesota. The Center City, Minnesota, facility worked with 6,000 clients in 1996, serving 2,000 residential primary patients. The largest of the Hazelden centers, it has 800 employees.

Intermediate care facilities are operated in St. Paul (where Fellowship Club St. Paul has been open since 1954) and New York to ease the transition of primary treatment patients back into their communities. Hazelden New York also has an intensive residential and extended-care program and an outpatient aftercare program.

Hazelden's second-largest treatment facility, Hanley-Hazelden Center at St. Mary's in West Palm Beach, served 1,534 clients in 1996 and has 100 employees.

More patients had come to Minnesota treatment centers from Illinois than any state other than Minnesota, so Hazelden Chicago was a welcome addition when it opened in 1996. Currently, 5,000 Hazelden alumni reside in the Chicago area.

Hazelden Addiction Counselor Training Program in Dallas is the most prominent of its kind in north Texas. Offering forty-six classes in the chemical dependency counselor field, the program had 1,271 students in 1996.

Patient aid is an important part of Hazelden's efforts to help people get the treatment they need. Through the work of its Development office, Hazelden is able to provide more than $3 million a year in assistance to patients, in the form of grants and loans.

Modern technology helps Hazelden introduce its programs to the world. Hazelden's Internet Web site (www.hazelden.org) promotes calendar events and services, provides a chat room for visitors, and offers E-mail greeting cards and an on-line bookstore.

Jerry Spicer, president and chief executive officer of the Hazelden Foundation since 1992, is a teacher, author, and former

Above: Recreation and exercise are often neglected by people suffering from chemical dependency. An important part of the Hazelden campus, the full fitness facility allows patients to learn how to make a healthy lifestyle part of their sobriety. Left: Quiet time for reading, reflection, and self-examination is a critical component in all Hazelden programs. © Jim Barbour

director of evaluation and research coordination for the Alcoholism Foundation of Manitoba. His books on chemical dependency include *The Minnesota Model: Does Your Program Measure Up?; An Addiction Professional's Guide for Treatment Effectiveness;* and *Evaluating Employee Assistance Programs: A Source Book for the Administrator and Counselor.*

While even the most optimistic people acknowledge that the pain and suffering caused by alcohol and drug dependency are not likely to disappear, Hazelden's staff continues to see its mission clearly. Seeking progress, not perfection, the staff aims to improve the quality of life for individuals, families, and communities affected by drug dependency and related treatable illnesses.

Hazelden's committed professionals see themselves on the front lines of the effort to raise the understanding of dependency as a treatable disease. Education, research, and training are important tools. More than anything, Hazelden's staff knows that respect, dignity, patience, and understanding are key to providing recovering people with truly effective care.

Confidential information about any of Hazelden's programs and locations may be obtained by calling (800) 257-7800.

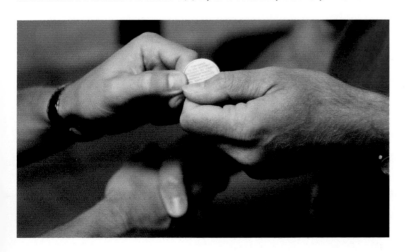

Patients finishing their stay at Hazelden are presented with a medallion, a reminder of their accomplishments. This presentation is a long-standing tradition, and one of the most moving ceremonies to take place in residential units. © Jim Barbour

AUGUSTINE MEDICAL, INC.

AUGUSTINE

MEDICAL, INC.,

USES ITS TEMPERATURE-

MANAGEMENT

EXPERTISE FOR ITS

BAIR HUGGER®

SYSTEM AND OTHER

INVENTIONS,

BRINGING COMFORT

TO MILLIONS OF

SURGICAL PATIENTS

Augustine Medical, Inc.®, pioneered the concept of forced-air patient warming in 1987 with the introduction of its Bair Hugger®–brand Total Temperature Management® system. With the success of Bair Hugger forced-air warming units and disposable warming blankets, the firm has grown in the past decade by designing, manufacturing, and marketing medical devices that are innovative, practical solutions for common health-care problems.

The company's founder, Dr. Scott Augustine, developed the Bair Hugger forced-air warming system after observing during his anesthesiology residency that patients were coming out of surgery uncomfortably cold. Today Bair Hugger warming therapy is the most commonly used patient warming modality throughout the world.

"For thirty or forty years, clinicians had been using water mattresses, cotton blankets, and airway heating and humidification to warm surgical patients, and there was no evidence that these things worked," Dr. Augustine says. "In my research I found that if the room temperature was high enough—85 degrees Fahrenheit or more—patients didn't get cold. However, at that temperature clinicians were uncomfortably warm. The Bair Hugger system creates a warm environment around the patient

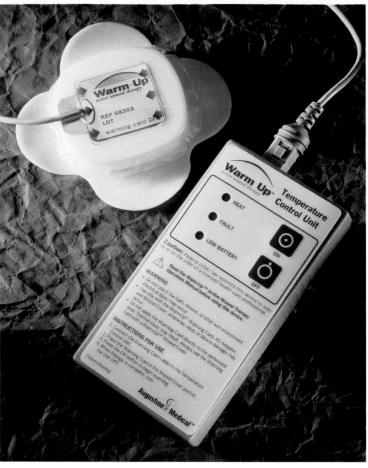

Warm-Up™ active wound therapy is a revolutionary wound care system for use on chronic pressure, venous stasis, and diabetic ulcers. Warm-Up therapy provides noncontact thermal wound therapy to assist the body's own healing process by maintaining warmth and humidity in the wound area.

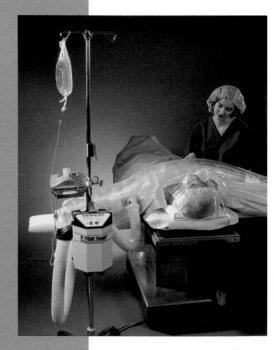

The Bair Hugger® Total Temperature Management® system includes a full line of blankets, forced-air warming and cooling products, and fluid warming products. Bair Hugger warming therapy is the most commonly used patient warming modality throughout the world.

to reduce the discomfort and risks of perioperative hypothermia." While the genesis of the product lies in reducing patient discomfort, recent clinical studies have pointed to enhanced outcomes resulting from perioperative warming. For example, maintaining perioperative normothermia—a core temperature of 37 degrees centigrade—has been shown to lower mortality rates, minimize the incidence of postoperative wound infections and myocardial infarction, reduce the use of blood products, and shorten length of hospital stay.

The Bair Hugger Total Temperature Management system includes a complete line of blankets, warming units, the 241® blood/fluid warmer, the Model 600 PolarAir® hyper/

hypothermia system for cooling and warming surgical patients, and the new Ranger™ blood/fluid warming system.

Augustine Medical's commitment to be a provider of innovative, practical solutions to common medical problems is played out in the company's slogan, "Bright ideas . . . that work." One of the newest products of this culture of innovation is Warm-Up™ active wound therapy, the only noncontact, thermal wound-care system available today. Warm-Up therapy capitalizes on Augustine Medical's expertise in temperature management and applies it to wounds that are hard to heal.

Augustine Medical's logo reflects its commitment to being a company with "Bright ideas . . . that work."

Warm-Up therapy is uniquely effective for chronic wounds such as pressure, diabetic, and venous ulcers. Wound beds are generally hypothermic. Warm-Up therapy warms wounds toward normal body temperature, resulting in increased blood flow and oxygen to the wound to help create an optimal healing environment.

The Warm-Up system consists of a flexible, noncontact wound cover, a warming card, a temperature control unit, and an AC adapter. The warming card connects to the disposable wound cover, giving warmth. The wound cover maintains a moist environment and does not disrupt healing tissues during cover changes. This is ideal for long-term care facilities, home care, and clinics. The device is having dramatic results in research worldwide. Wounds that have not closed during months of traditional treatments have improved in weeks.

Another example of Augustine Medical's "Bright ideas that work" culture is the GO₂™ glottic aperture seal airway. Designed to be less invasive than a tracheal tube, the GO₂ airway is easily inserted and aligns readily with the glottic opening, giving a clear view of vocal chords and creating an effective glottic-opening seal.

"This device—which will be commercially available after beta testing—will change the practice of airway management," Dr. Augustine says. "This is the first device to make an effective, gas-tight seal with the larynx—the opening to the airway." In 1992 Dr. Augustine was honored as Minnesota's Entrepreneur of the Year, and the Bair Hugger system received Medical Alley's "Outstanding Achievement in Health Care Product" award. In 1993 Augustine Medical was ranked seventy-second on *Inc.* magazine's list of the country's 500 fastest growing private companies, and Dr. Augustine was a regional finalist for the Inc. 500 list in 1994. In 1996 Augustine Medical was thirteenth among *Corporate Report Minnesota's* top-thirty-five Med-Tech companies in the state, and ninth on the list of Minnesota's fastest-growing medical technology companies.

Commitment to doing things right—a true commitment to excellence—is one of the company's corporate values. Equally important are its other values: communication, innovation, putting people first, and employee empowerment. One of its corporate goals is to "continue to build a company where people love their work."

"We try to create an open, honest work environment, which fosters maximum employee productivity," Dr. Augustine says. "As an entrepreneur, the key to success is to take the first step to implement an idea, and the first step is always the hardest. Once you make that step, as you encounter each hurdle you can find a way to overcome it." Clearly, customers respond to this culture. As a result, Augustine Medical's fiscal year 1998 net sales reached a record high—in excess of $40 million. The company is privately held and has been financed by several private stock offerings.

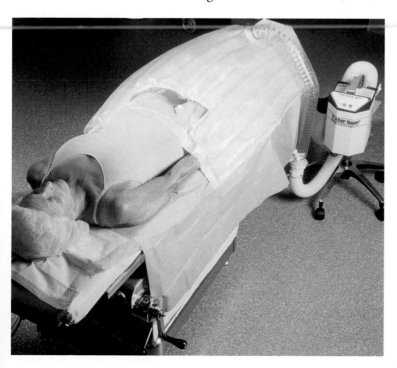

Recent studies show that patient warming reduces the incidence of postsurgical cardiac morbidity and myocardial infarction. Bair Hugger® cardiac blankets help protect patients from post-bypass after-drop.

LAKE REGION MANUFACTURING, INC.

TURNING POSTWAR

ENGINEERING SKILLS

TO NEW

APPLICATIONS,

ENTREPRENEUR

JOE FLEISCHHACKER

BUILT A MEDICAL

PRODUCTS COMPANY

THAT NOW SPANS TWO

CONTINENTS

Lake Region's headquarters facility is located on the shore of Lake Hazeltine in the Minneapolis suburb of Chaska.

Entrepreneur Joseph F. Fleischhacker founded Lake Region Manufacturing in 1947. © Dick Bobnick

The attitudes that helped shape this Minnesota company were forged during World War II, as a young engineer struggled to overcome design problems with the turbo chargers in U.S. bombers. Knowing that the lives of many of the crewmen hung in the balance, Joe Fleischhacker led a team of Honeywell engineers to correct the engine faults. Another of his teams designed certain precision gyroscopic controls with which they were able to greatly improve accuracy.

When the war was over, Fleischhacker and two partners decided to try their hands at business. Part-time at first, under the name Lake Region Manufacturing, they developed different products as they learned how to broaden their engineering expertise to satisfy market needs. Founded as a fishing lure company, Lake Region quickly evolved into water softeners and contract machining, with the whole Fleischhacker family helping to fill orders.

The transformation of Lake Region into a medical products provider was fortuitous. Fleischhacker was introduced to an upstart company that needed help producing small-diameter coils. The company was Medtronic; the product was the lead used with Medtronic's exciting new heart pacemaker. This was the challenge that would consume much of Fleischhacker's and his wife's time until a workable coil winder was perfected.

Medtronic was pleased with the results, and Lake Region soon had twelve employees and much demand for its work. Eventually, all four of the Fleischhacker children worked full-time for Lake Region. By the 1970s Lake Region was doing wire coating successfully, and became dedicated to manufacturing medical components. From making simple components and assemblies, the company began manufacturing completed guidewires used to direct catheters and other devices to their appropriate position in the body.

Lake Region Manufacturing was growing quickly, and in 1974 it moved to the Crosby Industrial Park in Chaska. Later it moved again, to a new manufacturing plant across the street on the shore of Lake Hazeltine, where there are now 700 employees. Another 200 employees work at Lake Region Medical, in Pittsburgh, Pennsylvania. Most recently, a plant employing 150 people was set up in New Ross, County Wexford, Ireland, in order to serve European and other global opportunities.

Today, more than fifty years after the company was begun, it still is a family-owned business. And it has become the world's largest original equipment manufacturer of high-quality guidewires and specialty wire-formed products—important parts in virtually every diagnostic, therapeutic, and interventional application.

The Wire Products Division is continually refining and expanding its product offerings through a dedicated partnership with its customers. It has more than 2,000 standard guidewire configurations for such clinical applications as cardiology, radiology, urology, gastroenterology, and critical care.

Guidewire configurations among Lake Region's standard and specialty products range from .010 to .095 inches in diameter, and from 10 to 550 centimeters in length. Specialty guidewires for cerebral angiography, site-specific fluid delivery and stent deployment, and custom guidewires for coronary angioplasty and other applications also are made by this division. Its custom-coil-winding and wire-forming products are used in cardiac pacing, electrophysiology, and gastroenterology, as well as peripherally inserted central-catheter (P.I.C.C.)-line and feeding-tube placements.

The Machined Products Division specializes in miniature, subminiature, and microcomponent medical devices. Among the division's manufacturing capabilities are Computer Numerical Control (CNC) turning and milling, secondary-operation machining, and specialty grinding. The resulting products are used in diverse applications such as cardiac pacing, ophthalmology, and dentistry.

Modern medicine's range of materials, including stainless steel, titanium, MP35N, Elgiloy, platinum-group metals, and other precious metals, are very familiar to Lake Region engineers. So, too, are Nitinol, Kovar, aluminum, brass and other alloys,

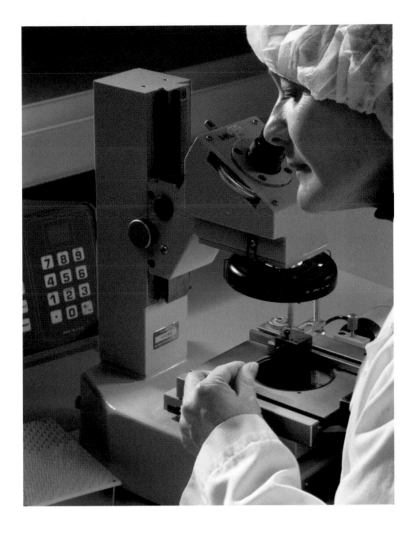

Lake Region's experienced technical staff and skilled workforce share a commitment to achieving the highest product quality and service excellence.

Lake Region conducts clinical preference evaluations, to give customers physician confirmation of products' procedural utility and value.

and space-age plastics. Specialty-use products often require specialty finishes, and the Machined Products Division provides high-speed centrifugal tumbling and polishing, microblasting, microbuffing and polishing, and titanium anodizing.

Selling as it does to the medical industry, which demands superior performance from suppliers, Lake Region assumes top quality to be fundamental. From design and prototype runs through full production, Lake Region uses Statistical Process Controls (SPC) and strict lot-control standards. SPC documentation with shipments certifies compliance with each component's specifications.

The high level of trust between Lake Region Manufacturing and leading medical-device companies has been earned through many years of close work with customers. Still, Lake Region considers these partnerships and its broad offering of innovative, value-added products simply to be a beginning. They are a measure of Lake Region's continuing mission of contributing to complex, changing technologies amid unpredictable global markets.

SOLVAY PHARMACEUTICALS, INC.

Solvay Pharmaceuticals, Inc., researches and develops medical therapies that offer hope in three of modern medicine's most challenging arenas: women's health, mental health, and gastro-enterology. One of the nation's fastest growing pharmaceutical companies, Solvay Pharmaceuticals has discovered and developed solutions that improve the health of millions of people.

Innovation and vision have enabled Solvay Pharmaceuticals to successfully develop and market treatments for osteoporosis, obsessive-compulsive disorder, mania associated with bipolar disease, cystic fibrosis, and ulcerative colitis. Ongoing research will broaden the ability of the company to help patients overcome these and other conditions.

Solvay Pharmaceuticals is a member of the Solvay Group of chemical and pharmaceutical companies, based in Brussels, Belgium. The group has operations in forty countries, employing 38,000 people. The headquarters of Solvay Pharmaceuticals are in Marietta, Georgia, and production facilities are in Baudette, Minnesota.

Solvay Pharmaceuticals is continually making strategic additions to its product line to meet patient needs. Since 1988 its research and development expenditures have grown dramatically.

"Our firm's corporate commitment to research and development is an important part of Solvay Pharmaceuticals Inc.'s continuing strategy to market innovative products that respond to a broad range of human health needs," says Solvay Pharmaceuticals CEO, David Dodd.

Solvay Pharmaceuticals invests in leading-edge facilities, information technology, and equipment. This commitment starts in the laboratory and continues throughout the company's two modern manufacturing plants in Baudette. One-

Solvay Pharmaceuticals, Inc.'s Main Street facility, established in 1933, is located in beautiful northern Minnesota.

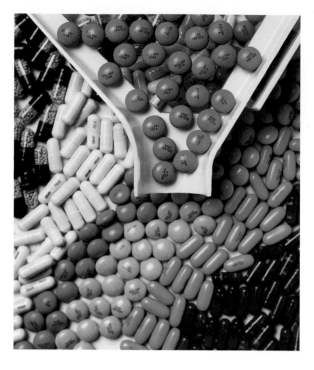

Solvay Pharmaceuticals manufactures and packages an array of sugar-coated tablets and capsules at its Baudette Main Street facility.

hundred-and-thirty-thousand square feet house high-speed, automated processing and packaging equipment, enabling the company to quadruple capacity in recent years and to respond promptly to changing production needs.

One-hundred-and-eighty highly trained employees use computerized production and packaging lines that generate nearly two billion dosage units per year. The Baudette facilities produce tablet, capsule, oral liquid, lotion, and rectal dosage forms.

Products include ESTRATAB® (Esterified Estrogens Tablets, USP) Tablets; LUVOX® (fluvoxamine maleate) Tablets; LITHOBID® (Lithium Carbonate, USP) Slow-Release Tablets; ROWASA® (mesalamine) Enemas and Suppositories; and CREON® (pancrelipase) Delayed-Release MINI-MICROSPHERES® Capsules.

"We are dedicated to being a responsible supplier of high-quality therapeutic products, to supporting the basic objectives of an improved health-care system, and to responding successfully to changes precipitated by managed health care," says the Solvay Pharmaceuticals CEO.

HEALTH RISK MANAGEMENT, INC.

BY DELIVERING

INTEGRATED

ELECTRONIC

MEDICAL AND

FINANCIAL

RISK-MANAGEMENT

SYSTEMS, HEALTH

RISK MANAGEMENT,

INC., PROVIDES

PRACTICAL SOLUTIONS

TO ISSUES OF

HEALTH-CARE

QUALITY AND COST

Health Risk Management, Inc. (HRM), headquartered in Minneapolis, is one of the largest independent health-care management companies in the country. With more than two decades of experience, HRM provides comprehensive health-care benchmarking information and develops and implements systems that unite the best medical practices with operational efficiency.

These electronically integrated health plan management services and systems are delivered throughout the United States, Canada, and New Zealand to a wide range of health-care-related organizations. HMOs, preferred provider organizations (PPOs), hospitals, provider networks, Medicare/Medicaid plans, employer and union self-insured plans, workers' compensation and disability plans, and numerous government entities look to HRM's tools and expertise to help manage medical and financial risk.

HRM's real-time management systems incorporate electronic data interchange (EDI) technology, handling the care process step by step—from the initial patient diagnosis through the final claim payment.

HRM has demonstrated that when you put quality first, savings follow. Based on that premise, the *QualityFIRST*®: Medical Risk Management System delivers quality-driven clinical management through interactive, evidence-based guidelines covering medical/surgical, workers' compensation/disability, behavioral health, and specialist referral care decisions. Data collection, documentation, and reporting capabilities provide organizations with a baseline for

HRM's dedicated professionals and advanced information systems provide twenty-four-hour access to integrated health-care services and information.

establishing quality benchmarks, evaluating performance, and measuring productivity.

Physicians and health plans use *QualityFIRST* to assure "best practice" consistency and optimal care decisions, manage resources, enhance productivity, and support continuous quality improvement.

"*QualityFIRST* helps facilitate consistency in health-care decision making across provider networks and enables efficient management of health-related and financial risks," says HRM president, Marlene Travis.

QualityFIRST is used in a stand-alone PC format or may be supported with HRM's medical and financial management services, including national provider networks and ISO-9002-certified administrative management services.

HRM also provides national quality benchmarking information for all health-care stakeholders—policy makers, providers, payers, and patients. Compiled annually, the *QualityFIRST Index*SM measures overall health-care quality across all fifty states. It is available to the public online at www.hrmi.com.

"Our goal is to furnish health-care providers and purchasers with the integrated financial and medical risk-management technologies and services they need to make health-care plans work effectively," Travis says.

Health Risk Management cofounders Gary McIlroy, M.D., chairman and CEO, and Marlene Travis, president, draw on more than two decades of experience.

© John Elk III

RELIGIOUS SERVICES

ROCHESTER FRANCISCAN ORDER

THE ROCHESTER

FRANCISCAN ORDER

WORKS AT HOME

AND ABROAD TO

PROMOTE JUSTICE, TO

ADVOCATE FOR THE

DISENFRANCHISED,

AND TO WORK FOR

PEACE IN THE WAY OF

SAINT FRANCIS

An act of nature in August 1883 changed the course of history in Rochester, Minnesota. When a tornado ripped through the small prairie town killing more than two dozen people, the country doctor, William Worrall Mayo, was overwhelmed with patients. He sought help from the Sisters of Saint Francis, who turned their six-year-old congregational center into a temporary hospital and cared for forty injured people.

After the last patient went home, Mother Alfred Moes, the founder and head of the Rochester Franciscans, met with Dr. Mayo and offered to build a hospital for him and his two sons, Will and Charlie. He doubted such a venture could succeed in a small town, but Mother Alfred persisted and promised that her order of sisters would raise forty thousand dollars to construct the facility.

They raised the money at great personal sacrifice. In 1889, Saint Marys Hospital opened its doors with Mother Alfred serving as the hospital's first administrator and the sisters as nurses. Five years later, Dr. William Mayo credited the growing hospital to ". . . the devoted and skillful care of the sisters. It is their funds that have built and maintained Saint Marys, and they have steadily endeavored to improve it in every possible way. All the credit for the successful treatment of patients at the hospital here is due to the ministrations of the devoted, skillful sisters in charge. We are but the sisters' agents."

A unique collaboration was under way, one that launched the medical mecca known worldwide today as the Mayo Medical Center.

Rochester Franciscans today continue to share their lives and ministries with many people, including these school girls in Bogotá, Colombia.

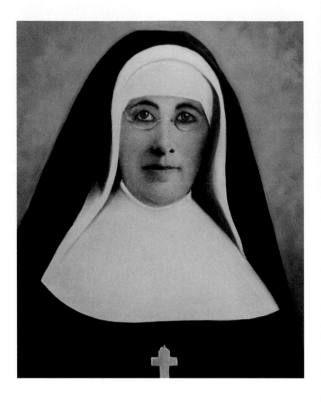

Mother Alfred Moes, foundress of the Rochester Franciscans, combined the ideals of Saint Francis of Assisi with practical action.

BEYOND THE STORM

The early spirit of the Rochester Franciscans continues to blossom. Today they are a vital community of 400 members; their ministries extend from Minnesota to many other states and foreign countries. Also present are more than 100 "cojourners"—people who share the sisters' values and spirituality.

The outreach of the Rochester Franciscans begins in their southeastern Minnesota home. Each year, more than forty thousand people enjoy the sisters' hospitality at their congregational center, Assisi Heights, which is situated on a hill and is visible for miles around. Visitors use Assisi Community Center's facilities for retreats, conferences, meetings, and solitude. Assisi Heights also serves as an ecumenical center with offices for area Lutherans and Methodists. Worship space is available, as well. In nearby Winona, Minnesota, Tau Center draws international scholars to its Franciscan studies program. The sisters' Holy Spirit Retreat Center on Lake Elysian near Janesville, Minnesota, offers visitors

solitude, a hermitage experience, and conference space.

THE SPIRIT OF CARING

The spirit of caring that brought about the great Mayo medical complex is imbedded in the sisters' history. Not content to establish and run Saint Marys Hospital, the sisters opened a school of nursing there and later worked to place the program in an academic environment. Rochester Franciscans served as nurses and administrators in other Midwest hospitals, and they founded some of the earliest hospice care centers in southern Minnesota.

Before building Saint Marys Hospital, the sisters primarily were teachers. They established academies in Owatonna and Rochester, where hundreds of children were empowered with knowledge and values. In the following century, these women helped establish fifty-three Minnesota parochial schools. Their work included post-secondary schooling. In 1894, they founded what would become the College of Saint Teresa in Winona, Minnesota, and helped many talented, bright young women blossom academically.

The sisters' role in education has diversified. Opening ventures in Bogotá, Colombia in the 1960s included helping form and staff the

School of Nursing at Javeriana University and founding two schools serving students from the range of economic backgrounds in the city. These schools continue to reflect the Franciscans' values of love and caring. They have been working with Harvard's Graduate School of Education on Teaching for Understanding, Multiple Intelligences, and Alternative Forms of Evaluation. Cambodians are benefiting from a school established by the Franciscans that teaches English to adults who then teach others.

TODAY'S PIONEERING SPIRIT

The indomitable spirit of Mother Alfred lives on in her order of sisters. Today's Rochester Franciscan is known for her spirit, her beliefs, and her actions. Many venture beyond the usual roles of nurses and teachers, working as pioneers in diverse, new ministries. Sisters work in the inner city, minister to prisoners, and are therapists and administrators, students and lawyers, artists and writers. They serve in churches and parishes as pastoral ministers, and on institutional and community boards. Still involved in Saint Marys Hospital, the sisters volunteer their services and give guidance on values and medical ethics.

Rochester Franciscans see God revealed in all creation, and they act on the challenges of peace, poverty, and care of the earth. They seek to promote justice, to advocate for the disenfranchised, and to work for peace in the way of Saint Francis.

THE NEW MILLENNIUM DAWNING

The Rochester Franciscans continue to share their values in collaborative ministries at the start of the new millennium. And Mother Alfred's words to Dr. William Worrall Mayo still define her Franciscan legacy: "With our faith and hope and energy, it will succeed."

SERVICES THAT BUILD SUCCESS

CHAPTER FIFTEEN

STANDING BEHIND **M**INNESOTA'S ECONOMIC VITALITY IS AN ARMY OF FINAN-

CIAL AND PROFESSIONAL SERVICES. **L**ENDERS AND LAWYERS, ACCOUNTANTS

AND ADVERTISERS, STATE OFFICES AND STATE-OF-THE ART DESIGNERS STAND

READY TO SERVE, PROTECT, AND STRENGTHEN **M**INNESOTA BUSINESSES BY

PROVIDING THE SPECIALIZED SERVICES THEY NEED TO EXCEL.

For starters, there are Minnesota's banks. Despite having only 2 percent of the nation's population, the state is home to 5 percent of the nation's banks. Led by the strength of U.S. Bank, formed from the recent merger of U.S. Bancorp and First Bank Systems, a $72 billion conglomerate ranking as the fourteenth-largest bank-holding company in the United States, Minnesota banks hold more assets than those in all but eleven other states.

The explosion of small businesses throughout the state has been ignited through a variety of financial sources, among them S.B.A. loans, venture-capital companies, and a host of public and private loans and grants. The U.S. Small Business Administration's (SBA) district office in Minneapolis was the busiest in the nation in 1995, providing 1,770 loans totaling $223 million. The SBA's Office of Advocacy also reports the First National Bank of Pipestone, Itasca State Bank of Grand Rapids,

Princeton Bank, and the Community First National Bank branches in Fergus Falls and Morris as being among the state's top small business lenders.

Venture-capital financing is especially popular in the state after the visible success of such homegrown companies as Cray Research, Control Data, International Dairy Queen, direct-marketer Damark International, and St. Jude Medical, the global leader in the design and manufacture of cardiovascular devices, all of which prospered as a result of venture-capital financing. Minnesota currently ranks eighth in the nation in venture-capital resources and has consistently appeared in top-ten rankings for both venture-capital pools and venture-capital disbursements for each of the past ten years.

Equity financing is plentiful here as well. Led by Minnesota investment banks Dain Bosworth and Piper Jaffray, recently acquired by U.S. Bank, Minnesota

Opposite: The IDS Center and Norwest Center towers add sparkle to the Minneapolis skyline at dusk. © Bob Firth/Firth Photobank. Above: At Minnesota's many fine banking institutions, couples, individuals, and companies receive the banking and financial-support services they need to realize their dreams. © Jon Riley/Tony Stone Images

THE ST. PAUL COMPANIES WERE ESTABLISHED IN 1853, MAKING THEM MINNESOTA'S OLDEST BUSINESS CORPORATION. THEY ARE CURRENTLY THE FOUR-TEENTH-LARGEST PROPERTY-LIABILITY UNDERWRITER IN THE COUNTRY, THE LARGEST MEDICAL LIABILITY UNDERWRITER, AND A LEADER IN NUMEROUS OTHER TYPES OF SPECIALTY COVERAGE.

companies make initial public offerings of stock at a rate double that of the rest of the nation and surpass all but a handful of states with their rate of secondary stock offerings. The line of private entrepreneurs with money to invest in fledgling companies is growing substantially as are the number of private and public loan and grant programs developed to assist small businesses with start-ups and expansions. The McKnight Foundation's six Initiative Funds were uniquely established at regional levels, placing funds, programs, and services in the hands of those who understood their need best, the residents of the area. The Department of Trade and Economic Development also maintains a funding pool that includes programs specifically designated for entrepreneurs in rural areas or areas of urban distress, and also offers limited guarantees for investors acting as private lenders.

Expanding Minnesota's position in the global marketplace was a priority of governor Arne Carlson. In his first five years of office, the governor visited ten of the state's top sixteen export markets and endorsed several initiatives fostering international

partnerships. The highly regarded Minnesota Trade Office houses one of the top international research libraries in the Midwest, and the office's staff, comprising experts in finance, marketing, custom regulations, and export documentation, offers several seminars each week to the business community on subjects relating to exporting. The Minnesota Trade Office also manages the World Trade Center Corporation through a unique public/private resources venture. The World Trade Center Corporation supports the state's international firms by maintaining a global database, a highly sophisticated conference center, videoconferencing facilities, and educational programs.

As a state with a well-deserved reputation as a leader in environmental practices and policies, Minnesota has also taken the lead with innovative legislation designed to streamline the environmental regulation process for

The Minnesota World Trade Center cuts an imposing outline as it rises above downtown St. Paul. Minnesota's top three export markets are Canada, Japan, and Germany. © Greg Ryan-Sally Beyer

businesses. Project XL, evolved from a partnership between the Minnesota Pollution Control Agency and 3M, allows businesses to conduct self-audits with standards that go beyond existing regulations and government to form partnerships with business instead of acting as an enforcer. The net result is a reduction of environmental management costs on both sides, coupled with uncompromised environmental protection.

Expertise is so abundant here it all but grows on trees. The state has unusually high concentrations in the fields of advertising, graphic design, commercial research, public relations, security and commodity brokers, architectural services, and computer and data processing. All of the country's major accounting firms maintain substantial operations in the state, and Minnesota's largest law firms have offices across the country and around the world. Industry specialists are common both in the large corporations and throughout the state's top-notch local firms.

Minnesota enjoys an exceptionally robust insurance industry. Fueled by the presence of Minnesota Mutual, one of the strongest life insurers in the country, with $16.2 billion in assets, and The St. Paul Companies,

A man checks the contents of a safety-deposit box in the secured interior of a bank. © Michael Rosenfeld/Tony Stone Images

which ranks 238th on the Fortune 500 list of largest businesses, the state's insurance companies provide reliable product, jobs, and growth. The industry's share

© Minneapolis Grain Exchange

MINNEAPOLIS IS HOME TO THE MINNEAPOLIS GRAIN EXCHANGE, THE LARGEST CASH EXCHANGE MARKET IN THE WORLD. AN AVERAGE OF ONE MILLION BUSHELS OF GRAIN, INCLUDING WHEAT, BARLEY, OATS, DURUM, RYE, SUNFLOWER SEEDS, FLAX, CORN, SOYBEANS, MILLET, AND MILO, ARE TRADED EACH DAY. THE EXCHANGE IS ALSO THE WORLD'S ONLY SEAFOOD COMPLEX. STARTED IN 1881 BY TWENTY-ONE LOCAL BUSINESSMEN CONCERNED WITH ESTABLISHING A FAIR METHOD OF TRADE, THE INSTITUTION STILL ENJOYS A GLOBAL REPUTATION FOR INTEGRITY AND HONESTY.

of the gross state product rose 15.4 percent in two years, making it one of the fastest growing in the nation, and added eight thousand employees to its base in the same period.

Recent trends in the state's real estate and construction sector divulge the presence of affordable housing and a demand for commercial space. The median price for an existing single-family home in the Twin Cities, the only region in the state where the median sales price exceeded $100,000, was $113,900 in 1996, still below the national average of $118,200. Office vacancy rates in the seven-county metropolitan area are at a thirteen-year low, but industrial vacancy rates in the area are beginning to climb after new industrial space was added in response to demand. Construction costs in Minneapolis mirror the national average. Costs to build in the rest of the state, however, are usually at least 10 percent below those in the metropolitan area.

THE INSURANCE INDUSTRY CONTRIBUTED APPROXIMATELY $12.6 BILLION TO THE ECONOMY OF MINNESOTA IN 1996. THE CHARITABLE CONTRIBUTIONS OF THE TWENTY-NINE MEMBERS OF THE INSURANCE FEDERATION OF MINNESOTA EXCEEDED $23 MILLION THAT SAME YEAR.

© Ed Taylor Studio/FPG International

Opposite: The contemporary Lutheran Brotherhood Building replaced the organization's 1956-built modern edifice. © Bob Firth/Firth Photobank. Below: An aerial view reveals a new residential development in Minnetonka. © Conrad Bloomquist/ Scenic Photo! Inset: An artist's depiction of a developing city, Minneapolis in 1881. © Corbis-Bettmann

Above: The I-394 flyover bridge in Minneapolis was built for high-occupancy vehicles. © Conrad Bloomquist/Scenic Photo! Right: The Marine Education Center at the Minnesota Zoo was designed by Hammel, Green and Abrahamson. Courtesy, Hammel, Green and Abrahamson. Below: In 1998, Minnesota Governor Arne H. Carlson met with Chinese President Jiang Zemin during a business trip to Beijing. © Minnesota Trade and Economic Development

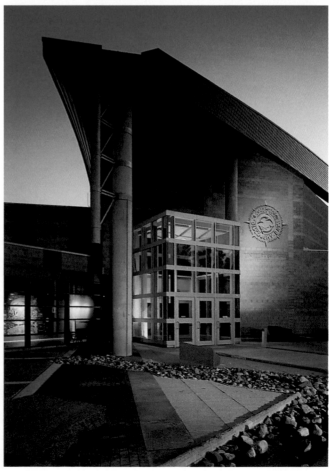

Above: Employees at Norwest Corporation work to provide banking, insurance, investment, mortgage, and consumer-finance services for their customers. Courtesy, Norwest Corporation. Below: Dayton's department store, this one along Nicollet Mall, is part of the Minnesota-based Dayton Hudson Corporation, whose stores include Target, Mervyn's, and Hudson's. © Dayton Hudson Corporation

REAL ESTATE, DEVELOPMENT, AND CONSTRUCTION

LESTER BUILDING SYSTEMS

LESTER BUILDING
SYSTEMS PROVIDES
FLEXIBLE BUILDING
SOLUTIONS
SUPPORTED BY
RESEARCH, PRODUCT
DEVELOPMENT,
AND ENGINEERING
EXCELLENCE

Lester Building Systems has been a vital and very visible part of the Midwestern landscape since 1947. From its modest beginnings in a 2,400-square-foot warehouse serving a three-county area around Lester Prairie, Minnesota, to its current 448,000 square feet of office and plant facilities serving the eastern two-thirds of the United States, Lester has grown to be an industry leader in engineered, nonresidential building construction.

For the most part, Lester's engineered structures are designed and manufactured using postframe construction techniques. Postframe construction is quite different than stud-frame, or "stick built," construction. Lester® structures are delivered ready to build, right down to the last piece of trim and screws, with a minimum of job-site interpretation and cutting. Lester pre-engineered buildings offer a number of benefits, including faster construction, reduced construction costs (both time and material), and unmatched flexibility.

Every Lester building is engineered for specific end-use, geographical, and climatological conditions. As a result of Lester's unyielding and legendary approach to engineering excellence, the

Lester buildings accommodate all sorts of needs, ranging from agricultural and livestock to commercial and equestrian, such as this large stable and riding complex.

company has an unmatched performance record—something of special note throughout Minnesota and the rest of the northern "snow belt."

Formed to take over a Stran-Steel franchise, Lester's of Minnesota, as it was called then, has seen many changes over the years. Throughout the 1950s, 1960s, and early 1970s, Lester's moved toward selling complete building construction packages. Hundreds of new employees were added and the markets Lester served expanded.

The Insl-Wall™ stress-skin panel was developed in 1960 and remains popular to this day. Insl-Wall panels put Lester's in the expanded-polystyrene business, which resulted in the formation of another company, Poly Foam. In 1965, Lester's became a licensee of Plywood Fabrication Service, which focused on introducing the concept of engineered structural plywood components to architects.

In 1968, Lester's introduced the Wingspan product line, which began the transition from the round wood poles used in traditional postframe construction to square posts. As a result of new products and an ability to serve various market requirements, Lester's material and construction sales increased from $1 million in 1960 to more than $5 million in 1968, and more than $10 million in 1972.

Alliances with national accounts like Purina Mills' "American Country Store" have fueled Lester's explosive growth in the commercial building market.

Faster, more efficient construction is a modern economic necessity. A growing number of well-known national companies with fast-track "build-out" plans depend on Lester and its independent builders to provide building solutions that ultimately allow these companies to be "under roof" and cash flow faster. The buildings shown here (from top: a day care center, a youth camp, and a golf course clubhouse/pro shop) were designed and manufactured using postframe construction techniques and were delivered ready to erect, right down to the trim and screws.

The late 1960s to late 1970s were marked by tremendous growth in agricultural markets. Lester's was uniquely qualified to meet this new demand. The result: sales rose to $60 million by 1979. However, the agricultural market's fast growth could not be sustained, and the "golden years" quickly shifted to a broad farm market depression for much of the 1980s. Lester's was able to weather the storm, but realized that it needed to broaden its markets. Thus, product development and marketing efforts aimed at the commercial market began in earnest.

In the meantime, Butler Manufacturing Company purchased Lester's of Minnesota in 1986, renamed the company Lester Building Systems, and began a rapid expansion into the eastern United States. Lester's was a natural fit for Butler, with its vast and experienced builder organization that sold and constructed larger steel-framed buildings and grain bins.

The purchase marked the start of distribution through local, independent builders rather than direct representatives as had been the case since 1947. Today Lester products are sold and erected through a network of nearly 500 independent builders.

However, a direct-selling construction company, Lester's of Minnesota, Inc., operating in and around the Minneapolis–St. Paul area, was carved out of Butler's purchase. This remains the last remnant of the original company.

Increased geographic distribution led Lester Building Systems to open additional facilities in Charleston, Illinois; Clear Brook, Virginia; and Ottawa, Kansas.

Product innovations continue to be the key to Lester's success. New framing systems with unique and real marketable benefits—the Uni-Frame® line of products—were introduced in 1991. An airy, rafter-style, dairy free-stall building was introduced in 1994 to tap into the market's trend toward larger, commercial-oriented dairy production. Rafter-style dairy buildings provide excellent airflow and prevent birds from "moving in" as they can with truss-style buildings. In 1995, Lester began to sell the R-Control® stress-skin panel—a completely modular framing/insulation system for commercial applications.

Lester's efforts to develop flexible solutions to meet the special needs of the commercial market began to pay off in the 1990s. A partnership with McDonald's Corporation for modular restaurant construction was established in 1995. In 1996 building programs were developed in conjunction with Purina Mills, Sears, and Land O'Lakes. As a result of these efforts, Lester initiated a National Accounts sales group within the company to further develop these and future relationships with large national companies with long-term, multisite "build out" plans.

Marc Hafer, president of Lester Building Systems, says, "Lester is in an excellent position for continued growth and expansion. We have a thriving and growing network of independent Lester builders. We have a well-respected construction company that continues to operate in the Minneapolis–St. Paul area. We have a dedicated staff of engineers and researchers to ensure product development to keep up with changing market environments." In short, Lester is poised to grow tremendously in the new millennium.

FAGEN, INC.

CIVIL, MECHANICAL,

AND ELECTRICAL

CONSTRUCTION

CONTRACTOR

FAGEN, INC.,

DESIGNS AND

BUILDS MAJOR

INDUSTRIAL PROJECTS

FOR COMPANIES

THROUGHOUT

THE NATION

In 1995 Fagen, Inc., built its new corporate office in Granite Falls, Minnesota, to make space for its expanded single-source design, procurement, and construction services.

To meet the industrial needs of the times, Fagen, Inc., a civil, mechanical, and electrical construction company, has evolved into a full-service design/build firm specializing in heavy industrial construction.

Fagen, Inc., is one of the largest merit-shop contractors headquartered in the Midwest and serves clients throughout the United States. Based in Granite Falls, Minnesota, the company has branch offices in Columbus, Nebraska, and Fargo, North Dakota.

In 1988, after twenty years of construction experience with other partnerships, entrepreneur Ron Fagen ventured out on his own and formed Fagen, Inc. As chief executive officer, his philosophy is one of dedication to the highest level of service, integrity, and honesty, and these principles are exemplified throughout the company. As a result, much of Fagen, Inc.'s workload is secured from previous clients.

One of Ron Fagen's first projects for his newly founded

Ron Fagen is the founder and chief executive officer of Fagen, Inc., and the driving force behind its ongoing success.

company was to participate in the expansion of the Boise Cascade Paper Mill in International Falls, Minnesota. Winter construction in "the nation's icebox" presented a challenge; nonetheless, concrete was successfully poured when the weather was forty degrees below zero. Today the mill remains a client of Fagen, Inc., for maintenance contracting services.

In 1990 Fagen, Inc., negotiated to build the first copper and brass facility to be built from the ground up in the United States in more than twenty years. The client, PMX Industries, Inc., of Cedar Rapids, Iowa, is a wholly owned subsidiary of Poongsan Corporation of Seoul, South Korea.

"I consider PMX a major, major project and quite a feather in my cap," says Ron Fagen. "We started in July and by the end of the summer we'd poured more than 23,000 cubic yards of concrete. That's about 3,900 truckloads. We'd spend as many as seventeen hours on a single "pour"—with trucks just lined up bumper to bumper."

One of the Minnesota contractor's biggest challenges on the PMX project was an eighty-seven-foot-deep vertical continuous-caster pit—

"probably the biggest hole in the Midwest." The project was a new brass-melt building. The excavation was complicated by rock, water, and the wettest year in Iowa's history. Ninety well points were required to keep the water table low enough to minimize flooding so the huge crater would not fill up during construction.

Fagen, Inc., also has been involved extensively in the meat-packing industry at sites in various stages of completion, expansion, and remodeling. IBP, Inc., John Morrell & Company, Excel, Tama Packing, Kenosha Beef, Swift, Armour, and Monfort, Inc., top the list of clients served. Fagen, Inc., provides shutdown crews for "fast-track" weekend work and projects involving long-term upgrades.

Always concerned with the agricultural economy that is the mainstay of the Midwest, Ron Fagen is a principal player in the ethanol industry. Fagen, Inc., has been involved in work on every major ethanol plant in the Midwest. The company remains politically active in the fight for ethanol incentives at the state and federal level.

Fagen, Inc., maintains a highly skilled workforce of approximately 400 to 600 craftsworkers from across the nation. Ron Fagen considers regard for the safety of the general public, employees, and the employees of subcontractors a supreme responsibility of all levels of the organization. Dedication to safety enables Fagen, Inc., to be hired by first-rate companies. Fagen, Inc., has been listed among the top 400 industrial contractors in the United States in the *Engineering News Record* rankings and has consistently received a 4A1 rating with *Dun & Bradstreet*.

Above, workers erect the steel frame of a millhouse built for Minnesota Corn Processors' Wet Mill in 1993 in Columbus, Nebraska.

A believer in promoting family activities, Ron Fagen hosts barbecues at various job sites, inviting all his own employees and their families and the clients' employees and their families. A seasoned aerobatic pilot, Fagen entertains the gatherings by performing various aerobatic maneuvers in his P51 Mustang, "Sweet Revenge." "Everyone works very hard to bring a project in on time, and gives up family time," Fagen says. "This is my way of giving something back to them as well as thanking the client."

With the establishment of Fagen Engineering, LLC, in 1995, single-source design, procurement, and construction services were added to Fagen, Inc.'s repertoire. The existing Fagen, Inc., corporate office became too small with this addition, so the expanded company's first design/build project was its own new corporate office. After just nine months for construction, a brand-new elongated diamond–shaped building stood prominently at the corner of Highways 212 and 23 in Granite Falls, Minnesota.

"I'm building for the future," Ron Fagen says. "The company will stay flexible enough to change with the industry. When I'm gone, I want Fagen, Inc., to be bigger and better than ever."

This vertical continuous-casting (VCC) pit was dug for a brass-melt building constructed for PMX Industries in Cedar Rapids, Iowa. The complex was the first copper and brass facility to be built from the ground up in the United States in twenty years.

MAXXON CORPORATION

As an innovator

and developer

of floor

underlayment

products, Maxxon

Corporation

provides solutions

for residential

and commercial

buildings world-

wide, whether

newly constructed

or renovated

Searching for better ways to do things is how innovators begin to question the status quo. Finding the answers is how great ones, like Maxxon Corporation, evolve into industry leaders.

Maxxon Corporation is an international provider of Gyp-Crete® brand high-strength gypsum cement and other construction underlayment products. It traces its beginnings to the early 1970s when Clyde Jorgenson and his brother Ron were in the drywall business. They paid close attention to the details of construction, particularly the industry's reliance on foamed concrete as a floor underlayment, despite cracking and dust problems.

After researching and testing alternatives, the Jorgensons devised a remarkable gypsum-based product they called Gyp-Crete. Sound-deadening and fire- and crack-resistant, it was immediately hailed as an alternative to foamed concrete.

A family of Maxxon® floor underlayment products is poised to carry Gyp-Crete, now the industry standard in multifamily residential and hotel construction, into the twenty-first century. Four other gypsum floor underlayments and a cementitious underlayment also fulfill specific construction needs.

Gyp-Crete 2000® and Dura-Cap® poured underlayments work perfectly in renovations where worn, uneven floors need to be smoothed and made flat. They can be poured to a three-inch depth over wood, concrete, and old floor coverings to fill the cracks and voids left after walls are removed.

Level-Right® self-leveling floor underlayment and its companion product, Level-Right FS-10, are low-cost solutions to uneven flooring in new construction and renovations. Also increasing the range of Maxxon applications is Maxxon's Acousti-Mat® sound-deadening rubber pad for use

Therma-Floor®, the ideal underlayment for radiant floor heat, is poured one and one-fourth- to one-and-one-half-inches thick over any brand of hydronic tube or electric heating cable.

between the subfloor and Maxxon's high-strength underlayments. Acousti-Mat actually inhibits sound transfer between stacked living units.

The innovative Infloor® heating system by Maxxon delivers clean, comfortable radiant heating from hot-water tubes in the subfloor. Therma-Floor® underlayment encases Infloor's tubes or cables in crack-resistant, noncombustible gypsum. It is poured only one-and-one-fourth-inches thick to maximize Infloor's responsiveness.

Maxxon products are tested daily in homes, apartments, and commercial buildings worldwide. Canada, Mexico, Puerto Rico, Panama, Taiwan, South Korea, New Zealand, and Hong Kong added to Maxxon's recent record sales and its mark of more than 1.5 billion square feet of successful underlayment solutions.

Always open to innovative methods of challenging the status quo, Maxxon supports and trains personnel at regional sales and service centers throughout its network. Its customers are the 170 applicators—the qualified construction subcontractors—who are close to their local markets, and whom Maxxon constantly encourages to "seek a better way."

Maxxon®, Gyp-Crete®, Gyp-Crete 2000®, Dura-Cap®, Therma-Floor®, Level-Right®, Infloor®, and Acousti-Mat® are registered trademarks of Maxxon Corporation, Hamel, Minnesota.

Maxxon Corporation's Level-Right® Plus multipurpose self-leveling floor underlayment is ideal for thin- or thick-topping applications over concrete.

© Bob Firth/Firth Photobank

© Bob Firth/Firth Photobank

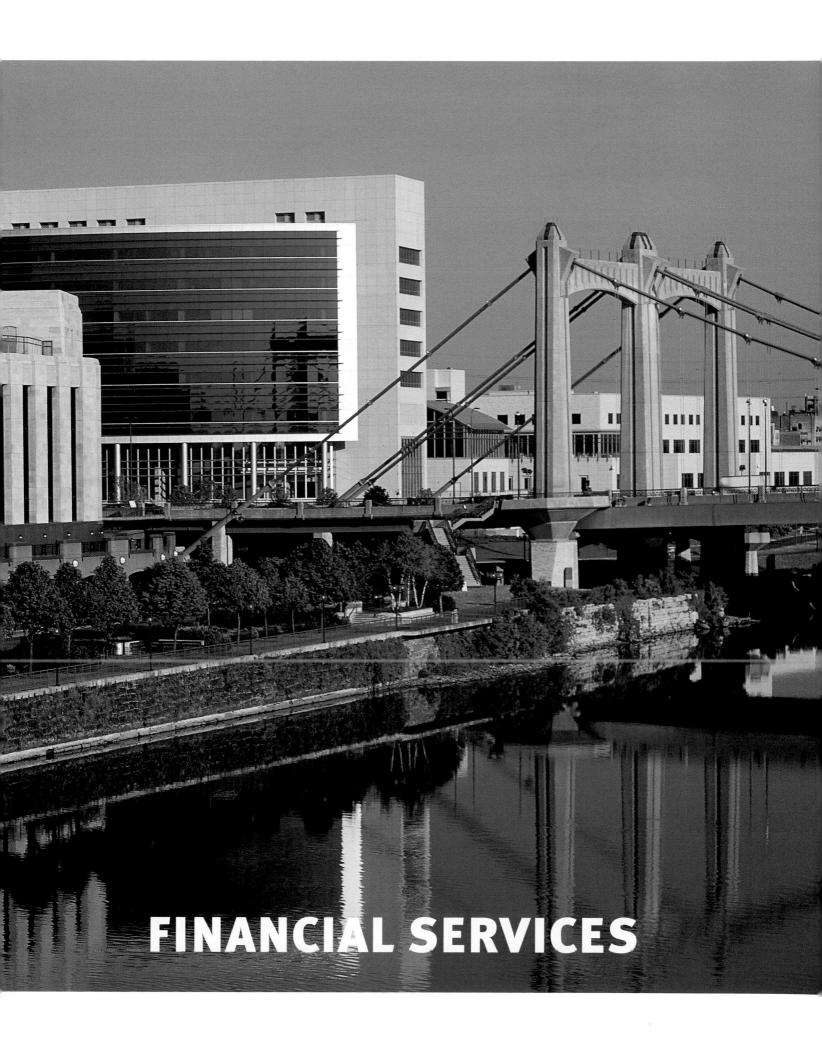

FINANCIAL SERVICES

NORWEST CORPORATION

WITH NEARLY

FOUR THOUSAND

FINANCIAL STORES

THROUGHOUT THE

UNITED STATES

AND GLOBALLY, THE

STRONG CUSTOMER

COMMITMENT BUILT

BY NORWEST

CORPORATION

HAS PRODUCED

TEN YEARS OF

RECORD EARNINGS

A financial services company with assets of $96 billion, Norwest Corporation provides banking, insurance, investment, mortgage, and consumer finance at 3,847 stores in all fifty states, Canada, the Caribbean, Latin America, and many other locations around the world.

In the late 1980s Norwest reinvented itself after some challenging years. For decades, Norwest had a very strong service culture. On top of that, it built a strong credit culture to manage risk. It began diversifying risk by industry, geography, and product. It also decentralized decision-making, giving managers more autonomy, and adopted a retail approach to marketing its financial services.

Reflecting its new sales-driven culture, Norwest stopped using the word "branch" and started using the word "store." This sent a message to Wall Street to view Norwest as a retailer, deserving a higher price-to-earnings ratio. Norwest also made a concerted effort to communicate to its employees, now called "team members," that the company was developing a sales culture. Norwest banks not only began operating like stores, they began looking like stores. For example, service counters were placed at the entrance to help customers with quick transactions and refer them to the appropriate salespeople.

"First, we focus on earning 100 percent of every creditworthy customer's business," says Norwest CEO Richard Kovacevich. "Next, we work to 'out-national the locals and out-local the nationals.' That means offering a broader product line and better products than our local competitors, and at the same time, out-performing our national

The Norwest Center is 772 feet high—a dramatic landmark on the Minneapolis skyline.

competitors by focusing on personal, hometown service. We decided we're not in the banking business—we're in retail financial services. We started thinking and acting like retailers, not bankers," he says.

As part of its effort to reinvent itself, Norwest created a training and professional development arm, called Norwest University. Today it has eleven campuses throughout its sixteen banking states, offering courses in all facets of sales and service.

Norwest also gave stock options to its 58,000 team members. Its first stock options for team

In 1989 noted architect Cesar Pelli designed the fifty-seven-story Norwest Center in downtown Minneapolis, headquarters for the $96 billion financial services company.

members, called "Partnershares," vested in just eleven months, generating a pretax gain for team members of $66 million.

Norwest offers customers a variety of channels, such as stores, ATMs, telephone banking, interactive video, the Internet, and kiosks. Its goal is to integrate all channels and match them to the preferences of its customers.

"We're using technology to be closer to our customers, understand their needs better and faster, and deliver real value at less cost," Kovacevich explains. "Banks are not just in the lending business anymore—they're in the value-added information business. The winners in our industry will use technology to make it easier for customers to manage their money anywhere, anytime they please.

"We view technology as the means to an end, serving customers when, where, and how they want to be served. It's not a means for replacing people, it's a tool to help people be more effective and efficient. Used the right way, it can personalize, not depersonalize, customer service," says Kovacevich. "Technology is indispensable, but we believe the best computer ever created is the human mind."

Serving customers to the "Nth Degree" is critical to Norwest's success.

Norwest is truly a community-oriented company. In 1997 Norwest team members in the Twin Cities donated more than 100,000 hours of community service, and the Norwest Foundation gave $5.1 million to nonprofit organizations in Minnesota. Nationwide, Norwest invested $22 million in nonprofits in 1997. In a national competition, *George* magazine named Norwest one of "America's 10 Most Generous Companies."

Among Norwest's recent achievements:
• Ten consecutive years of record earnings
• Norwest's profits/earnings ratio is now greater than that of McDonald's; and for the first time, greater than the Standard & Poor 500 average
• Ranked by *Fortune* magazine as the most admired super-regional bank in the nation and among the top 10 percent of all companies in the United States
• The *Wall Street Journal* named Norwest on its honor roll for outstanding stock performance, a recognition received by just thirty-one companies in the world
• For the past five years, Norwest has been the top SBA (Small Business Association) lender in Minnesota.

"We believe the company with the best people wins," says CEO Kovacevich. "If our people care more than people we compete against, then we'll transmit to customers that energy, that enthusiasm, that great service— what we call 'going to the Nth Degree®.' We believe that commitment and motivation are even more important than products, technology, and cutting costs."

A Thanksgiving day fire in 1982 destroyed Norwest's headquarters. It was the most costly downtown office building fire in U.S. history.

BANK WINDSOR

What happens when a metropolitan bank treats its customers with the same friendliness normally associated with small-town Minnesota banks and makes those customers the sole focus of its business? In the case of Minneapolis-based Bank Windsor, what happens is impressive growth and success over a short span of years, generated by a loyal group of satisfied *individual* customers.

It's no accident that Bank Windsor has adopted what cofounder Samuel Kaplan, a prominent Minneapolis attorney, calls an "informal style and bias for quick response to its customers" given the fact that the bank's roots are in rural Minnesota. In 1988 Mr. Kaplan, his law partner Ralph Strangis, and a group of other investors purchased a tiny bank in the farming community of Nerstrand. They added capital to the bank and continued to operate it, as they do to this day. However, they moved its principal offices to Minneapolis, where they created Bank Windsor.

At Bank Windsor, customers are greeted by their first name and invited to discuss their banking business over a cup of coffee, not at a traditional banking station.

From the outset, this was to be a different kind of bank, devoted solely to serving the personal and business banking needs of individuals—entrepreneurs and corporate executives, real estate developers and investors and professionals. At Bank Windsor there were, and still are, no teller windows in the office, only desks where a receptionist and personal bankers greet customers by their first names. This ambience even deterred a would-be bank robber a few years ago—confused by the nonbank appearance, he left and robbed another bank.

While many banks offer private banking, Bank Windsor makes this style of banking its principal business. Focusing on the individual enables the bank to know its customers very well. In turn, it can respond positively and quickly to requests for both business and personal loans. Thus Bank Windsor can readily approve business and real estate loans that normally would face time-consuming reviews at other financial institutions. Yet the bank's loan loss experience is outstanding because of its close client relationships.

How well the bank delivers on its promise of excellent relationships can be seen in the results of a recent survey of all customers. On a scale of 1 (average) to 3 (excellent), customers' overall rating of their satisfaction with the bank was 2.8.

Customer satisfaction comes in part from the continuity of staff in key contact positions. At many banks, personal banking is a training stopover known for its turnover. At Bank Windsor, more than half the staff has been with the bank for most of its existence.

Along with satisfied customers, Bank Windsor's growth is the best measure of its success with its focused personal banking strategy. When the bank was acquired in 1988, it ranked a lowly 638th among all Minnesota state banks with $2.5 million in assets. At the end of 1997, Bank Windsor ranked 41st among Minnesota banks with total assets of $158 million and deposits of $131.8 million.

BANKWINDSOR

THE FLYNN COMPANIES

AN AWARD-WINNING

AGENCY, THE FLYNN

COMPANIES PROVIDES

FINANCIAL SERVICES

FOR INDIVIDUALS

AND BUSINESSES,

USING A WIDE

VARIETY OF

INSURANCE AND

INVESTMENT PROGRAMS

Founded in 1975, The Flynn Companies has a long history of helping clients develop the financial strategies that lead to success and reward.

The Flynn Companies is a General Agency of New England Life, which was chartered in Boston in 1835. Captain John Todd, first cousin of Mary Todd Lincoln, bought a policy from New England Life in 1848, while serving at Fort Snelling. New England Life sold its first insurance policy in Minnesota in 1846—twelve years before Minnesota became a state.

The philosophy of The Flynn Companies is to always provide the best product for its clients. Although New England Life is its primary insurance company, The Flynn Companies also represents some fifty other insurance companies. A full-service financial services company, The Flynn Companies offers the full spectrum of financial products through the New England Securities Broker Dealer.

The Flynn Companies is familiar with the nuances of many and varied financial products and services, and the ever-changing legislative and economic factors that may affect a customer's financial position. Its agents work with customers to provide solutions designed to help meet financial goals.

As a Registered Investment Adviser Firm, The Flynn Companies offers total financial planning

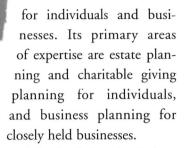

The Flynn Companies is a General Agency of New England Life, whose long history of providing successful financial strategies is reflected in this advertisement from the St. Paul Daily Pioneer *dated 1854.*

for individuals and businesses. Its primary areas of expertise are estate planning and charitable giving planning for individuals, and business planning for closely held businesses.

The firm's founder, Robert G. Flynn, CLU (Chartered Life Underwriter), ChFC (Chartered Financial Consultant), is a graduate of Marquette University. He entered the United States Marine Corps as a second lieutenant, and served during two tours in Vietnam as a helicopter pilot. In 1968 he joined New England Financial and was appointed Agency Manager in St. Paul in 1975, and General Agent in 1978. Flynn was named Agency Manager of the Year in 1978. In both 1978 and 1979, Flynn received the Group Agency of the Year Award.

The Flynn Companies has been nominated many times for, and is a four-time winner of, the President's Trophy. This is the top award given to New England Financial agencies on a national basis. The agency also has received the Ship's Bell Award for policyholder services, the Judge Willard Phillips Award for agent training, the Agency Builders Award, and the Heritage Award for quality service.

"We are an agency that cares about our clients," Flynn says. "Our representatives use a broad array of insurance and investment products and services, and develop financial solutions that create real value for our customers."

Since 1975 The Flynn Companies has developed financial solutions that create real value for its customers.

LUTHERAN BROTHERHOOD

President and CEO Robert P. Gandrud leads Lutheran Brotherhood in its mission to serve the financial and fraternal needs of Lutherans and their congregations, institutions, and communities.

Upon first hearing the name "Lutheran Brotherhood," some people are more than a little confused. Church? Social services organization? Men's group? Few would guess that this Minneapolis-based fraternal benefit society with its unusual name is one of the largest financial services organizations in the United States.

But even more distinguishing than its name is Lutheran Brotherhood's mission—its commitment to helping Lutherans achieve financial security and be good stewards of their resources and gifts. It is Lutheran Brotherhood's mission that sets it apart from other financial services organizations.

Lutheran Brotherhood was created in 1917 as a fraternal mutual aid society for Lutherans. Its purpose was to help Lutherans "bear one another's burdens" by sharing financial risk and preparing prudently for the future through insurance protection. This mission of service remains unchanged.

Lutheran Brotherhood and its affiliated companies today manage more than $20 billion for its 1.1 million members (product owners) and offer a portfolio of financial products and services that includes life insurance, annuities, variable products, disability income insurance, long-term care insurance, and mutual funds, among others.

Lutheran Brotherhood was built on the quality and performance of its financial products, and on

Copper-colored glass characterizes the seventeen-story Lutheran Brotherhood Building in downtown Minneapolis.

an uncompromising standard of putting members' needs first.

Products and services are delivered to Lutherans via a professional 1,600-member field force. These individuals work closely with clients to ensure that appropriate strategies are developed to meet their short- and long-term needs, including retirement planning, estate protection, education funding, charitable giving, business continuation plans, and many other life needs.

With more than $45 billion of life insurance coverage in force, Lutheran Brotherhood is playing a key role in the financial security of Lutherans across the United States.

Independent insurance analysts have consistently given Lutheran Brotherhood high ratings that reflect its strong financial position. This success can be traced to unwavering commitment to financial solvency and strength, and the trust members place in it.

Through its charitable and benevolent programs and resources, Lutheran Brotherhood aids its members, their congregations, institutions, and communities. These programs include disaster relief; educational scholarships; matching gift programs for Lutheran congregations, schools and ministries; and financial and administrative support for Lutheran Brotherhood's 969 branches (local service groups made up of Lutheran Brotherhood members). Each year these branches put Lutheran Brotherhood's fraternal resources into service, multiplied by millions of hours of volunteer service.

"Being a good steward is our business," says Robert P. Gandrud, president and CEO of Lutheran Brotherhood. "It's who we are, and it's what we do."

© Bob Firth/Firth Photobank

© Bob Firth/Firth Photobank

PROFESSIONAL SERVICES

COLLE & MCVOY MARKETING COMMUNICATIONS, INC.

In 1935 Alfred Colle, a successful printing salesman, quit his job and founded an advertising agency, the Alfred Colle Company. His friend, Kirk McVoy, joined him a year later, and the firm became Colle & McVoy Marketing Communications, Inc. Throughout its formative years, signature accounts—including Weyerhaeuser, Electric Machinery, Tennant, and Polaris Industries—defined the agency's character, culture, and mission to provide "100 percent commitment to the client."

The agency has since expanded that commitment by offering clients an integrated approach to marketing communications, including advertising, public relations, market research, database marketing, and interactive media. Having built a solid reputation for serving agribusiness, business-to-business, and consumer clients, the agency has grown to include national giants such as 3M, Novartis, DEKALB, Pfizer Animal Health, Winnebago, Caterpillar, Cenex/Land O'Lakes, and GE Capital.

What's more, the agency has taken the kind of commitment it has to its clients one step further—to its employees. Colle & McVoy established an Employee Stock Ownership Plan (ESOP) in 1989 and is proud to be one of the only independent marketing communications firms in its market that is 100 percent employee-owned.

"The ESOP offers employees an opportunity to have a stake in the financial prosperity of the agency," says Jim Bergeson,

Located in the 8500 Tower in Bloomington, Minnesota, the Colle & McVoy Marketing Communications offices offer a spectacular view of Normandale Lake.

chairman and CEO. "Success for the client and for the agency translates into success for employees. The two are interchangeable."

Colle & McVoy was named the Minnesota ESOP Company of the Year in 1993, 1995, and 1997, and went on to become the 1997 National ESOP Company of the Year—the first time a marketing communications firm or a Minnesota company has ever earned that distinction.

While the ESOP has become embedded into the Colle & McVoy culture, so has the firm's "Connect. Compel." creative philosophy. "We 'connect' with our clients' audiences by spending time talking, listening, and really understanding them," Bergeson says. "Then we 'compel' the audiences by combining our knowledge of our clients' products and services with a solid understanding of what our clients' customers really need. The outcome is communication that is strategically focused and results-oriented."

Succeeding in its mission to empower employees and to provide creative communications solutions for its clients, Colle & McVoy is thriving . . . and keeping its founders' principles in good hands.

Shown are Colle & McVoy's president, Phil Johnson (on the left), and chairman and CEO, Jim Bergeson.

Cŏlle & McVoy

GAGE MARKETING GROUP

"SKIP" GAGE SAW

THAT REAL

INNOVATION FOR A

TRULY INTEGRATED

MARKETING

COMPANY MEANT

ORCHESTRATING

ALL ELEMENTS IN

THE MARKETING MIX,

FROM STRATEGY

THROUGH

DEVELOPMENT

TO EXECUTION

When a good idea is pushed by an entrepreneur with absolute conviction, the results can be stunning—and quick. That is how industry observers characterize the growth and performance of Gage Marketing Group, which redefines "integrated marketing" by offering everything from conceptual and strategic planning through program development and execution. Gage then fuses its broad array of marketing applications with technology to create information-based marketing solutions that deliver maximum efficiency and impact. The Minneapolis-based company was started in 1991, and by 1997 Gage Marketing's sales reached $130 million.

Edwin C. "Skip" Gage, the firm's founder, president, and chief executive officer, points out that, "Marketing professionals must always be on the lookout for changing needs and changing solutions." Gage's own vision for successful marketing is three-faceted: He sees the future bound in integrated marketing. He is willing to invest in experienced, high-caliber managers and personnel. And he wants his company to be unique by both developing and executing marketing programs.

Gage Marketing Group serves many of the leading companies in the United States, including three-quarters of the Fortune 100. Its broad spectrum of marketing functions includes:

- Direct
- Promotion
- Database and Internet
- Sweepstakes, games, and contests
- Point-of-purchase display
- Teleservices
- Fulfillment
- Lettershop and print personalization
- Events
- Travel

For its performance of such services, the company has received industry tributes: It was ranked second among the nation's marketing services agencies by *Ad Age* and cited as the third largest business-to-business agency by *Business Marketing*.

Using his unique vision of integrated marketing, Edwin "Skip" Gage built the Gage Marketing Group into a $130-million powerhouse in just six short years. Today, amazingly, about half of all U.S. households each year are involved in some way with a Gage program.

Gage Marketing Group's 2,100 employees and multiple offices and operations centers across the world enable the company to deliver marketing services to many leading companies, including 75 percent of the Fortune 100 firms.

A Web site Gage Marketing created for a client was rated "one of the ten best" by *Inter@ctive Week*.

Gage Marketing has 2,100 employees. Corporate headquarters are in Minneapolis, and there are marketing offices across the country, in Detroit; Cleveland; Bentonville, Arkansas; St. Louis; and Newport Beach, California. Marketing offices outside the United States are in London, England, and Cologne, Germany. In addition, there are operations centers in Minneapolis; Detroit; El Paso; Kankakee, Illinois; Juarez, Mexico; and Winnipeg, Canada.

As a result of the activities taking place at these facilities, each year about half of all U.S. households are involved in some way in a Gage-designed promotion. Gage point-of-purchase displays are seen in 50,000 U.S. retail stores; millions of consumers can be reached at any moment via Gage's Internet marketing capabilities; and every day more than 20,000 incoming calls and 2 million orders are processed and fulfilled.

Gage Marketing is dedicated to mastering the substance of tomorrow's business needs. Striving to continue on as one of the world's largest, truly integrated marketing companies, it feels its objective of "remarkable growth" will be the natural outcome of putting customer needs first and providing information-based marketing solutions that deliver maximum efficiency and impact.

Visitors are welcome at Gage Marketing Group's Internet Web site: www.gage.com.

LIFETOUCH INC.

FOR MORE THAN

SIXTY YEARS,

LIFETOUCH INC.,

HAS BEEN CAPTURING

THE SPIRIT OF TODAY

AND PRESERVING

MEMORIES FOR

TOMORROW WITH

TOP-QUALITY

CHILDHOOD,

STUDENT, AND FAMILY

PHOTOGRAPHY

Lifetouch Portrait Studios, located at JCPenney and Target stores, capture childhood memories through professional portraits.

In 1936 two young entrepreneurs began photographing school children, one country schoolhouse at a time. Their energy and vision launched a Minnesota-based photography enterprise that evolved into Lifetouch Inc. with operations today in all fifty states, Canada, Mexico, and Puerto Rico. Lifetouch portraits are proudly displayed in homes and offices around the world—everywhere memories are kept and treasured.

As one of the largest employee-owned photography companies in the world, Lifetouch fosters a team spirit within the organization that attracts talented and dedicated men and women. Collectively, the nearly 16,000 Lifetouch employees continue the tradition of providing customers with the kind of high-quality products and service that build long-term relationships.

Lifetouch is "Photography for a Lifetime," serving early childhood, school, and family

New photographic technologies for Lifetouch are developed at the corporate headquarters, based in suburban Minneapolis.

accessible for the whole family. The Lifetouch school yearbook formation process, which has gained national recognition, is at the core of Lifetouch Publishing. Lifetouch Church Directories produces pictorial publications that become organizational tools and a means for historic preservation in churches.

Lifetouch has always added value to emerging technologies for the photographic industry. Utilization and application of new technology has made Lifetouch a leader in photography, printing, manufacturing, and processing. And now, Lifetouch Development Inc. is projecting Lifetouch into the future by its creation and development of new markets and products for the imaging industry.

"The smiles in the portraits of children and families are at the very heart of Lifetouch," says Paul Harmel, president and chief executive officer. "Our mission is to preserve these memories with portraits for a lifetime."

The Lifetouch Inc. world headquarters is located at 11000 Viking Drive, in Eden Prairie, Minnesota. The phone number is (612) 826-4000.

markets. That family focus is clearly established with employees and customers and continues to be a point of differentiation.

Lifetouch National School Studios photographs daily in schools and preschools, working in concert with families and educators to preserve memories from childhood to high school graduation. With more than 500 locations nationwide, Lifetouch Portrait Studios in JCPenney and Target locations are easily

Lifetouch ®

CLEAN-FLO INTERNATIONAL

No other natural resource is as important to our communities as clean water, yet its supply is threatened by global industrial and agricultural pollution. In response to the critical need for clean lakes, rivers, and reservoirs, engineer Robert L. Laing founded Clean-Flo International in 1970. Laing holds patents in electronics, limnology, and agricultural chemistry, and he sees solutions to the diminishing supply of clean water worldwide.

The basis for Clean-Flo's environmentally friendly restorative system is the physics of seasonal water changes. In cool climates, every spring and autumn, bodies of water "turn over." That is, the oxygen-rich top layer of water sinks, allowing the unoxygenated lower layer to rise and neutralize its toxic gases. Clean-Flo forces the process continuously and "nudges it" with additional natural buffered precipitants and natural bacteria to remove weed and algae food, and to kill disease bacteria. The Clean-Flo "continuous laminar flow inversion/oxygenation" system is many times more effective than ordinary diffused-air systems.

Starting with seventy-eight-acre Crystal Lake in Robbinsdale, Minnesota, in 1972, Clean-Flo has restored more than 2,000 bodies of water plagued by low oxygen, organic sediment and muck, weeds, algae, and disease bacteria. The company has salvaged many lakes, rivers, and ponds, including Indianhead Lake in Edina, Minnesota; Sylvan Lake in Palatine, Illinois; Rice Lake in Frederick, Wisconsin; and Lake Weston in Orlando, Florida.

England's Buckingham Palace hired Clean-Flo International and SGS Environment of Liverpool to restore the royal lakes.

Located in Golden Valley, Minnesota, 100-acre Sweeney Lake sparkles during the artificial-inversion process.

As Clean-Flo's reputation spread, it took on larger lakes, ocean bays, wastewater treatment lagoons, aquaculture, rivers, drinking-water reservoirs, disease bacteria, and odor-removal projects.

Clean-Flo began providing services to international clients in 1989, completing notable projects in France (where restoration of L'Helpe River earned that country's two highest environmental awards), Japan, the Philippines, India, and Korea. Clean-Flo systems presently operate in the lakes at Buckingham Palace in London.

None of those, however, matches the scope of Clean-Flo's Kaohsiung, Taiwan, project involving the 8.4 million-cubic-meter Feng-Shan reservoir, which was terribly contaminated by pig farming. With 400 Clean-Flo diffusers in place, the vast reservoir was once again made clean, saving the government of Taiwan $586,000 in annual potable water treatment expenses.

"What," says company president Laing, "could be a finer legacy from the Land of Lakes than clean-water technology?"

AAA MINNESOTA/IOWA

Although most people probably know AAA best for its long history of providing road service and maps, these are just two of the many travel services AAA offers. In fact, today AAA is one of the largest leisure travel companies in the world.

"During our many years of service to the public, AAA has sought to continually evaluate services in an effort to anticipate and stay ahead of the needs of our members," says AAA Minnesota/Iowa president and CEO Duane J. Crandall. "We want to expand our efforts to provide quality services, convenient resources, and peace of mind in order to develop lifetime relationships with our members and provide benefits for every stage of their lives."

AAA's services are centered in four primary areas. Its wide range of automotive services includes roadside assistance and endorsement of selected auto service facilities under its AAA Approved Auto Repair Program. As a leisure travel agency, AAA offers air, hotel, car rental, cruise, and tour bookings, plus numerous discounts and routing assistance for automobile travel. In addition, AAA offers a variety of insurance products. Through its agreement with PNC Bank, AAA has created the nation's largest branchless bank, providing electronic and telephone access to a variety of financial services.

AAA Minnesota/Iowa was the first AAA organization in the country to integrate voice and data technology for day-to-day operations in its twenty-four-hour Member Service Center. This system will allow the organization to efficiently handle more than one million calls annually.

The national AAA organization was founded in 1902. The original Minnesota State Automobile Association was formed in 1907. In the early years, these clubs were primarily road clubs and charged annual dues ranging from one to three dollars per member. The Minnesota State Automobile Association, later known as AAA Minnesota, became AAA Minnesota/Iowa in January 1997, when it merged with AAA Iowa. It is a nonprofit organization that now serves more than 700,000 members. With more than forty offices in two states plus the Member Service Center, AAA Minnesota/Iowa serves all of Minnesota, except for Hennepin County, and all of Iowa.

"For almost a century AAA has been a strong public voice both locally and nationally," says Crandall. "During the past two decades, we've spoken out on a number of important issues, including triple-trailer trucks, drunk driving, gas taxes, and toll roads.

"AAA Minnesota/Iowa representatives will continue to serve on local and national committees and meet regularly with key legislators and other elected officials in an effort to influence public policy."

Almost immediately after the first horseless carriages appeared on America's roads, motorists began to realize the need for organizing automobile clubs.

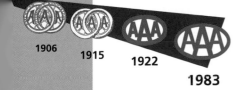

1906   1915   1922

1983

1997

MADE IN MINNESOTA

CHAPTER SIXTEEN

WHAT DO SNACK FOODS, MOTORCYCLES, ELECTRICAL COMPONENTS, HEARING AIDS, HARDWOOD MOLDINGS, AND IN-LINE SKATES HAVE IN COMMON? THEY'RE ALL PRODUCTS PRODUCED BY MINNESOTA'S FASTEST-GROWING MANUFACTURING INDUSTRIES. WHILE MANUFACTURING INDUSTRIES ACROSS THE NATION DECLINED NEARLY 5 PERCENT FROM 1985 TO 1994, EMPLOYMENT IN MINNESOTA MANUFACTURING INDUSTRIES GREW MORE THAN 10 PERCENT IN

the same period, and the numbers are still climbing.

The strength of manufacturing in Minnesota can be found in its diversity. The state's manufacturing base is a mix of major national and international firms with homegrown enterprises, a blend of large corporations and small factories and shops, and a variety of traditional and emerging industries. The base is also distributed throughout the entire state, from the metropolitan areas to the rural towns and communities. This diversity has helped insulate Minnesota from the wide swings in employment experienced elsewhere in the country. Also contributing to the success of manufacturing is the strength of the state's export markets and their exceptionally high labor-force participation rate.

Minnesota's largest manufacturing industries are industrial machinery (including computers), printing and publishing, processed foods, scientific instruments, paper and allied products, fabricated metals, and electronic and electric equipment. IBM, Cray Research, Control Data, Unisys, Taylor Corporation, Deluxe Corporation, General Mills, Pillsbury, Hormel Foods, Medtronic, St. Jude Medical, Boise Cascade, Blandin Paper, and Rosemount are just some of the major manufacturers with headquarters or a significant presence in the state. Rubber and plastics, food and kindred products, transportation equipment, and millwork are among the roster of quickly emerging manufacturers. Altogether, the manufacturing sector accounts for the highest share of Minnesota's $124 billion-plus gross state product, which continues to grow at a rate far higher than the national average.

Manufacturing and Minnesota in the same sentence immediately brings to mind the state's premier manufacturing company, Minnesota Mining and Manufacturing,

Opposite: Colorful fishing-lure heads receive their eyes at the Blue Fox Tackle company plant in Cambridge, Minnesota. © Greg Ryan-Sally Beyer. Above: The 3M headquarters in St. Paul houses the company that gave the world such innovations as Scotch Tape and Post-it Notes. 3M has an unusual corporate policy that inspires creativity in its scientists: They are allowed to use up to 15 percent of their on-site work time to devote to inventive projects that keep their conceptual fires burning. © Greg Ryan-Sally Beyer

DAHLGREN AND COMPANY IN CROOKSTON IS A LEADING INTERNATIONAL SUPPLIER OF RAW AND ROASTED SUNFLOWER PRODUCTS. DAHLGREN OFFERS A VARIETY OF KERNEL AND IN-SHELL SNACK FOODS FOR HUMAN CONSUMPTION, ALONG WITH SEVERAL TYPES OF BIRDSEEDS.

better known around the world as 3M. Founded in 1902 by a group of five businessmen, the company began with the mining of a mineral deposit for use as a grinding abrasive. Finding little success, the company relocated to Duluth and concentrated its efforts on sandpaper products. After a 1910 move to St. Paul and the subsequent development of both the world's first waterproof sandpaper and first masking tape, the company charted a steady course of technical progress, introducing the world to products it would shortly be unable to fathom being without, among them Scotch Tape, Scotchguard fabric protection, magnetic audiotape, videotape, the Thermo-Fax copying process, and Post-it Notes. Today, the company is the state's leading high-technology firm and employs more than twenty-three thousand Minnesotans.

Another manufacturing giant and industrial leader with Minnesota roots is Honeywell, founded more than one hundred years ago with the invention of the automatic thermostat for home heating. The company now has sites in ninety-five countries and is the global leader in control technology. Approximately 45 percent of Honeywell's business is still related to home and building controls, but the company has expanded and is now also the world's leading manufacturer-supplier of industrial control systems as well as avionics systems for commercial, military, and space markets. Other manufacturers that call Minnesota home are H.B. Fuller, the world's largest adhesive manufacturer, and Tennant, the premier designer, manufacturer, and marketer of nonresidential floor-maintenance equipment and floor coatings.

Plastics, polymers, composites, and new end uses for agricultural products top the list of up-and-coming industries. Employment in Minnesota's plastics industry has risen 15 percent since 1991 and is currently sixteenth in the nation. Much of the growth in this industry has come from small towns and companies with a few dozen to several hundred employees. Engineered Polymers, for

In Belle Plaine, Minnesota, the Hanlon brothers are bringing back the Excelsior-Henderson motorcycle. Here, in the background is the 1931 Excelsior Super X, in the foreground, the 1999 Excelsior-Henderson Super X prototype. © Excelsior-Henderson

example, has a workforce of 377 in the tiny town of Mora, population 2,900. In Mankato, Phenix Biocomposites has pioneered a highly engineered composite material known as Environ. Used in the construction and furniture industries, the material, which looks like natural stone but can be cut, fabricated, and finished in a similar fashion to hardwood, is made from soybeans and recycled paper.

In a state known for water, it's no surprise to find a company concerned with the growing water pollution problem. Aeration Industries International in Minneapolis developed an innovative aspiration aeration technology and today is the world's largest manufacturer of aspirator aeration equipment, with installations in all fifty states and in eighty-five countries. Colonial Craft in St. Paul is a leading millwork manufacturer that has also become the first company of its kind to receive green certification, ensuring that all its products are produced in an environmentally friendly way. A pioneer in the movement, Colonial Craft has ushered environmental responsibility to the forefront of the wood-products industry.

Elsewhere in the state, there are plenty of surprises to be found. In the old-dog, new-trick category, Polaris

In southeast Minnesota, some brightly colored farm equipment stands by. The manufacture of farm and garden machinery is a growing sector in the state. Employment in this area increased 33.2 percent between 1985 and 1994. ©John Elk III

ECONOMIC VITALITY IS REACHING EVERY PART OF MINNESOTA. SINCE 1990, THE NUMBER OF MANUFACTURING JOBS IN GREATER MINNESOTA HAS BEEN RISING FOUR TIMES FASTER THAN IN THE TWIN CITIES METRO AREA. THE INDUSTRIAL GROWTH CREATED BY MAJOR MANUFACTURERS AND FORTUNE 500 COMPANIES HAS SPREAD TO THE SUPPLIERS AND SUBCONTRACTORS THAT SUPPORT THEM. IN FACT, OVER 60 PERCENT OF THE NEWLY CREATED JOBS IN THE EARLY 1990S AROSE IN BUSINESSES WITH FEWER THAN ONE HUNDRED EMPLOYEES.

Courtesy, Deluxe Corp.

PLYMOUTH, MINNESOTA, IS HOME TO THE REXTON CORPORATION, ONE OF THE WORLD'S LEADING MANUFACTURERS OF HEARING AIDS. SONAR, IN EAGAN, HAS USED 3M TECHNOLOGY TO BECOME ANOTHER RECOGNIZED INNOVATOR IN THE INDUSTRY.

Plaine, brothers Dave and Dan Hanlon are resurrecting a legend. Their Excelsior-Henderson Corporation is once again manufacturing the Excelsior motorcycle, arguably once the most elite of the American made. Then there's Red Wing Shoe Company. Named for the city where it has its headquarters, the company has remained somewhat of an enigma since its beginnings in 1905. While the American shoe-manufacturing industry has plummeted over the decades after taking serious hits from foreign competition, Red Wing Shoe, which manufactures a wide variety of rugged and industrial shoes and boots, has continued to experience steady and sizable growth.

Industries, a leading manufacturer of snowmobiles, all-terrain vehicles, and personal watercraft in Roseau, is introducing its latest product, a motorcycle. The innovative Victory is aiming to earn recognition as the best-handling cruiser on the market. Several hundred miles to the south in the sleepy farm community of Belle

What else is manufactured in Minnesota? Well, high school graduates ordering graduation announcements or class rings, FBI agents loading ammunition, figure skaters and hockey players lacing up world-class custom skates, office workers reaching for an expandable file, golfers appreciating the beauty of the world's most prestigious courses, and the Rock and Roll Hall of Fame architects ordering those magnificent expanses of glass, all have connections to Minnesota manufacturers. Minneapolis-based Josten's is the world's premier

Opposite: A man works at the engine rebuilding and repair company Bolduc Aviation Specialized Services at the Anoka County Airport. © Greg Ryan-Sally Beyer. Below: A man checks the operations in the press room at Precision Associates, a Minneapolis company that manufactures O-rings. © Greg Ryan-Sally Beyer

THE MINNESOTA JOBS SKILLS PARTNERSHIP NOT ONLY PRO-MOTES COOPERATION BETWEEN THE STATE'S EDUCATIONAL INSTITUTIONS AND LOCAL BUSINESSES BUT ALSO PROVIDES FINANCIAL ASSISTANCE TO COMPANIES UPGRADING THE SKILLS OF ITS WORKERS, ALL IN AN EFFORT TO HELP MINNESOTA BUSI-NESSES TRAIN THEIR WORKFORCES TO MEET THEIR PARTICULAR NEEDS. CASE IN POINT: WHEN FRIGIDAIRE, THE HOME-FREEZ-ER MANUFACTURING COMPANY, INTRODUCED ROBOTICS TO ITS ST. CLOUD MANUFACTURING SITE, IT DID SO VIA A TRAINING PROGRAM JOINTLY CREATED AND IMPLEMENTED BY PRIVATE TRAINERS FOR THE COM-PANY, INSTRUCTORS FROM A LOCAL TECHNICAL COL-LEGE, AND THE FACULTY FROM ST. CLOUD STATE UNIVERSITY SCHOOL OF ENGINEERING.

manufacturer of graduation products; Federal Cartridge Company in Anoka is the ammunition industry's leading innovator; Riedell Shoe Company in Red Wing is the nation's largest manufacturer of figure and other skates; Smead Manufacturing in Hastings developed the "band-

less file" and is the leading producer of filing supplies; Bloomington-based Toro Company, the lawn-mower and snowblower manufacturer, is also the preferred provider of golf-course maintenance equipment, includ-ing automatic irrigation systems, in the world; and Owatonna's Viracon leads the world in the production of high-performance architectural glass. Oh, and odds are, anyone needing corrective lenses will be wearing an optical product developed or manufactured by one of the numerous optics companies in Stearns County.

All of Minnesota manufacturers have been given a recent boost by the state legislature. The once burden-some workers' compensation system has been reformed, the sales tax on capital replacement equipment is being eliminated, and property taxes on commercial and indus-trial property have been reduced. Their biggest boost, however, continues to come from that strong Midwestern work ethic displayed day in, day out by their employees.

Below: Check printing, here at Deluxe Corp., is one of the many businesses that make printing and publishing the second-largest manufacturing sector in Minnesota. Courtesy, Deluxe Corp. Opposite: The clustering of flour mills in turn-of-the-century Minneapolis earned that city the nickname Mill City. This advertisement is circa 1900. Courtesy, General Mills

Above: 3M Trizact Abrasives are used by metal-working customers to finish metals used in hand tools, golf clubs, and other products. © Steve Niedorf/3M. Below: Assembly-line workers polish auto bodies in a Ford Motor Company plant in Minnesota in 1935. © Minnesota Historical Society/Corbis

Workers in Minnesota can boast of low absenteeism rates and high levels of industry-specific skills, as well as commendable work habits. With a robust economy and historically low unemployment rates, employers here, already feeling the squeeze of a shortage of workers, have lost no time in joining with available community resources to develop such employment initiatives as school-to-work programs, job training, and an aggressively proactive welfare-to-work posture.

LIFE WITHOUT POST-IT NOTES IS HARD TO IMAGINE. BUT THE PRODUCT ALMOST DIDN'T MAKE IT INTO THE MAINSTREAM. AFTER FAILING TO CAPTURE CONSUMERS' IMAGINATIONS IN TEST MARKETING IN 1977, POST-ITS WERE THEN GIVEN AWAY AS FREE SAMPLES BY 3M—A BOLD MARKETING STRATEGY THAT WORKED.

ORDERS ROLLED IN, AND BY 1980, THE LITTLE CONVENIENCES DEVISED BY 3M CORPORATE SCIENTIST ART FRY WERE POPULAR NATIONWIDE. IT WASN'T LONG BEFORE THEY CAUGHT ON IN CANADA AND EUROPE.

© Steve Niedorf/3M

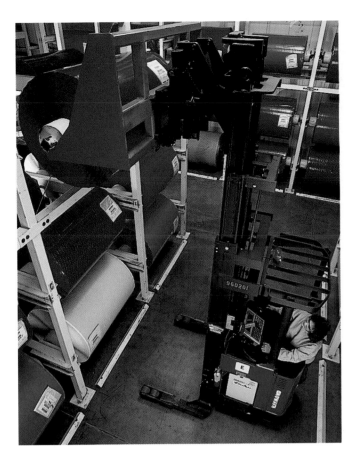

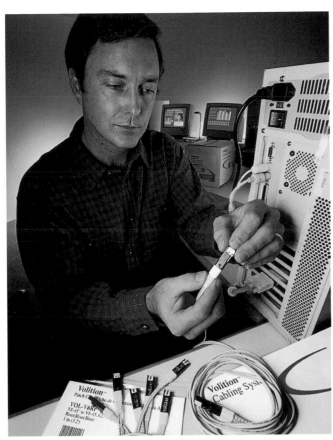

Clockwise from top left: Many 3M facilities employ solventless manufacturing processes to help meet 3M's environmental, health, and safety goals. The 3M Volition Fiber Optic Cabling System has a unique, easy-to-use fiber-optic connector. 3M also makes products for the electronics, electrical, and communications industries. 3M is also a global leader in fluorochemicals. All photos© Steve Niedorf/3M

Above: Toro employees in Windom build consumer products that are distributed worldwide. The Windom plant produces garden tractors and snow throwers. Below: Toro customers and distributors from around the world learn how to service and repair Toro's commercial equipment in the company's Technical Training Shop at Toro's headquarters in Bloomington. Both photos © Toro Company

Clockwise from top left: Honeywell's process controls are in action in industrial plants across the globe. The cockpit of Boeing's 777 has a full set of cutting-edge Honeywell avionics. Both photos © Honeywell. Careful work is required in a window-manufacturing company. © Marvin Windows & Doors. Dahlgren quality extends to finished products with climate-controlled warehouses. © Dahlgren & Company, Inc.

MANUFACTURING

TWIN CITY FAN COMPANIES, LTD.

Fans? People seldom think of fans unless they're uncomfortably hot, and Minnesotans have less reason than many to think of fans at all. Ironically, one of the world's leading makers of fans is located in suburban Minneapolis.

Twin City Fan Companies, Ltd. (TCF), manufactures and sells centrifugal fans and blowers, axial fans, propeller fans, and power roof ventilators ranging in size from ¼ HP exhaust fans to 2,000 HP industrial units. Related products include dampers, air-makeup units, and door heaters. Of the company's 800 employees, 130 work at its Minneapolis headquarters, which is home to all its corporate, engineering, and sales activities as well as its test laboratory.

The principle of how fans work remained unchanged for centuries. Only recently, and mainly in this generation, have fan technology and creative applications pushed one another along. As technology became innovative, so too did people's need for fans. A simple device, the fan now seems a necessary part of life—in our homes and hospitals, where we work, shop, and play, even where our environment is cleaned.

The Twin City Fan Companies, Ltd., corporate headquarters is located in Minneapolis. Relocated in 1993, the facility contains TCF's test and research laboratory and corporate offices.

Twin City Fan can trace its product roots to 1874, when Clarage, the traditional name in centrifugal fan design, started operations in the United States. In 1926 the motor-repair company Piqua Electric Manufacturing made its first "Aerovent" fan, then operated for the next sixty years as Aerovent Fan Company. The first fan produced by a company called Twin City Fan & Blower appeared in 1974.

Meanwhile, since 1955 Charles Barry had been working with his father, Ben Barry, at another fan company to learn all aspects of fan manufacturing. Ben Barry was a pioneer in the air-moving industry and later became a founder of Twin City Fan & Blower. His tutelage gave Charles a

Clarage radial tip fans are designed for stringent petrochemical applications and API 560 and 673 specifications for use in processing crude oil into gasoline.

full appreciation of the engineering requirements of fine centrifugal fans. Having owned Twin City Fan & Blower since 1973, the Barrys acquired Aerovent in 1993 and Clarage in 1997 and proceeded to establish them as internationally known names.

Charles Barry, now company chairman, understands that experience, imagination, and caring are important in establishing a successful company. "That's how you pick your people, run your company, put out your product, and make friends out of customers." It was hardly surprising that in 1996 he credited his employees for building TCF into a world leader and instituted an Employee Stock Ownership Plan (ESOP) to reward them with a share in company ownership. TCF also cares for its community, making the United Way, scholarships, and other charity donations part of its corporate culture of sharing.

Building success upon success, annual net sales of Twin City Fan now exceed $100 million.

A LESSON LEARNED

Company president and chief operating officer Zika Srejovic relates an early experience that was a defining moment in TCF's history. One of his customers processed and bottled sauerkraut. Fans were necessary to vent the work areas, and they did do that. But shortly after the installation, the manager called to report "the sauerkraut fumes are eating my fan."

"It seems we didn't know how volatile the fumes were that would be processed through the plant's ventilation system," remembers Srejovic, "and the acid level was high enough to be corrosive."

Fumehood Exhaust Fans are specifically designed with a phenolic coating for fume treatment and exhaust applications in chemical labs, and for various processes involving corrosive solvents.

That was a valuable lesson. As a result, orders now are evaluated for the type of application and size of area to be exhausted, as well as the nature of the environment. If necessary, construction materials are amended. "We always ask what can, or ought, the fan do for the customer. Horsepower, speed, air volume, sound, and vibration are important considerations. Temperature and environment are, too," Srejovic says. "The better we know our customer, the better we can produce a fan that perfectly meets their needs."

Those needs are seemingly endless. Wherever there is material handling and conveying, manufacturing, livestock to raise, produce to grow or store, or common areas to provide with filtered air, Srejovic knows he has an opportunity.

TCF sells to two basic markets, the industrial market and the commercial plan and specification market, both of which are broad and whose end-users sometimes overlap. The industrial market includes manufacturers who use fans for agriculture, air cleaning, ventilation, cooling, heating, combustion air supply, filtration and drying systems, fume hoods, spray-paint booths, and exhaust systems. The commercial plan and specification market installs fans in commercial buildings, schools, hospitals, state and federal buildings, multiple dwellings, and industrial plants.

One high-profile customer of TCF ventilation equipment is the ship *Trump Casino,* built by Atlantic Marine, Inc., which installed forty-two Aerovent direct-driven vaneaxial fans. The fans were chosen for their reliability in marine-duty applications and because they perform quietly, a necessity when used in close proximity to sleeping quarters, restaurants, and other public areas.

Even skiers enjoy the benefits of TCF products, which are found in snowmaking machines.

The ship Trump Casino houses forty-two Aerovent vaneaxial fans, which provide the compact, quiet, marine-duty service needed in oceangoing vessels for air conditioning and other processes.

FOCUS ON PLANNING

It is not enough to build a fan that works. TCF also focuses on how it plans its products. Its goals include the following:

- ENGINEERING FLEXIBILITY—TCF gives individual attention to each customer by designing custom fans for specific applications when needed
- QUALITY—TCF Clarage company is ISO-9001-certified
- RELIABILITY—TCF products are tested by industry standards and warranted for reliability and performance
- SERVICE—TCF provides highly qualified sales representatives who give technical help from more than 100 offices across the United States and Canada. On-site field service also is available
- COMPETITIVE PRICING—TCF offers the best value and competitive prices among products of equal standards

OMNIPRESENT, YET INVISIBLE

A hospital, where a quiet, sterilized environment with precisely regulated temperature is critical, is an obvious example of a setting in which TCF's services are invaluable. So, too, are the computer and semiconductor industries in which fans must meet exacting requirements for particle filtration and vibration. Stairwell pressurization systems, where some fans serve an important fire-safety function, are yet another example of areas with special requirements.

Fans in automotive spray-painting areas need frequent cleaning, so TCF designed a swing-out version of one of its models for easy access to the fan impeller. Because saving energy is important in commercial buildings, TCF developed variable-volume fans so air volume and energy consumption adjustments can be made at times when needs are lower.

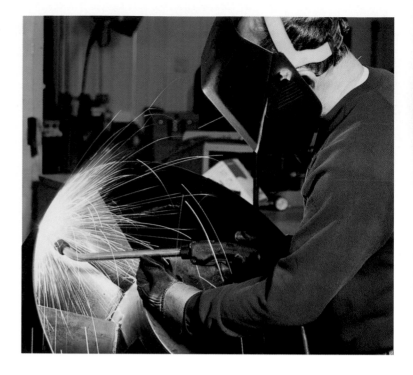

Gas Metal Arc Welding (GMAW) guns have cut costs, boosted productivity, and improved product quality.

Water treatment and pollution-control systems also require highly dependable fans capable of moving gases and particles, often at high temperatures and for extended periods. TCF is proud of its record in construction technology and knowledge of alloys that enables it to produce superior specialty fans.

Individual uses are too numerous to list, but the roster of areas where TCF fans are sold is an indicator of their scope: North and South America, Central America, the Caribbean, Europe, the Middle East, Asia, and the Pacific Rim. And who does the selling? Twin City Fan Companies, Ltd., operates seven separate international fan companies:

- **Twin City Fan & Blower**—centrifugal fans and blowers for air- or material-handling in industrial and commercial applications
- **Aerovent**—axial and centrifugal fans, roof ventilators, and air-makeup units since 1926
- **Clarage**—centrifugal fans, mechanical dust collectors, and repair and rebuild services; a standard in fan design and industrial applications since 1874, especially in petrochemical and power plants
- **Fiber-Aire**—fiberglass centrifugal roof and wall ventilators
- **TC Axial**—axial fans and roof ventilators

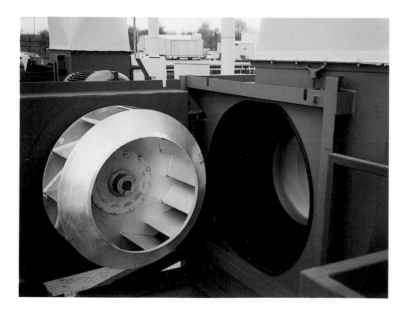

Twin City Fan & Blower swing-out fans are designed specifically for applications where frequent cleaning of the fan impeller is required, such as in automotive spray-paint booths.

- **TC Ventco**—centrifugal fans and power roof ventilators for commercial applications
- **Azen Manufacturing, Pte., Ltd.**—located in Singapore, manufactures marine-duty fans, as well as all types of centrifugal and axial fans

Twin City Fan is proud of its superior engineering expertise and continually improving manufacturing technology. Manufacturing is done at TCF's South Dakota plants in Aberdeen, Brookings, Elkton, and Mitchell; and in Birmingham, Alabama; Dayton, Ohio; and Singapore. The company has 600,000 square feet of manufacturing and warehouse space in addition to its 43,000-square-foot headquarters building in Minneapolis. Qualified service technicians can completely rebuild or repair any type or brand of fan as well as perform balancing or precise vibration analysis in-house or on site.

STRINGENT TECHNICAL QUALITY STANDARDS

Product quality assurance and research and development are done at the Air & Sound Test Laboratory at TCF's Minneapolis headquarters. The Air Movement and Control Association (AMCA) registered laboratory specializes in testing the performance of axial fans, propeller fans, and centrifugal fans and blowers. Situated next to undeveloped parkland, away from industrial noise sources, TCF engineers and technicians can accurately test even small fans in the laboratory. TCF's test laboratory includes the following:
- 73,000-cubic-foot, semi-reverberant room
- sound testing using 1/24 octave band analyzers
- three separate air-flow test chambers that meet AMCA standards
- air-flow capacities to 63,000 CFM
- air testing of axial fans up to 72-inches in diameter, and power to 50 BHP
- high-inertia mounting plate for precise vibration and modal analysis

Latest technologies such as Finite Element Analysis (FEA) are used by Twin City Fan design engineers to evaluate stresses and assure that fans will withstand high rotating speeds.

The laboratory can be compared to a music mixing and mastering studio, except as TCF analyzes product-sound power levels in eight octave bands, the intended result is a reduction of sound. Technicians electronically graph acoustical characteristics of fans using a substitution method of sound analysis through which products are measured against a known reference sound source. Any discrepancy is then reengineered.

Likewise, the air performance of fans is tested, as are power consumption, vibration characteristics, and strain limits that affect operating speeds. Finally, laboratory engineers study product endurance capabilities at different temperatures, wear patterns, and potential for metal fatigue in an effort to eliminate any problem before a product is shipped.

Because it is a leading manufacturer in the "air movement" industry, Twin City Fan welcomes its role as an educator in that industry. Company engineers serve on many AMCA committees to establish useful standards within the industry, especially in the areas of safety and energy conservation.

TCF offers customers and engineers their Fan Selector®, Microsoft® Windows®–based software program, which provides quick and accurate fan selections and information to help choose the most suitable fan. To obtain complete information about TCF's products, customers may visit the Twin City Fan Web site: www.twincityfan.com.

Engineers perform tests in Twin City Fan's test and research laboratory to evaluate performance of fans for air volume, pressure, power, and sound levels to assure the customer that the fans will perform as designed and tested.

TEMPCO MANUFACTURING COMPANY

WITH FIFTY YEARS

OF EXPERIENCE,

TEMPCO

MANUFACTURING

COMPANY PRODUCES

PRECISION STAMPINGS,

FABRICATIONS,

AND ASSEMBLIES

OF MATERIALS

FOR CLIENTS IN

JUST ABOUT EVERY

INDUSTRIAL SECTOR

Tempco Manufacturing Company produces an array of precision stampings, some of which are shown here.

For use in widely differing products—from sophisticated high-technology equipment to simple children's toys—Tempco Manufacturing Company provides low-cost, top-quality stampings, sheet-metal fabrication, and assemblies.

Tempco was founded in 1945 when Peter J. Cronen Sr. and his wife, Mildred (Billie), started a metal stamping company in their south Minneapolis garage. Sons Peter and Timothy were seven and five years old. Currently, Timothy is president of marketing and Peter is president of manufacturing. The third generation of stockholders are Daniel Cronen (vice president and chief financial officer), Kimberly Douville (human resources), Phillip Cronen (estimating and sales), and, at the Sarasota, Florida location, Paul Cronen, John Cronen, and Christie Pearl. Others employed are Parish Cronen and Peter J. Cronen IV.

The company has grown steadily as it has made tooling for more than 60,000 jobs. Tempco also has developed thousands of programs for sheet-metal fabrication on its CNC (computer numeric control) turret presses.

Tempco works closely with its customers to produce stamping dies to meet their needs, and offers customers

Mildred (Billie) V. Cronen (1917–) and Peter J. Cronen Sr. (1912–1977) are the founders of Tempco Manufacturing Company.

cost-saving production alternatives. The firm generates considerable savings in the manufacturing of parts for client orders by producing its own stamping dies and tools. The costs for Tempco's temporary or semipermanent tooling are 80 percent to 90 percent less than those for permanent dies, and the quality is equal or superior to the quality of conventional dies.

The diverse product categories of Tempco's customers include high technology, agribusiness, appliances, automotive, chemicals, computers, dairy equipment, defense, door and window hardware, electronics, food processing, laboratory equipment, laundry equipment, material handling, office equipment, photography, toys, trucks, valve components, vending, and more.

To meet the demands of these industries, Tempco's production stampings include blanking, piercing, forming, and drawing in most materials. It works in aluminum, brass, beryllium copper, phosphor bronze, Monel metal, steel, stainless steel, plastics, fibers, phenolics, nickel, silver, and space-age alloys. These stampings can be produced on more than 175 presses with capacities up to 460 tons. Tempco produces millions of pieces from its dies in materials as thin as 0.002 inch, while maintaining tolerances that often exceed industry standards.

The company has the ability to form, draw, and assemble the large sheet-metal fabrications that its four CNC turret presses produce. There is a large welding department assisted by robotic welding capabilities for all customers' assembly and fabricating needs. The cosmetic needs of each job are handled by finishing techniques performed by skilled personnel with four straight-line sanding machines.

Tempco's dedicated workforce is committed to quality. Each worker is trained to identify, analyze, and solve some of the problems in their work; to present solutions to management; and, whenever possible, to implement solutions themselves.

"Quality is our first priority. By using the latest inspection equipment, we are able to assure that parts are made precisely to every customer's specifications," says Tempco marketing president Timothy Cronen. "Tempco has been handling quality needs for fifty years."

The combination of Tempco's extensive facilities and its experienced personnel equips it to meet customer requirements. Its facilities include more than 100,000 square feet of production area. Tempco constantly upgrades equipment to meet the demands of modern industry. Employees are continually trained in the latest stamping technologies.

All of Tempco's tooling is produced in-house. It excels at cost-effective design conversions from castings, forgings, two-piece assemblies, and screw machine parts. Customers are helped in determining the most efficient, cost-effective approach to tooling. Tempco maintains and replaces nonpermanent dies without charge to customers. In addition, it updates these dies to eliminate obsolescence. Tooling storage is free.

Tempco provides large and small original equipment manufacturers (OEM) with a wide variety of low-cost stampings and top-notch engineering know-how.

The firm's precision secondary operations include anodizing, broaching, countersinking, counterboring, embossing, drilling,

The principals of Tempco Manufacturing Company are (from left): Peter Cronen Jr., president of manufacturing; Timothy A. Cronen, president of marketing; and Daniel W. Cronen, vice president and chief financial officer.

grinding, hand-deburring, heat-treating, milling, painting, plating, rounding of edges, reaming, riveting, stencilling, spot welding, shaving, tapping, tumbling and finishing of all kinds, wire-feed welding, spray welding, PEM® nut insertion, and assembly.

Tempco understands the importance of on-time delivery for its customers. It makes every effort to be faster than any other stamping source without sacrificing quality. To satisfy short-term demand, customers can receive partial shipments.

There are knowledgeable Tempco representatives throughout the country. In-house account executives handle customers' day-to-day needs. The company assigns each customer its own account executive who will assist them in all their requirements.

"We believe our emphasis on personalized service and our understanding of customers' needs makes Tempco Manufacturing unique in our field," Peter Cronen says.

Shown here with examples of customer AIR-serv, Inc., end products are (from left): Ted Klimek and Mark Bradshaw, Tempco engineers; Gary Nelson, AIR-serv purchasing manager; Bruce Childs, AIR-serv operations director; C. Mike Olson, Tempco superintendent; and David Bobert, AIR-serv owner.

ST. PAUL METALCRAFT, INC.

KNOWN FOR ITS

HIGH-QUALITY, COST-

EFFECTIVE CASTINGS

AND EXCELLENT

SERVICE, ST. PAUL

METALCRAFT OFFERS

A RANGE OF CAPABILI-

TIES IN CUSTOM,

PRECISION-TOLERANCE

THIN-WALL-ZINC

AND ALUMINUM-DIE

CASTINGS

Many of its customers regard St. Paul Metalcraft, Inc., as a leader in die casting. Those customers, however, represent such a broad array of industries that the company's founder is one of only a few who can name them all.

Computer components, communications, aerospace, and hardware door products all are familiar to John T. Walker, who founded the company in 1960. But then, so are pumps, electric motors, and military ordnance products.

Walker started his career as a tool and die maker and is recognized for both his die casting expertise and his ability to meld a superior team of executives and craftsmen. Not surprisingly, he also is recognized for his infallible instinct for discovering niche opportunities in diverse industries.

Since 1964 St. Paul Metalcraft has enjoyed the convenience of its location in Arden Hills, a northern Twin Cities suburb. It occupies 86,000 square feet of space, making it large enough to handle demanding die casting projects. St. Paul Metalcraft strives to provide personalized service to all clients, demonstrating a loyalty to customers that begins with its employees. Of its 150 employees, 41 have been with the company for more than twenty years.

Just as its diverse product involvement has been part of St. Paul Metalcraft's strategic plan, so too has been its international base of customers. Besides shipping to

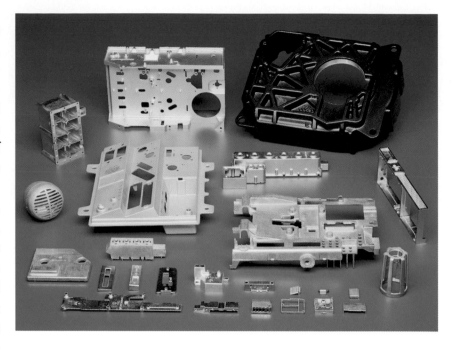

St. Paul Metalcraft, Inc., provides only the highest quality castings for its customers.

thirty-five states, the company also has customers in Canada, England, Germany, Israel, and Malaysia that are among those who are committed to St. Paul Metalcraft not only for its high-quality, cost-effective castings and excellent service, but also for its range of capabilities in custom, precision-tolerance, thin-wall-zinc and aluminum-die castings.

The die casting services include computer-aided design and manufacturing, construction and maintenance of dies, full-service machining, tumbling, and vibratory finishing. A quality-assurance program monitors each and every step in the process.

Sixteen die cast machines can handle aluminum from 280 to 800 tons and zinc from 20 to 500 tons. From less than an ounce, the aluminum castings can range up to eight pounds, and zinc castings to six and one-half pounds. St. Paul Metalcraft currently produces more than 200,000 castings weekly.

Early supplier involvement and production of intricate designs is not the end of commitment for the company's skilled engineers, who maintain a close relationship with clients' projects throughout the entire process. They work with tooling craftsmen to ensure that customer specifications and

John T. Walker, who is known for his die-casting expertise, founded St. Paul Metalcraft, Inc., in 1960.

any changes are successfully met. No aspect of workmanship is overlooked. St. Paul Metalcraft is in compliance with ISO-9002 standards. The commitment to quality assurance begins with an employee-wide attitude of success and extends from vendor selection through product delivery.

Early in his career, Walker developed a process that could provide enormous savings to customers. When St. Paul Metalcraft was a reality, he began making unit dies to give his customers the benefit of quick tooling changes, short runs, a fast response, and savings on tooling costs. With what it calls a "master unit die chase," St. Paul Metalcraft can run eight different customers' multicavity molds at the same time in a single casting shot. This technique is equally effective with zinc as aluminum. Setup time alone can be reduced by up to 80 percent using this process.

Customers appreciate the concept; more than 75 percent have benefited from the use of unit dies, which save time and money from design through production. This innovative spirit exemplified by Walker, and continually promoted by him, has enhanced his company's image among customers as a leader in die-casting technology.

Walker and his employees are constantly alert to environmental requirements of good corporate citizenship. St. Paul Metalcraft was among the earliest of area companies to totally redesign its water purification system. It now processes system water to a cleaner level than what it takes in. Thanks to strict compliance with environmental and safety regulations, the company has achieved substantial cost savings while increasing its operating efficiencies and improving the quality of products and services.

This six-station, multicavity unit die-master chase offers St. Paul Metalcraft's customers the benefit of lower tooling costs and short-run capabilities.

Clients in the field of sportscraft constituted 30 percent of St. Paul Metalcraft's business in 1997. Communications and office equipment each accounted for about 12 percent, followed by hydraulics, instrumentation, and other sectors. Aftermarket parts and accessories, ordnance, and industrial and computer components, along with home and building hardware, also made up significant areas of its business.

Industry watchers recognize that St. Paul Metalcraft's aims are firmly set on future manufacturing needs. The company has planned important organizational changes to assure continued growth and increased productivity. Walker recently sold the company to "The Leggett and Platt Aluminum Group." With the drive to remain technologically current and a goal of total customer satisfaction, St. Paul Metalcraft will continue to push the industry standard in die casting. Its mission statement says it all: "St. Paul Metalcraft, Inc., is dedicated to providing *real solutions* for our customers."

ST. PAUL METALCRAFT, INC.
QUALITY POLICY

A UDITING OUR QUALITY AND PRODUCTION SYSTEMS.

C ONTINUOUSLY IMPROVE OUR PROCESSES.

T RAINING OF EMPLOYEES TO BE FORMAL AND DOCUMENTED.

I SO 9002-1994 AS BASIS FOR OUR DOCUMENTED QUALITY SYSTEM.

O N-TIME DELIVERY TO OUR CUSTOMERS.

N EED TO ENABLE ALL EMPLOYEES TO BE RESPONSIBLE FOR THE QUALITY OF THEIR WORK.

UFE INCORPORATED

For industrial customers who require precise and reliable products, UFE Incorporated provides complete custom engineering and manufacturing services, from design through production

UFE Incorporated's corporate headquarters is located in Stillwater, Minnesota.

Our mission at UFE is to deliver custom engineering and manufacturing services utilizing advanced technologies to our customers worldwide," says Orville D. Johnson, UFE chairman. "Through continuing innovation we have established UFE as an industry leader that meets the high standards of our customers."

UFE Incorporated, located in Stillwater, Minnesota, provides product engineering, mold manufacturing, injection molding and contract assembly services to precision-oriented customers around the world. UFE began operation in 1953 with three employees in 2,000 square feet of the old Stillwater train depot. As one of the first producers in the world of precision plastic gears,

For this Hewlett-Packard inkjet printer media chassis, UFE Incorporated provided design assistance, plastic part production, and final assembly.

UFE's early customers included Eastman Kodak, Bell & Howell, and 3M.

Through the years UFE's highly skilled and trained workforce has been the foundation for the company's continued growth and its enduring reputation as a customer-focused innovator. Today UFE's more than 750 employees work at its facilities in Minnesota, Wisconsin, Texas, Singapore, and Mexico.

To achieve continued growth in an increasingly competitive environment requires a unifying force for clear strategic direction. UFE's Concepts for Guidance provides this unifying force. Prominently displayed throughout the organization, this statement of basic concepts creates quality through method as UFE pursues its mission and expands its vision to reach its goal of industry leadership and rewarding employment opportunities for its workforce. UFE's unified methodologies, developed over forty-five years of experience, become the company's core strength for managing and delivering large, complex programs for customers such as 3M,

Becton Dickinson, Delphi, Hewlett Packard, IBM, S. C. Johnson, and Thomson Consumer Electronics.

Providing top-notch, quality service to these and all other customers is paramount to UFE's strategic business units—Product Engineering, Mold Manufacturing, Injection Molding, and Contract Manufacturing.

UFE Product Engineering provides complete mechanical and electromechanical product design services with a focus on manufacturability and reliability. With extensive experience in designing products in ways that enable concurrent manufacturing, UFE's Product Engineering business assists customers in improving cost and time to market.

UFE Mold Manufacturing is a technology leader in engineering, manufacturing, and developing precision injection molds. This business unit was a pioneer in the application of computer-aided mold design linked to machining processes. UFE Mold Manufacturing's strength, enhanced by a total company experience in molding processes and materials, provides unique technical capabilities to support its customers.

UFE Injection Molding employs an extensive depth and breadth of experience in worldwide production of precision thermoplastic components for OEMs in a variety of demanding industries. This UFE business unit works with all engineering grade resins and specializes in fine tolerance components, custom precision gears, and complex insert molded components.

UFE Contract Manufacturing is a total responsibility resource for customers requiring subsystem or complete product assemblies. It responds and adapts to its customer's needs by providing component sourcing, logistics management, production process development, and ongoing production.

Top: Example of precision gear transmission produced by UFE Incorporated.

Above: "Hands-on" product design provides capable results.

While each UFE business unit provides a unique service, customers often combine services to obtain a seamless progression from product concept to final assembly. Selecting any or all of the services offered by UFE adds a dimension of versatility to a customer's capabilities. Using UFE to augment their engineering and manufacturing capacity allows the customer to focus on their own core competencies and on meeting the needs of their marketplace.

To further support their customer's capabilities and growth, UFE has long been committed to maintaining the highest possible quality standards. Evidence of this commitment can be found in UFE's numerous quality certifications and accreditations including ISO-9001, ISO-9002, QS-9000, Ford-Q1, FDA/GMP, CE, and the GM Mark of Excellence.

The future of UFE will be driven by the foundations of excellence established at the company's very beginning. UFE's central values are, and will continue to be, the key element of its Concepts for Guidance. UFE's commitment to quality, continuous improvement, economy, and productivity provides the customer a solid economic value. UFE understands that its keystone value of customer satisfaction ultimately depends upon achieving relationships where all parties benefit. And all of UFE's vital stakeholders—customers, suppliers, employees, and investors—enjoy a relationship supported by values of fairness, fulfillment, teamwork, and citizenship.

Regarding UFE Incorporated's plans for the future, Martin N. Kellogg, president, states: "Our final value is one of durability in all that we do. UFE's stakeholders desire to be united for excellence over the long term. Thus we invest today in each other for a mutually rewarding future."

SMEAD MANUFACTURING COMPANY

A LEADER IN RECORDS

MANAGEMENT, SMEAD

MANUFACTURING

COMPANY HAS COME A

LONG WAY SINCE ITS

1906 FOUNDING—YET

ITS GUIDING

PRINCIPLES ARE STILL

TO SERVE CUSTOMERS'

NEEDS WITH THE

HIGHEST QUALITY

PRODUCTS AND TO SET

THE STANDARDS FOR

THE INDUSTRY

Charles Smead and his staff of production and office personnel began the company in a small room in Hastings, Minnesota, in 1906.

Ever since Charles Smead invented the bandless filing envelope in 1906, the Smead Manufacturing Company has been dedicated to helping its customers meet the demands of an ever-changing world of information. As a provider of total filing solutions, Smead is committed to its leadership role in the records management industry.

Charles Smead began with a single product, the bandless file. As a replacement for files secured with the quickly deteriorating rubber bands common at the time, metal clips were attached to the innovative "bandless" file, providing a welcome improvement. Smead continues to manufacture the bandless file, along with thousands of modern filing products that are designed to make records management more efficient and economical. Innovative new concepts and products continue to help simplify and expedite the management of ever-increasing quantities of records.

Charles Smead began the company with a staff of six in a small room above the local newspaper office in Hastings,

Ebba Hoffman and her daughter, Sharon Avent, share the philosophy that quality products and loyalty to customers and employees are what make Smead the leader in the filing-products industry.

Minnesota. Shortly after founding the business, however, he died. In 1916 an employee of Smead named P. A. Hoffman purchased the company, and he and his son Harold successfully led its growth. Hoffman began a tradition of leadership that has continued for three generations and is currently as strong as ever.

Today Smead Manufacturing Company is 100 percent women-owned. Ebba C. Hoffman, who has served as president and chair of the board since the death of her husband, in 1955, is joined in ownership and daily management of the company by her daughter, Sharon Lee Hoffman Avent, senior executive vice president.

More than 2,300 people now operate Smead production facilities and distribution centers, which are located in Georgia, Minnesota, Ohio, Texas, Utah, and Wisconsin.

The company's loyalty to its employees is reciprocated by the very personal way in which they dedicate themselves to Smead Manufacturing Company customers.

"Smead customers rely on the stability, consistency, and personal service that naturally accompany our staff members' long-term commitment," says Hoffman.

Smead's innovation in the filing-products industry started when Charles Smead introduced the bandless file, shown at right.

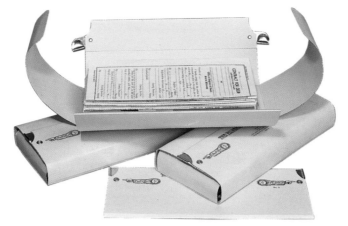

Smead's innovation in the filing-products industry started when Charles Smead introduced the bandless file, shown at right.

Although there have been many changes since 1906, the company still adheres to the principle of providing only the highest quality products that best serve its customers' needs. Smead continually researches, develops, and manufactures new products to meet the changing needs of large, small, and home-based businesses. As techniques for organizing and storing information evolve, end users keep Smead informed of products that help them do their jobs more efficiently.

Dedication to advancement in records management is a hallmark of the Smead Manufacturing Company. From the introduction of color-coded indexing and efficient shelf-filing techniques to the company's comprehensive line of new software systems using electronic tracking, imaging, and bar code technologies, Smead continues to set the standards for state-of-the-art records management.

Among the company's most innovative products is Smeadlink™, an integrated document management software application for imaging, Computer Output to Laser Disk (COLD), PC documents, faxes, and hard copy (both paper and microfilm). Smeadlink customers can select from various modules to meet their current needs.

Regardless of the storage medium, Smeadlink customers index, manage, work from, and maintain documents in a single software application. This integrated approach provides an unprecedented combination of document management solutions. The modules are fully integrated with each other and also with applications currently in development or projected for the future. This consistency prepares customers for easy transition to the next generation of document management solutions.

Smeadlink was uniquely designed to provide a comprehensive solution for managing electronic and paper documents. This design has the benefit of allowing new technologies to be added seamlessly to the system. Users are never aware of the technology involved; they simply search and retrieve the document. The scalable, modular design allows users to select and size modules according to their individual business needs.

Smead president Hoffman is known for her hard work, common sense, and staunch loyalty to employees, dealers, and the community. The company's success is grounded in her management expertise, her understanding of the importance of manufacturing quality products, and her relationship with the dealers who handle the company's products. As a working single mother who has always maintained a positive attitude, Ebba Hoffman is a role model for aspiring businesswomen.

Hoffman still works every day. Just as she has for forty years, she reviews the mail and keeps current with all aspects of the company. Rather than resting on her laurels, she is—characteristically—guiding Smead Manufacturing Company into the future as the company develops new paper and electronic filing products.

According to Hoffman's daughter Sharon, who works at her mother's side, "My mother is my best friend. She's very concerned about her employees and their welfare, and how, as a company, we're perceived in the industry. We've always had a quality product. These are her main goals and the ongoing goals of our company."

Smeadlink is an integrated document management software product that allows users to select from modules to meet their current needs, while simultaneously preparing users for the next generation of document management solutions.

MID-CONTINENT ENGINEERING

Mid-Continent Engineering (MCE), a Minneapolis-based turnkey manufacturing organization, is dedicated to providing a full range of services: precision machining, cell manufacturing, sheet-metal fabrication, welding, industrial painting, and assembly. MCE serves a focused group of industries: commercial aircraft, defense, and high-tech medical diagnostic equipment.

Entrepreneurship has been a guiding theme since MCE's modest beginning, in 1949, when Arthur J. Popehn started the company in his basement. Initially it was a small-scale stamping and tooling business. The company's earliest customers included Univac, Honeywell, and Control Data.

Since then, MCE has grown steadily. It employs 150 workers and occupies a 138,000-square-foot facility. Popehn's small business has developed into an operation of multiple capabilities, such as three-, four-, and five-axis CNC (computer numeric control) milling, sheet-metal fabrication, welding

MCE is a major supplier to the commercial aircraft industry, serving companies such as Boeing and Northrop.

and spot welding, complex assembly, plating, and painting.

Popehn, a manufacturing innovator, developed operational capabilities to better serve his customers. He shifted the company's focus to the defense industry in the 1970s, contributing to such well-known projects as the Phoenix Missile antenna arrays with Hughes Aircraft, onboard-ship applications through Univac and General Electric Aerospace, and rugged cabinetry for the Aegis surface ships and Trident submarine programs. In 1974 Popehn decided to concentrate his efforts on Hiawatha Rubber, his offshoot rubber-molding company. In 1977 MCE was sold to another entrepreneur, Charles Marvin.

Marvin further broadened MCE's manufacturing capability, and increased the company's emphasis on high quality, overall marketing, and customer service. He diversified the business from its 95 percent concentration in the defense industry to a focus divided among three major sectors: 45 percent commercial aircraft, 40 percent defense, and 15 percent high-tech medical. All three of these industry disciplines require the highest levels of quality and service. Today MCE customers include Boeing, Northrop, and Lockheed Martin, as well as GE Medical Systems and 3M Medical Systems.

Under Marvin's leadership and his broadening of employee training and participation, MCE

MCE supplies critical components and assemblies for the Aegis program. In 1996 MCE received the Lockheed Martin/Navy Aegis Award for Excellence.

implemented the principles of W. Edwards Deming, including Statistical Process Control (SPC), and Total Quality Management. In 1998 the company introduced a Lean Manufacturing Program to achieve further cost control and continued operational improvements. In addition, MCE is implementing the ISO-9002 quality standard and internationally accepted registration process.

MCE's corporate mission statement is a living statement supported by employees and always evolving. Currently it reads, "To improve continually our people's skills in the manufacture of high-quality, custom-built parts and complex assemblies—mechanical and electromechanical; and in providing associated services on schedule and at market and cost-driven prices, to meet our customers' expectation."

MCE adds value for its customers with its core competencies and by manufacturing precisely to specification. Its broad range of internal capabilities is further enhanced by special operations, such as heat treating, five-axis profiling, spot welding, and hot/cold joggling. MCE specializes in complex assemblies and the management of major programs. Its twenty-three machining centers can handle parts up to fifty feet in length.

MCE has a long history of working with its customers on design-assist programs and improving the ease of manufacturing their products. Offerings include full CAD/CAM manufacturing capabilities and experience-based design for manufacturing. MCE has built its business through the outstanding service it provides, the integrity of its staff, and by offering customers the best overall solutions and capabilities.

Reflecting its commitment to quality in meeting its customers' requirements, MCE has received many quality awards including "Advanced Technological Assembly" approval from Boeing and "Accurate Fuselage Assembly" approval from Northrop Aircraft. In 1996 MCE was awarded the Lockheed Martin/Navy Aegis Award for Excellence.

"Modern equipment and added capabilities have enabled seven-times growth in sales

Shown (from left) are Charles Marvin (owner), Sanders Marvin (board member), Pete Sievert (lead man), Art Popehn (founder), and Charles Marvin Jr. (board member), as they discuss a job for VMC 200B Machining Center.

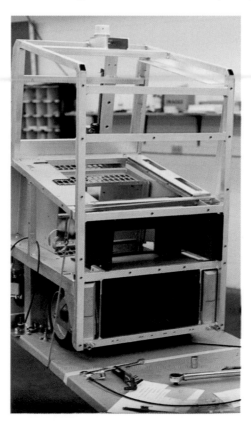

since 1977," says CEO Marvin. "With the range of capabilities we offer, we can provide complex, critical levels of assembly, rather than just piece parts. This means customers can greatly reduce their investment in activities they consider non-core competencies. MCE's resources are wide-ranging, prime-quality, cost-effective solutions for our customers' mechanical, component, and assembly requirements."

"Mid-Continent always has offered high levels of technical support to our customers," he says. "We like to be involved with product design early in the process so any unnecessary cost can be designed out of components and assemblies. This lets our customer be more competitive, and at the same time, it strengthens our customer relationship. Our attention to continual improvement is what makes MCE special and has helped our growth."

A mobile, ultrasound cart assembly is an example of the high-level assemblies manufactured for MCE's medical-customer base.

LIBERTY DIVERSIFIED INDUSTRIES

The roots of Liberty Diversified Industries reach all the way back to 1918, when a Russian immigrant named Jack Fiterman began supporting his family by collecting, refurbishing, and reselling old wooden crates and burlap bags. His small business, which he named Liberty Carton Company, grew over time and ultimately became a leader in corrugated packaging.

Today Liberty Carton is just one of several companies that form the privately held and still-growing Liberty Diversified Industries (LDI). Michael Fiterman, president and chief executive officer of LDI and a grandson of the founder, and chairman of the board, Ben Fiterman, the son of Jack Fiterman, have been instrumental in building LDI into an organization that has grown far beyond its founder's dreams.

With its headquarters in New Hope, Minnesota, LDI has operating divisions across the state in Becker, Bloomington, Golden Valley, and

LDI's Valley Craft division manufactures high-quality material-handling equipment and office storage systems, which are marketed by Safco Products.

Liberty Paper manufactures and markets recycled linerboard and specialty packaging papers, keeping more than 150,000 tons of old corrugated containers out of landfills each year.

Lake City, as well as in Lenexa, Kansas; Baldwyn, Mississippi; and Fort Worth, Texas.

Liberty Carton has divisions that serve important niche markets. One division sells shipping containers for bulk freight; protective packaging for electronic equipment; and circuit-handling equipment. Another division has carved a niche in the fast-growing decorative-packaging market, serving customers involved in retail and direct-mail marketing. It is nationally recognized for its corrugated protective packaging and displays. Its Northern Package division, in Bloomington, Minnesota, also is a manufacturer of corrugated packaging and is known for its high-quality four-color package printing.

Another LDI company, Safco Products, was formed in the 1960s in response to customer demand for corrugated office products. Today Safco is a leading marketer of storage and organizing products and furniture for offices, art and engineering firms, and industrial and recycling businesses.

Valley Craft, acquired by LDI in 1979, specializes in high-quality metal fabrication. Product lines include carts, hand trucks, and hydraulic lifting equipment for materials handling.

LDI's Diversi-Plast Products is the world's largest manufacturer of corrugated plastic, a unique fluted-core sheeting. With plants in New Hope, Minnesota, and Baldwyn, Mississippi, Diversi-Plast's products support the packaging, building materials, and materials-handling industries.

With Liberty Paper (LPI), LDI comes full circle in the box-recycling business. This high-technology mill recycles used corrugated containers into Kraft linerboard for new containers and specialty papers for the packaging industry. It also manufactures its own unique linerboard in Dream Catcher™ colors.

LDI Fibres procures the raw materials LPI uses to manufacture paper. It works closely with brokers and mass merchants, buying and selling fibers and ensuring a consistent source of supply for the Liberty Paper mill.

Diversi-Plast, an LDI subsidiary, is the world's largest manufacturer of corrugated plastic.

As the umbrella organization for all LDI companies, Liberty Diversified provides marketing, legal, human resources, accounting, management information systems support, and transportation services to its manufacturing and marketing subsidiaries.

LDI employees pride themselves on their ability to listen to customers and respond creatively to their needs with new products and solutions. This attitude is reflected in some of the unique products developed by employees, including such diverse inventions as a corrugated-plastic roof-vent system; moisture-barrier paper; a hydraulic attachment for lifting fifty-five-gallon drums with a forklift; an adjustable wire tote for printed circuit boards; a tray-forming machine for making corrugated-plastic trays; a hand truck specially designed to move file cabinets; and a modular system of receptacles for collecting and segregating recyclable materials.

Looking ahead, Liberty Diversified Industries is committed to expanding to meet customer expectations and provide a secure, progressive organization where employees can find opportunities to grow. Says president Mike Fiterman, "We are proud of our Minnesota roots and look for continued expansion in the state."

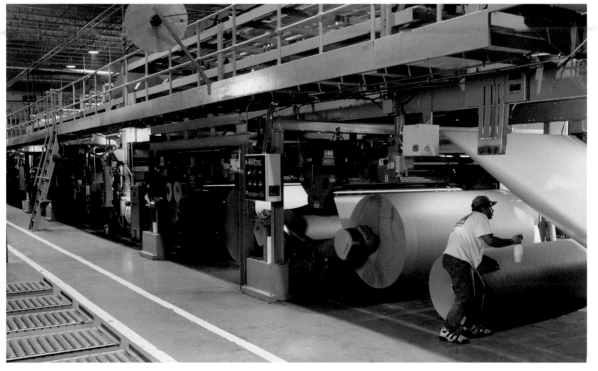

Liberty Carton Company is one of the Midwest's largest independent manufacturers of corrugated packaging material.

DAYTON ROGERS MANUFACTURING

Founded in 1929, Dayton Rogers Manufacturing is an industry leader in the production of value-added, precision metal formed parts and assemblies. The company pioneered the concept of short-run tooling.

Dayton Rogers is distinguished by its superior service and the unique, high-quality products it manufactures. The company's staff assists customers through innovative engineering services that include conceptual design assistance, prototype development, and after-sale technical services.

"Our philosophy of business is focused on forging long-term customer relationships," says company president John Seeger Jr. "We use 'value engineering' to become a strategic ally with our customers, working

Dayton Rogers Manufacturing produces an array of parts, some of which are shown here, with its precision metal forming process.

closely with them and their particular marketplace. We use communications tools such as the Internet and videotape to educate our customers and help them to make the best possible use of our products and services. The more open the relationship between customer and supplier," Seeger observes, "the more rewarding the entire process becomes."

With nearly seventy years in the development and fabrication of precision metal forming, the engineers at Dayton Rogers draw on a wealth of experience to help customers achieve their requirements. Superior stampings result from the combined efforts of a skilled design team comprising both Dayton Rogers's staff members and customer staff members. The earlier that this synergism occurs, the better—preferably in the design stage.

This circa-1900 oak ice box was made by the Seeger Refrigerator Company, a firm run by John Seeger Jr.'s grandfather and father that inspired Seeger's own entrepreneurial spirit.

With headquarters in Minneapolis, Dayton Rogers has facilities in New York, Ohio, Florida, Texas, and California. Its six plants together offer more than 260,000 square feet of manufacturing space for prototype development and production facilities.

Each full-service plant is able to blank, pierce, form, and draw in all types of cold-rolled steel; stainless steel; aluminum; brass; nickel; nickel alloys; and other materials that are cold-workable. All secondary procedures can be added, including heat-treating, finishing, plating, painting, silk-screening, or any other processes required. Material thickness can range from 0.005 inches to 0.500 inches. The company serves diverse industries: medical equipment, electronics manufacturing, telecommunications, and office equipment.

The proximity of Dayton Rogers's plants to major markets expedites quotations, services, and finished parts. Most customers' stampings are no more than an overnight run by common carrier from Dayton Rogers's strategic plant locations.

Company president John Seeger Jr. was influenced by watching the way his grandfather and father ran their businesses. He admired his family's entrepreneurial spirit, and continues building the company his father purchased from the D. A. Rogers family in 1961. However, he is adding one further step—that of focusing his efforts on encouraging employee involvement in shaping the business.

"Once we concentrated our efforts on employee involvement to improve the manufacturing processes, we were able to meet increasing customer needs and grow as a business," Seeger says. "We're still of the opinion that people buy from people—and the better people are treated, the better they will treat customers. We treat our employees well, and they treat our customers well."

The precision metal formed parts produced by Dayton Rogers are a marriage of form and function designed to perform a specific job at minimal cost. Appearance of the finished product is a major emphasis. Precision metal formed products are designed to last the life of the unit to which they are assembled. By using Dayton Rogers design assistance, precision metal formed parts can replace costly cast or machined items. Seeger says, "Just knowing the best way to approach a problem can save valuable lead time and result in better parts at lower cost."

The Dial Toaster, patented in 1925 by Mr. Dayton A. Rogers, provided the spark that gave birth to a new company and process within the metal stamping industry: short-run tooling.

Just as Dayton Rogers pioneered the concept and development of short-run tooling, the company has remained on the leading edge of production technology, utilizing CAD-CAM, Statistical Process Control (SPC), and other computer-aided manufacturing operations. But along with these new technologies, the company maintains an extensive inventory of standard tooling and fixtures that can be used to achieve manufacturing economies.

Quality control is an integral part of Dayton Rogers's manufacturing credo. To ensure uniform quality throughout a run, first-article and random inspections are conducted according to a customer's specifications, using state-of-the-art coordinate measuring equipment. Dayton Rogers's quality assurance department works in coordination with sales, engineering, and purchasing to ensure that materials and specifications precisely follow a customer's order.

"Monitoring as we do allows us to deliver to customers the most dimensionally perfect stampings in the industry," says Seeger. "It is one of many steps that we take to ensure the customer's complete satisfaction."

Laser-cutting equipment speeds the production of precision metal formed parts.

UMC, INC.

UMC, Inc., is

an organization

of people dedicated

to providing

quality services

associated with

the production

of precision-

machined parts

and assemblies

When Terry Tomann used the word "ultra" to describe his new company, he meant it as a personal challenge. He wanted his firm to represent high quality—to exceed usual manufacturing standards. Thus was born the Ultra Machining Company (UMC).

UMC's origins were not fancy. Tomann simply set up two milling machines in his garage. Then he went to work. The result of his skills and perseverance was more work, due to word-of-mouth recommendations and repeat business, and in 1972 Tomann moved to a spacious plant near Minneapolis.

Today UMC is trusted by its customers, who include aviation and medical products companies, and general industry. Tomann's insistence on state-of-the-art CNC (computer numeric control) equipment ensures the best technology required for the customer. That attention to detail is partly responsible for UMC's ISO-9002 certification.

The types of industries UMC serves are among the most exacting

anywhere. UMC engineers work side-by-side with customers through a project. With a computerized quoting system, MSE™ (Machine Shop Estimation) and networked computers, up-to-date information is accessed through UMC's job-tracking system, Vantage™. These are some of the tools set up to help ensure the continuing high degree of accuracy and efficiency UMC's customers have come to expect.

UMC has successfully anticipated market changes. By the time defense industry growth slowed in the 1980s, UMC already had realigned the precision skills it developed for that industry, turning them to the medical products sector. A majority of UMC's work now is in making surgical tools, piece parts and assemblies.

UMC's eagerness to fulfill its customers' expectations led to the creation of an area dedicated to their unique manufacturing needs. But it is UMC's expertise with such difficult-to-machine materials as stainless steel, titanium, hastelloy and inconel that is the mainstay of its reputation.

Among the features UMC offers are:

- Nine CNC turning centers with bar feed and live tooling capability;
- Twelve CNC milling centers, fourth-axis capabilities and pallet changers;
- Machined components and assemblies;
- CAD/CAM, SPC capabilities;
- Computerized inspection equipment; DCC; Zeiss Eclipse CMM; calibration systems; estimating; Vantage job-tracking; and
- Citizen M20-7-axis-capable CNC Swiss turning; Charmilles Technologies Robofil 310-wire EDM; auto thread allows the machine to run unattended.

UMC continues to strive to meet the original challenge of providing "ultra" high-quality parts and assemblies for its customers.

WE•NO•NAH CANOE, INC.

MIKE CICHANOWSKI

BEGAN BUILDING

CANOES AS A

BOY IN HIS

PARENTS' GARAGE.

FORTY YEARS LATER,

HIS COMPANY'S

WATERCRAFT EXCEL

IN LIGHTNESS,

PERFORMANCE,

AND DURABILITY

To characterize We•no•nah Canoe is difficult because it presents many seeming contradictions. It is an established manufacturer whose products are sold internationally, yet it is a family business with just fifty employees in a small Minnesota town. We•no•nah's canoes and kayaks embody traditions of the earliest American explorers, yet they present technology rivaling the aerospace industry.

The company's founder, Mike Cichanowski, is another contrast: he looks like a woodsman but is an acclaimed composite-materials engineer.

Mike began canoeing as a Boy Scout on the Mississippi River at Winona. Paddling those vast expanses daily made him want a better canoe than the bulky, aluminum or wood-canvas ones that were standard fare. Since he couldn't afford to buy a superior canoe, he laboriously built one from edge-glued cedar strips following a published design.

His canoe performed well, but Mike sought further gains. So he revised the design and built another, then repeated that process many times. Each canoe performed differently, and slowly Mike acquired the skills of canoe designing and testing. He also learned to work with composite materials—fiberglass, at first, because it could produce fine canoes faster than cedar-strip construction.

While in college in 1968, Mike formed a very small company to build canoes. It has now grown to include many of the country's most talented hull designers and builders, plus several nationally ranked paddlers,

A canoe trip on Minnesota's famed Boundary Waters Canoe Area Wilderness typically involves paddling long distances with a heavy load, interspersed with portaging the canoe frequently. Several We•no•nah models are well suited to such trips, and two (including the Minnesota II, above) are designed specifically for this use.

including Mike. This group has reshaped the frontiers of canoe performance, creating a huge selection of exceptional canoes in the process.

Today We•no•nah builds light, yet durable hulls using Kevlar,® Tuf-weave® (a company invention), or Royalex®. The innovative use of these materials has prompted several awards, including Canoe Manufacturer of the Year (twice) and the "ACE" award for excellence in composites fabrication. A central theme of the company's philosophy is that a canoe's design should suit its owner's needs ideally. To accomplish this, We•no•nah offers more than twenty-five canoe models, plus sixteen for kayaks. The designs reflect great diversity of size and purpose, some being highly versatile, others very specialized.

To suit the typical trip in Minnesota's Boundary Waters, for example, We•no•nah has designed several canoes to carry heavy loads over long distances easily—and to weigh as little as thirty-nine pounds!

These watercraft, like all We•no•nah's products, spring from Mike's lifelong devotion to paddling. Many talented people now contribute to the creation of a new model, but only one decides when it merits release the same person who, as a Boy Scout forty years ago, refused to accept an ordinary canoe.

Mike Cichanowski is the founder and owner of We•no•nah Canoe, Inc. His company produces about 6,000 canoes a year using high-tech composite materials. The canoes are sold throughout the United States and in Canada, Europe, and Japan. We•no•nah also builds and sells kayaks in the United States under license from Current Designs, a Canadian company.

WARNER MANUFACTURING COMPANY

Warner Manufacturing Company has been bringing creativity and quality to the hand tool marketplace for more than seventy years. From founder Harry Warner's first wallpaper steamers to the company's newest tools, Warner consistently delivers superior quality, innovative design, and outstanding value.

Warner uses only the best materials in the production of its hand tools. Value is built into every Warner tool through new and efficient manufacturing practices that keep the quality high while reducing cost.

"There is a resurgence in the area of home improvement. Today's building materials are produced to make construction and decorating easier for do-it-yourselfers. On the other hand, we also see an upturn in professional contractors serving two-income families who are too busy to do home improvements themselves. Whether it's the homeowner or the contractor who uses them, Warner tools are designed to do the job well, to make it easy to do, and to keep the cost down," says Guy Warner, the company's current

chairman of the board of directors and the founder's grandson.

Warner is proud of the company's long history of growth, innovative products and programs, and the responsiveness it provides to its customers. "My grandfather started this business, and it was his dedication and hard work that made it a successful family business," Warner says. "My own father started bringing me to work when I was six years old. My vision for the company is that it always remain owned and controlled by a Warner descendant."

Warner makes its own wood and injection-molded components, and fabricates, finishes, and assembles the tools it provides to its customers. Over the past

WARNER™

several years, Warner has replaced its traditional assembly lines with cellular manufacturing. These manufacturing cells are designed to provide the customer with a high-quality product, on time, at a competitive price.

Warner Manufacturing Company has developed a very responsive customer delivery system. This system gives the customer the ability to send orders to Warner by computer via Electronic Data Interchange (EDI). The system also provides customers with the opportunity to receive Advance Ship Notices (ASN), so they can better manage their product distribution into their retail outlets. The overall system has given Warner the ability to respond very quickly to its customers' requirements, and to give its customers superior product tracking and improved inventory control.

"For companies like ours serving the retail market, the value of the product goes beyond the tool itself," Guy Warner says. "We continuously strive to provide our customers with a total program that gives them added value through creativity and innovation."

Warner Manufacturing Company—a world leader in the manufacturing of high-quality professional and home handyman tools for drywall, painting, masonry, tile, and wallcovering work—has introduced many innovative tool designs that have become standards in the industry.

CYTEC FIBERITE

Since being founded as a private enterprise in 1947 Cytec Fiberite® has grown to become one of the world's largest suppliers of advanced composite materials.

When the creators of new technologies write material specifications, it's a challenge to suppliers to "qualify" a new product. Qualification is a demanding, costly process and only the best materials are candidates. Cytec Fiberite products are among those most often selected for qualification. The products are high-performance, pre-impregnated fabrics, unidirectional tapes, and filament roving. Cytec Fiberite products have been qualified for most major

military and civilian aircraft, and most major space structures launched since 1967.

Cytec Fiberite also has supplied the sporting goods industry with composite materials for golf club shafts and fishing rods, tennis rackets, windsurfer masts, snow skis, and bicycles.

Cytec Fiberite relies on excellence in planning, high quality, and financial stability as the key components of its role as an industry leader. Research has enabled Cytec Fiberite to understand the technical relationship between product and application, which has led to such developments as 977 toughened graphite epoxy, and the 954 family of cyanate resins. Acquiring composite products and technology from B. P. Chemical (Hitco) and Amoco has allowed Cytec Fiberite to expand its offerings.

Manufacturing Products Of Tomorrow, Today

CYTEC FIBERITE INC.

501 West Third Street
Winona, MN 55987-2854
(507) 454-3611

TICONA CELSTRAN®

Founded in 1980 as Polymer Composites, Inc., and today known as Ticona Celstran, this global manufacturer is a world leader in fiber-reinforced thermoplastic composite materials.

Celstran's products combine fibers (glass, aramid, carbon, or stainless steel) with matrix resins, such as nylon, polypropylene, or polyurethane, making new materials with unique properties. The resulting products have both stiffness and toughness—often of a high enough degree to replace metals. In addition, parts made from these materials are usually lighter in weight than parts of comparable strength made from other materials. Other benefits include improved fatigue properties, low co-efficient of thermal expansion, and resistance to corrosion.

The Ticona Celstran headquarters facility in Winona, Minnesota, opened in 1991.

Celstran makes more than 100 products and custom formulations at plants in Winona, Minnesota, and Kelsterbach, Germany, and by licensing agreement in Japan. Its products are used in virtually every sector of consumer and industrial manufacturing, including automobiles, computers, electronics, appliances, power tools, and sporting goods.

Celstran's Winona facility houses manufacturing, research and development, quality assurance, technical support, sales, and global administration.

CENTURY MFG. CO.

Long before anyone thought of corporate mission statements, Century Manufacturing built its own out of sheet metal and electrical parts. In 1937 Century's founders manufactured and sold their first product, a unique dial welder. It simplified arc welding by allowing a welder to simply turn a dial to set the amperage level. As the popularity of the dial welder grew, so did the company's customer base. The easy-to-use dial welder established Century's corporate mission—to build innovative products that make work easier and safer.

Innovation and attention to customer needs has served Century well over the past sixty years. When competition grew in the 1950s, Century responded with a welder that worked faster and with more electrode types. Century also introduced a new compact battery charger with enough power to start an engine. In the 1960s Century created one of the first welders with a 100-percent duty cycle and continuous, infinitely variable amperage settings. Customer suggestions at Century-sponsored welding clinics led to more innovations, including welders that operated at lower amperages and battery chargers with built-in testers.

New developments in the automotive industry also prompted new Century products. When unibody construction was introduced in the 1970s, Century created the first 115-volt wire-feed welder for use by body shops faced with repairing unibody automobiles. In response to environmental concerns, Century created products for servicing vehicle-cooling systems while safely recovering and recycling antifreeze.

Today Century employs more than 400 people at its Bloomington, Minnesota, headquarters. The company was acquired by Pentair, Inc., in 1996, becoming part of Pentair's vehicle-service equipment (VSE) business, with Lincoln Automotive. Pentair is a diversified manufacturer with nine subsidiaries and nearly 10,000 employees around the world.

"The combination of Century and Lincoln gives us a powerful presence in both the retail and professional automotive markets," says Winslow Buxton, Pentair chairman, president, and CEO. "We can take advantage of synergistic opportunities in product development, marketing, manufacturing, and distribution as we expand globally."

Century Manufacturing is organized into four product divisions: *Century* makes battery chargers, Booster Pacs, and welders for consumers. *Solar* is a leader in the production of professional automotive-service supplies, including battery chargers and pro-Booster Pacs; wire feed, MIG, arc welders, and plasma cutters; and service equipment for antifreeze/coolant and air-conditioning systems. *Viper* offers unique professional automotive air conditioning service equipment and accessories, while *Cobra* offers air-conditioning service equipment for industrial, commercial, and residential markets.

Booster Pacs are one of Century's newest and most popular product lines. Consumers can use a portable Booster Pac to jump-start their cars by themselves. The Booster Pac is also a convenient 12-volt power source for operating a cellular phone, television, radio, lantern—almost any 12-volt appliance—for hours. The wide product line includes 24-volt models for starting trucks, and a portable, cordless, and rechargeable 130-amp wire-feed welder.

"Century Manufacturing has enjoyed more than sixty years of growth in Minnesota," says company president, Steve Bentson. "We attribute this to a balance of good people, advanced manufacturing facilities, and innovative, high-quality products."

Century's products include battery chargers, welders, plasma cutters, air-conditioning and antifreeze service equipment, and Booster Pac— a twelve-volt portable power supply.

VTC INC.

VTC Inc. designs

and manufactures

integrated circuits

for data-storage

applications,

including disk-

drive read/write

preamplifiers, for

which it holds a

dominant share of

the world market

The privately held semi-conductor company VTC Inc. is a proven leader in providing high-quality, high-performance integrated circuits to the data-storage industry. Headquartered in Bloomington, the company designs and manufactures integrated circuits for computer hard-disk drives, an essential component of business and home computers worldwide. VTC specializes in read/write preamplifiers and mixed-signal circuits.

VTC has pioneered major advancements in data storage, with a continuous stream of innovations to help its customers stay at the leading edge of disk-drive technology. Today VTC's circuitry can be found in drives sold by the world's leading disk-drive manufacturers including Seagate, Quantum, Western Digital, and Maxtor.

When it was formed, in 1984, with the purpose of producing high-performance semi-conductors, VTC purchased a division of Control Data that had been dedicated to building integrated circuits for disk drives for nearly twenty years. From 1984 until 1990 VTC marketed a variety of integrated circuits that were used in applications ranging from laptops to aerospace computers.

VTC's facility for fabricating six-inch wafers is capable of handling 3,500 wafer starts per week using proven bipolar and bi-CMOS processes.

In 1990 VTC's president, Larry Jodsaas, and vice president of finance, Greg Peterson, bought the company from Control Data. They decided to concentrate VTC's marketing efforts on its primary area of expertise—making integrated circuits for data-storage applications. This new strategic effort resulted in immediate sales growth and increased profitability.

Along with this new focus, VTC also put into operation a companywide quality-improvement plan for both service and products. The company currently embraces statistical process-control (SPC) procedures throughout its operation, and is ISO-9001 certified. VTC empowers employees to continually evaluate manufacturing processes that can effect improvements and to follow a proactive course of action in their work.

In the years since 1990, when VTC implemented its strategic change, the company's employee complement has grown from 225 to more than 600 today. In addition to a sales office in California, VTC has support centers in Colorado and California and distributors in Japan, Singapore, and Korea.

"At VTC we're all very proud of our long-standing reputation for good customer service and our strong leadership position in the disk-drive industry," says Larry Jodsaas. "Our customer-comes-first philosophy has helped us achieve impressive revenue growth during the 1990s. Today we hold a dominant share of the world market for read/write preamplifiers."

VTC's 165,000-square-foot headquarters is centrally located in the Twin Cities next to major interstate highways, seven minutes from the airport.

MAMAC SYSTEMS, INC.

Founded in 1981 by its CEO, S. Asim Gul, Mamac Systems, Inc., produces a complete line of sensors, transducers, and control peripherals for heating, ventilation, and air-conditioning (HVAC); energy management; industrial automation; and cogeneration applications.

Sensors and transducers detect and measure a change in a physical variable, such as temperature, pressure, or humidity. In a closed-loop control system, a computer-based controller uses a sensor to measure a variable and computes its value relative to a programmed set point; if the value is higher or lower, the controller manipulates a device—such as opening or closing a valve—that returns the value to the set point. The controller monitors numerous input points in real time, twenty-four hours a day, seven days a week, maintaining multiple processes within operating parameters without human intervention. A controller also may be used to log values measured by the sensors, or to activate an alarm when a variable ranges outside its set point.

In the late 1970s Gul recognized that the advent of microprocessor-based control systems would

Mamac Systems manufactures a complete line of high-performance, moderately priced sensors, transducers, and control peripherals in its state-of-the-art production facility. The facility houses research and development, semiconductor fab operation, PC-board assembly, final assembly/calibration, distribution, sales, and marketing departments.

revolutionize industrial and environmental control systems. Before microprocessors, closed-loop systems were controlled by minicomputers, which were cumbersome and expensive; only critical applications were automated.

While the world was first beginning to recognize the computing capabilities of microprocessors, Gul envisioned a low-cost microprocessor-based control system bringing automation to many applications for which automation had previously not been economically justifiable. In the early 1980s Mamac Systems began to develop, manufacture, and distribute a complete line of 100 percent solid-state, reliable, affordable precise sensors that would be compatible with all automated control systems.

From one employee in 1981, the company has grown to more than one hundred employees worldwide, with manufacturing plants on three continents, and global sales and distribution. Mamac

MAMAC SYSTEMS®
MONITOR • DECISION • CONTROL

Systems is one of the few technology companies that was created when the founder invested his own personal funds and single-handedly designed, manufactured, and sold the initial product offering. The company is still wholly owned by its founder, and all funding for research and development, sales and marketing, and capital equipment is handled internally.

Mamac has conducted significant research and development to make high-volume, low-cost, highly reliable products. It now offers more than one hundred different types of sensors, transducers, actuators, and control peripherals. More than 80 percent of sales are to major other-equipment manufacturers (OEMs) of control systems, such as Honeywell, Johnson Controls, Trane Company, Carrier, and Lennox. Mamac products are also used by large companies such as IBM, Hewlett Packard, Boeing Company, Lockheed, Merck, Abbott, Dupont, Intel, Ford, Chrysler, and General Motors, for sophisticated in-house control systems.

Mamac Systems has designed numerous types of sensors to handle various system needs. Today Mamac's pressure sensors are used to pressurize clean rooms and hospital operating rooms. Its low-pressure sensors have kept the Hubert H. Humphrey Metrodome in Minneapolis inflated since the day it opened. High-pressure sensors measure steam pressure or control air-conditioning compressors, supermarket refrigeration systems, or tank levels. Temperature sensors are used for pipes, air ducts, rooms, and incubators. Rugged humidity sensors are deployed throughout buildings such as hospitals, pharmaceutical firms, and electronics companies. Electropneumatic transducers and actuators control valves, dampers, and other mechanisms. Ambient light sensors control lighting in areas from parking lots to atriums; sunlight is measured and lighting is brightened or dimmed accordingly.

Mamac sensors are being used more and more to automate, from the most simple to the most sophisticated control applications worldwide. Uses for sensors include: pressurizing sophisticated electronic clean rooms; controlling comfort and other environmental factors in hospital operating theaters, factories, offices, and classrooms; testing missiles and rocket engines; growing tulips in Holland; growing mushrooms; monitoring incubators in chicken hatcheries; monitoring and controlling turkey farms to increase the yield per bird; keeping foods in supermarkets frozen; dehumidifying indoor swimming pool environments; measuring precise fume-hood air flow to make sure noxious gases are not released; measuring the leak-rate of automobile gas caps to minimize the Greenhouse Effect; and washing and drying dishes in large commercial applications.

In the early 1990s Mamac Systems began developing microelectromechanical systems (MEMS) technology, using processes developed by the semiconductor industry, to manufacture extremely small sensors and transducers. In the mid-1990s Mamac pioneered technologies to micromachine silicon capacitive pressure sensors and bulk-polymer humidity sensors. It now is a recognized world leader in micromachined silicon sensors. All Mamac processes are done in-house, where the company has a sophisticated "class-100" clean room for micromachining sensors at the wafer level. Using state-of-the-art semiconductor fabrication operations has lowered the cost of micromachined sensors and enabled the company to mass-produce reliable high-performance sensors not previously available. Facilities are available to service Mamac's customers: wet etching of silicon with chemicals; plasma dry etching; photolithography; low-pressure and chemical vapor deposition; anodic, electrostatic, and eutectic bonding; surface metrology to submicron level; wafer dicing; wire bonding; die attaching; and all testing and calibration processes.

Mamac Systems is committed to being a technology leader, and founder Gul strongly believes that micromachined MEMS sensors are the technology of the future. Based on this, the company is committed to ongoing research and development, creating new sensors that will further reduce cost and enhance reliability and performance.

All Mamac's semiconductor fabrication operations and PC-board operations are done in Mamac's state-of-the-art, forty-thousand-square-foot facility in Eden Prairie, Minnesota. To reduce cost and improve quality, Mamac uses advanced calibration and computer-controlled manufacturing systems, most of which it custom-designed. The company also has four wholly owned subsidiaries, in Canada, the United Kingdom, Australia, and Singapore. The Canada and Singapore subsidiaries are sales and distribution offices. The United Kingdom subsidiary has assembly, testing, and manufacturing capabilities, to service Mamac's European customers. The Australia subsidiary assembles and distributes products throughout Asia. In this way, Mamac Systems can offer its customers global sales and distribution from a single source. Last year more than 20 percent of Mamac sales were to overseas customers.

MAMAC SYSTEMS LOCATIONS

UNITED STATES
7400 Flying Cloud Drive
Minneapolis, MN 55344-3720
(612) 835-1626 or (800) 843-5116
Fax: (612) 829-5331

UNITED KINGDOM
Baird House, Units 6 and 7
Dudley Innovation Centre
Pensnett Estate, Kingswinford
West Midlands DY6 8XZ
01384-271113; Fax: 01384-271114

AUSTRALIA
4 Armiger Court, Unit 2
Holden Hill, S. A. 5088
08-8395-4333; Fax: 08-8395-4433

CANADA
155 McIntosh Drive, Unit 5
Markham, Ontario L3R ON6
(905) 474-9215; Fax: (905) 474-0876

SINGAPORE
5611 North Bridge Road
03-06 Eng Cheong Tower 198782
65-3927273; Fax: 65-3927276

DUININCK COMPANIES

With diversified businesses from heavy highway construction and plastic pipe manufacturing to specialty foods and a vacation resort, Duininck Companies looks confidently toward the new millennium

From the blacktop of our nation's highways to the Black Hills of South Dakota, the four divisions of the highly diversified Duininck Companies have made their mark on the American landscape. These divisions comprise a heavy highway construction company, a plastic pipe manufacturer, a specialty food company, and a mountain vacation resort near Mount Rushmore. The common thread that ties together the Prinsburg-based firm is the exceptional group of people behind every Duininck product and service.

"If we as a company have found success, it is because of our exceptional employees," says Harris Duininck, who is a member of the family's second generation partners. "Currently we are fortunate to have, in some cases, the third generation of families working for our company. It is the passion of our employees for quality that brings excellence and reward to us all."

The Duininck Companies began in 1926 when Henry Duininck founded a small company that graded roads. Henry was joined by his brothers, Amos and Wilbur, and the first generation of Duinincks formed a partnership that has continued through three generations. This original division of the business continued to flourish as the founders' children became the second-generation partners. Now in the hands of the third generation of the Duininck family, this division, with facilities in Minnesota and Texas, continues to be the primary generator of revenue among the four businesses. The company's ability to diversify into new areas derives from the strength of the Duininck family's original business.

DUININCK BROS., INC.–MINNESOTA

Providing 300 jobs to Minnesota workers, this Prinsburg-based division processes and places mineral aggregates and bituminous asphalt for local, state, and federal highways. This division also does a wide variety of privately funded projects for corporate clients. The Duininck Bros. Minnesota operation has grown to include three portable asphalt plants, four crushers, two wash plants, and a small-scale grading operation. A single division of the Duininck Companies that is almost as diverse as the overall company itself, this division also has crews capable of underground pipe installation, bridge building, and heavy lifting (operating under the name Anderson Crane). A subgroup, DBI Golf, builds championship golf courses throughout the Midwest. The firm develops the courses from raw land, building every phase of the project, including the final grow-in stages of the entire course. Duininck also does extensive remodeling projects for many public and private links.

DUININCK BROS., INC.–TEXAS

The 300 Duininck Bros. employees of Grapevine, Texas, provide bituminous and concrete paving for local, state, and federal highways,

Asphalt paving is one of several types of construction performed by Duininck Bros., Inc., located in Minnesota and Texas. Other related work by the firm includes concrete paving, aggregate production, underground utility construction, and grading construction.

Prinsco Inc.'s twenty-four-inch PE Dual-wall GOLDFLO, at right, is one product in a broad line of plastic products ranging from corrugated PE pipe, sizes three inches to twenty-four inches, to septic tanks. All Prinsco products are used in commercial, residential, and agricultural applications.

PRINSCO INC

and a wide variety of large-scale private work for corporate customers throughout Texas, including many commercial and regional airports. In an effort to expand its market, this Dallas-based group became its own entity, separating from the Minnesota organization in 1983. This group operates three portable-asphalt plants, one portable-concrete plant, and a large grading operation. It also does other related construction, such as underground utility work.

PRINSCO

Prinsco was founded in 1974 in Prinsburg, Minnesota, as an automated manufacturer of concrete drainage pipe. Today it has evolved to become one of the nation's leading manufacturers of corrugated polyethylene pipe. Prinsco uses the most modern manufacturing machinery in the United States, including new state-of-the-art blow-molding equipment. It has established its strong reputation by maintaining the strictest quality control on all products and by offering them at a fair, competitive price.

Polyethylene (PE) is a high-density plastic that is used in making corrugated pipe for gravity-flow applications. Prinsco's lines of GOLDFLO and GOLDLINE pipe, made in three-inch to twenty-four-inch diameters, single wall or dual wall, have both residential and commercial applications. Its product line includes drainage pipe and culverts, geotextile fabrics, septic tanks, sump basins, and storm drains. PE is the perfect material for these applications since it is not affected by acid or alkali, frost, peat, muck, fertilizers, soil-treatment chemicals, or other effluent contaminates. Its corrugated surface gives strength to the pipe walls while reducing the weight of the pipe, making it a cost-effective alternative to concrete and steel pipe. Its GOLDFLO pipe is designed with a smooth interior that offers greater flow rates than pipe with a corrugated interior. This design feature allows construction crews to use a smaller diameter pipe, which means lower costs. GOLDFLO is strong enough to handle the job, but light enough to be installed without heavy equipment. Construction with GOLDFLO pipe requires less manpower and equipment than ordinary pipe, reducing installation costs significantly.

Prinsco's GOLDLINE pipe, which is corrugated on the inside and the outside, is designed for gravity-flow drainage construction. GOLDLINE is a flexible pipe that is used primarily in enhancing the drainage conditions on agricultural, residential and commercial sites. Since it is very lightweight, it is easy to handle and install.

Prinsco has distribution centers in Iowa, Missouri, Nevada, Colorado, and Texas. The company's more than sixty employees work around the clock, producing and selling millions of feet of pipe throughout the United States.

INDIAN HARVEST SPECIALTIFOODS, INC.

An entirely different side of the Duininck Companies' corporate personality, is Indian Harvest Specialtifoods, Inc. Indian Harvest

Indian Harvest supplies the finest restaurants across the nation with unique grains and beans that make dining a very enjoyable experience. Indian Harvest products now are available to consumers through catalogs and the Internet and in a variety of retail stores.

was founded in the 1970s in Bemidji, Minnesota, as a whole-grain food marketer. Duininck Companies took over Indian Harvest in 1987 after Duininck had built a large processing and packaging facility in Colusa, California. Indian Harvest now processes wild rice and other grains that are blended, packaged, and marketed in a vertically integrated sales operation. Its customers include upscale restaurants, retail outlets such as grocery stores, catalog sales to the general public, and industrial users. Its products are sold under a variety of brand names including Indian Harvest, Guest Chef, and Voyager Trading.

To market its products, Indian Harvest maintains a Web site (www.indianharvest.com) offering cooking tips, profiles of guest chefs, links to fine food and wine sites, and a shopping page offering unique and healthy whole-grain and rice blend products; and circulates a newsletter for food-service professionals. Its product line includes heirloom beans—rich in history because, through the efforts of dedicated individuals in the genetic preservation movement, the original tastes of cultural beans, such as Red Calypso, Good Mother Stallard, Black and Red Nightfall, Tiger Eye, New Mexico Red Appaloosa, Pebble, and Speckled Brown Cow beans have been retained; the beans are cultivated for years to attain their exceptional appearance and flavor. The complete product line also includes exotic grains, unique pasta, and wild rice. Indian Harvest grains are a tasty addition for many dishes, including soups, salsas, and salads.

The thirteen-thousand acre Hart Ranch—"where the West begins"—features a vacation resort, championship golf course, and a residential and townhouse area located on the way to Mt. Rushmore, where the rolling prairie is interrupted by the beautiful Black Hills.

HART RANCH VACATION RESORT

Amidst the breathtaking natural beauty of Mount Rushmore in the Black Hills of South Dakota, the Hart Ranch Vacation Resort provides endless entertainment in a relaxing atmosphere for family enjoyment. The thirteen-thousand-acre Hart Ranch, located near Rapid City, is a private five-star-rated membership resort with 5,000 members. The resort and the Hart Ranch Development Company offer a wide range of amenities, including championship golf, swimming, trail rides, rodeos at its sixteen-thousand-square-foot indoor arena, hiking trails, tennis, and minigolf. Wonderful views of the Black Hills take in buffalo herds and other native animals. The Hart Ranch includes townhomes and houses in the "ranchette" area, situated along the eighteen-hole championship golf course. The ranch is a great place to unwind from the stress of everyday life.

THE DUININCK PHILOSOPHY

"All of our diverse businesses are managed by on-site managers under the umbrella of the Duininck Companies," says Harris Duininck. "Each division is run as an independent entity, which allows each one to be in control of its own destiny. This structure gives each division individual ability to respond quickly to change—a key word for business as we move toward the new millennium."

© Steve Niedorf/3M

HIGH MARKS IN EDUCATION

CHAPTER SEVENTEEN

FEW STATES DISPLAY A DEDICATION TO EDUCATION THAT EQUALS THAT OF MINNESOTA. FROM PRESCHOOL OPTIONS TO POSTGRADUATE OFFERINGS, HIGH-QUALITY EDUCATIONAL OPPORTUNITIES ABOUND. MINNESOTA CURRENTLY RANKS SECOND IN THE MIDWEST AND NINTH IN THE NATION IN PER CAPITA STATE AND LOCAL EDUCATIONAL EXPENDITURES AND COMMITS MORE EDUCATIONAL DOLLARS PER PUPIL AND LESS PER ADMINISTRATIVE COSTS THAN THE NATIONAL AVERAGE.

Minnesota's focus on education starts young. In conjunction with its focus on families and early-childhood issues, the state has developed strong resources in the area of quality child-care providers and preschool education. Twenty-five years ago, Rochester was one of the first communities in the nation to develop a child-care resource and referral network, and its founding executive director, Tutti Sherlock, continues today to be a national authority and advocate.

For the past decade, Minnesota's high school graduation rate has consistently been among the top five in the nation. The state's ranking in the 1996–1997 school year was fourth, according to the U.S. Department of Education. The state's ACT and SAT college entrance exam scores are also among the best in the country and have continued to improve over the past six years.

Several factors together help place and keep Minnesota's students at the summit of the national charts. First, nearly 80 percent of the state's elementary and secondary students participate in a gifted or talented program in their school. These programs are offered in a wide variety of subjects, allowing students enrichment opportunities on everything from math and science to drama and creative writing. Second, the state has created a public school open enrollment program that allows elementary and secondary students to enroll in public school districts other than the ones in which they reside. Students from small towns with limited upper-level science or foreign-language programs, for instance, are free to enroll in neighboring metropolitan areas to pursue a curriculum more suited to their needs. Likewise, students in larger schools may opt to pursue their education in a more

Opposite: Designed by Cass Gilbert, the Northrop Mall on the Minneapolis campus of the University of Minnesota represents the mind and spirit of the university. © Bob Firth/Firth Photobank. Above: Also on the mall, students take their studies outside on a beautiful spring day. The University of Minnesota is promoting funding initiatives to position itself as a leader in molecular and cellular biology and in media and communications. © Greg Ryan-Sally Beyer

MAKING THE GRADE: MORE THAN 84 PERCENT OF 1993 NINTH-GRADERS IN MINNESOTA GRADUATED IN 1997, NEARLY 16 PERCENT HIGHER THAN THE NATIONAL AVERAGE OF 68 PERCENT. OVER 71 PERCENT OF MINNESOTA'S HIGH SCHOOL GRADUATES PURSUE SOME FORM OF HIGHER EDUCATION WITHIN FIVE YEARS OF GRADUATION. AND IN 1997, MINNESOTA HAD THE THIRD-HIGHEST AVERAGE SAT COMPOSITE SCORE IN THE NATION: 1,174.

personalized environment by transferring to a smaller school. Not content to rest on its accomplishments, the Department of Education is currently implementing graduation standards into the already comprehensive secondary curriculum.

Technology also plays an important role in giving Minnesota students a competitive advantage. According to the 1997 "Technology in Public Schools" survey, Minnesota students have greater access to computers than do students in forty-five other states. In two years, the state has jumped from a ranking of eighteenth in the nation in this category to its current fifth-place status. Eighty-six percent of Minnesota's students have Internet access, making them second in the nation. The state government continues to finance advancements in this

area in their long-range technology plan. Last year alone, the legislature allocated $90 million for new and ongoing technological initiatives.

Minnesota's commitment to technology in the classroom is perhaps nowhere more evident than it is in Crookston. There, in a community of under ten thousand people some one hundred miles south of the Canadian border, the local branch of the University of Minnesota, once dubbed "Moo U" because of its heavy emphasis on agriculture, was in danger of extinction due to declining enrollment. Fewer of Minnesota's sons and daughters were pursuing a future in agriculture, and the school seemed destined to becoming another farming casualty. Before simply closing their doors and chalking it up to the times, the school's administrators surveyed regional employers on the No. 1 skill they sought when hiring new employees. The answer? Computer literacy. So, in a bold and unprecedented move, in lieu of closing the doors, the administration wired the classrooms, labs, libraries, and dorms and created the first university in the country to provide every full-time student with his or her own notebook computer. Three years and as many technological upgrades later, enrollment was up 22 percent.

Elementary schoolchildren board a bus in the south-central city of North Mankato. Public elementary and secondary students in Minnesota enjoy a pupil-teacher ratio of 17.3 to 1, slightly better than the national average. © Joe Miller Photography

Above: Since 1982, the U.S. Department of Education has recognized seventy-four Minnesota schools for excellence through its Blue Ribbon Schools Program, including thirty elementary and forty-four secondary schools. © Telegraph Colour Library/ FPG International. Right: In the 1920s, these two college-age women tried their hand at football at Gustavus Adolphus College in St. Peter. © Minnesota Historical Society/Corbis

The growth at Crookston reflects an upswing in the number of higher-education students statewide. The increase in the number of bachelor's degrees awarded by Minnesota colleges and universities from 1980 to 1994 has outpaced that of the rest of the nation. In 1996, Minnesota ranked twelfth in the nation and second in the Midwest for the percentage of residents over the age of twenty-five that held bachelor's degrees or higher. In 1995, the state's public colleges and universities united to form a marketing system known as MnSCU (Minnesota State Colleges and Universities), bringing together twenty-one community colleges, thirty-four technical colleges, and seven state universities.

Above: A choir sings at a Minnesota high school graduation. Minnesota's high school graduation rate is consistently among the nation's highest. And in 1997, Minnesota seniors earned the fifth-highest ACT scores and the third-highest SAT scores in the country. © Bob Firth/Firth Photobank. Below: All's quiet in the stacks at Moorhead State University, part of the Minnesota State Colleges and Universities system, which encompasses sixty-two educational institutions.© Glenn Tornell, Publications, Moorhead State University

TWENTY-SEVEN PERCENT OF ALUMNI OF MINNESOTA'S PRIVATE COLLEGES GO ON TO START THEIR OWN BUSINESSES, AND 47 PERCENT PURSUE AN ADVANCED DEGREE.

The flagship educational institution is the University of Minnesota, one of the most comprehensive universities in the country and prestigiously ranked among the nation's top twenty. Founded in 1851, the University of Minnesota is both the state's land-grant university, with four campuses, and a major research institution. Its courses in engineering, economics, and geography are rated in the top ten nationally, as are several of its medical fields of study, including psychology, dentistry,

Old Main inspires respect on the campus of St. Olaf College, a Lutheran college founded in 1874 in Northfield. The 350-acre campus graces a wooded hilltop. © Bob Firth/Firth Photobank

pharmacy, and health-services administration. In addition to the campuses in the Twin Cities and Crookston, the university has campuses in Duluth and Morris. The campus in Duluth offers undergraduate and graduate degrees and has been ranked among the top three Midwestern universities by *U.S. News and World Report.* The strong academic quality found on the Morris campus has received numerous recognitions in national publications.

Minnesota is also home to outstanding private colleges. In fact, one-third of all four-year degrees granted in the state each year are to graduates of one of the state's sixteen private colleges. St. Olaf, founded by Norwegian immigrants in 1874, is highly regarded for its musical programs as well as its science and English departments. The school is perpetually considered a good value in education and is situated on a beautiful 350-acre campus in Northfield. Just a few miles away from St. Olaf is Carleton College, one of the top liberal arts colleges in the nation. The school ranks in the top five of those with undergraduates who go on to seek Ph.D.'s. Carleton alumni have graduated to notable careers in business, commerce, law, medicine, education, and the arts.

TWENTY PERCENT OF MINNESOTA
PRIVATE COLLEGE STUDENTS ARE
FROM FAMILIES WHO EARN
$20,000 PER YEAR OR LESS,
AND HALF FROM FAMILIES WHOSE
ANNUAL INCOME IS LESS THAN
$40,000. ONE IN EIGHT IS THE
FIRST MEMBER OF THEIR FAMILY TO ATTEND COLLEGE.

Augsburg College in Minneapolis has a unique focus on public service that starts on the first day of school, when incoming freshmen volunteer at neighborhood nonprofit organizations. The science department at Gustavus Adolphus College hosts the annual Nobel Conference, which to date has attracted more than seventy Nobel laureates to its campus in the small town of St. Peter. St. John's and its sister college, St. Benedict's, are among the

Right: Student Kyla Whitecrow and instructor Gordon Savela work in the chemistry lab at Rainy River Community College. © Grandmaison Photographic Studios/Rainy River Community College/MnSCU. Below: Students enjoy a break from class at Mankato State University. © Joe Miller Photography

nation's premier Catholic colleges and are known for their highly competitive academic atmosphere.

Excellence in education also extends to technical training in Minnesota. The state's technical schools routinely join regional employers and design programs to meet the specific needs and skills of the area. Private technical colleges Dunwoody Institute and Brown Institute are nationally recognized for their specialized training. Graduates of these two institutes are prepared for long-term careers in a variety of technical fields.

THE MINNESOTA AIR TRAFFIC CONTROL TRAINING CENTER IN EDEN PRAIRIE, BEGUN IN CONJUNCTION WITH THE FAA, IS THE ONLY ATC IN THE NATION ENTIRELY DEDICATED TO THE DEVELOPMENT OF AIR TRAFFIC CONTROL SPECIALISTS. STUDENTS MUST ALREADY HAVE A COLLEGE DEGREE TO BE ADMITTED.

Courtesy, Metropolitan Airports Commission

Above: MnSCU also offers advanced art education. ©Jeffrey Grosscup/SSU-Marshall/MnSCU. Below: Sunlight warms the tower at the University of St. Thomas. © Steve Jordan/Univ. of St. Thomas

© Bob Firth/Firth Photobank

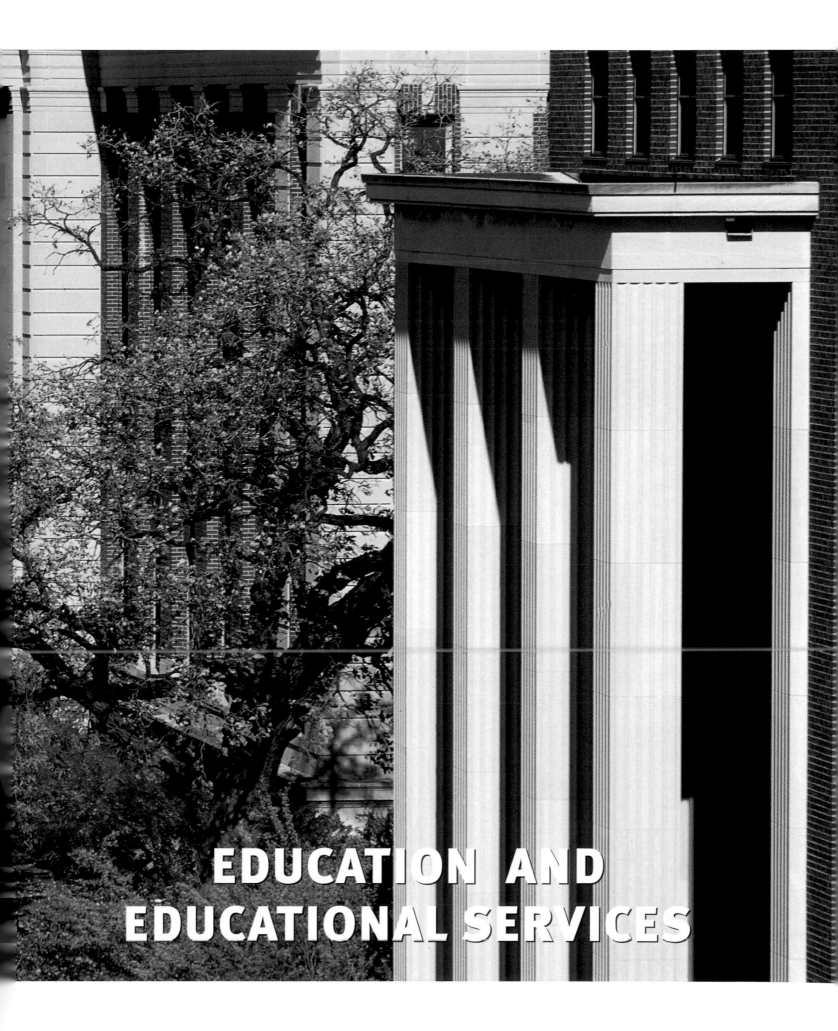

EDUCATION AND EDUCATIONAL SERVICES

UNIVERSITY OF MINNESOTA
CARLSON SCHOOL OF MANAGEMENT

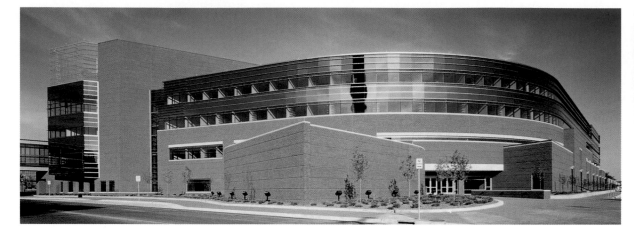

THE CARLSON

SCHOOL OF

MANAGEMENT

OFFERS DIVERSE

BUSINESS PROGRAMS

WITH COMMUNITY

AND INTERNATIONAL

INVOLVEMENT FOR

FULL-TIME STUDENTS

AND WORKING

PROFESSIONALS

The cornerstone of the Carlson School of Management's transformation to a world-class institution is its new $45 million building complex. Construction was supported largely by local businesses, alumni, friends, and the state of Minnesota—a true public/private partnership that reflects the school's diverse mission as a learning institution. Traditionally, the Carlson School has invited community businesspeople to participate with the school at every level, from serving on its prestigious Board of Overseers, to classroom lecturing, to presenting case studies for analysis by faculty researchers.

After talking with more than 150 business leaders directly and involving more than 900 businesspeople and alumni in focus groups, the school developed a strategic plan to transform the institution, with an immediate focus on the school's daytime Master of Business Administration (MBA) program. The new building was an essential part of that change.

In determining its strategic advantages, the Carlson School quickly realized that its location in a thriving economic community with many Fortune 500 firms and dozens of other midsized and entrepreneurial ventures was an untapped opportunity. Programs were

The Carlson School of Management is housed in a state-of-the-art $45 million complex constructed in 1997 on the University of Minnesota's West Bank campus.

amended to emphasize "experiential learning." Overseers often serve as mentors to MBA students, giving students a glimpse of life in the executive suite. Some serve on advisory boards to academic departments or research groups. Others speak to classes or participate in the school's Top Management Perspectives series, in which executives discuss current business issues.

Alumni also have been invited to contribute their services. To create a stronger partnership with its local alumni, the Carlson School has revitalized its Alumni Advisory Board, approximately twenty-five alumni who advise the school on long-range planning and other matters. This change in the school's curriculum and its approach to learning has not gone unnoticed by corporate recruiters. Graduates of the Carlson School are in great demand and starting salaries for its MBA graduates have climbed dramatically.

The school's improvements in its physical facility and its academic programs have been made in and amid competition from other education programs, and the Carlson School continues to flourish. Its daytime MBA program is ranked twenty-seventh nationally and the undergraduate program thirteenth nationally by *U.S. News & World Report* in 1998. Its "Techno MBA" program

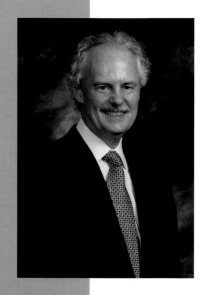

Carlson School Dean David Kidwell says the institution is well on its way toward becoming one of the nation's premier graduate and undergraduate business schools.

was ranked fourth best by *ComputerWorld*. The Carlson School also has been included in *Success* magazine's list of "The 25 Best Business Schools for Entrepreneurs."

Reflecting the globalization of business, the Carlson School offers a multifaceted international business initiative, including more than a dozen exchange programs. Exchanges with partner institutions in Europe, Latin America, and Asia Pacific enable students to study abroad for an academic quarter and receive MBA credits. For students who can't participate for a full quarter, two-week schedules are available. To increase its global presence, the school also is developing joint MBA programs in partnership with other premier educational institutions in other countries and in collaboration with Minnesota-based businesses.

Like its MBA program, the Carlson School's curricula for undergraduate students emphasize a combination of both theory and practice. To maintain its high standard, the school recruits freshman of outstanding ability. These students are encouraged to develop leadership skills by combining their academic career-development work with volunteer activities in the community. In the Emerging Leadership Program, a

The Carlson School's new building complex includes thirty-three classrooms, thirty-five meeting rooms, the latest in computer-based technology and a soaring central atrium designed to provide students with a strong sense of community.

program designed to enhance the undergraduate student experience, students devote seventy hours to community service, leadership, diversity, and career-development projects.

Academic links to the business community are provided for Ph.D. candidates as well. In numbers, doctoral students make up the smallest group of students of the Carlson School. However, the academic caliber of these future scholars and teachers is ranked in the top tier nationally.

Numerous other ventures have added to the Carlson School's prestige. In 1993 the school founded the Quality Leadership Center, now named the Juran Center for Leadership in Quality, to conduct research on work site quality-improvement issues and disseminate information to businesses. This center has received several highly competitive National Science Foundation research grants. In 1997 the Carlson School founded the Entrepreneurial Studies Center to promote entrepreneurial research and education. In 1998 a new strategic planning process and a significant lead donor gift combined to launch a major expansion of this effort.

The Carlson School's Executive Development Center provides top-quality, intensive training in general and specific management areas. One of the center's resources is its Quorum, a board of sixty-five human resources executives who provide ideas for new programs and evaluations of completed programs.

The Carlson School of Management's Minnesota Executive Program is a focused, short-term course designed for senior executives. It focuses on strategic planning and decision-making skills.

"Our goal for the future is to offer a daytime MBA program that is pre-eminent among the nation's public business schools and other top-ranked graduate and undergraduate business programs," says Dean David Kidwell. "This effort, in combination with all our other programs, is the next step to solidly placing ourselves among the ranks of the premier business schools in the country."

Classroom experiences frequently include interaction with top management from international firms and many of the largest and most important companies in the Twin Cities.

JOSTENS

From its small beginnings as Otto Josten's jewelry and watch repair business in Owatonna, Minnesota, Jostens has emerged as a world leader in helping people celebrate the important events in their lives. Jostens innovations in the scholastic jewelry, yearbook, graduation products, school photography, and recognition industry have helped preserve the memories of a lifetime for millions of people.

For most of its history the company's focus has been on students. Generations of school graduates recognize Jostens as the company that helped them commemorate their high school achievements. Today Jostens uses the power of its brand name to reach out to customers at other times in their lives. In schools, through businesses, and in other ways, Jostens is helping customers celebrate life's important events, recognize achievements, and build lasting affiliations.

In the college market, for example, Jostens is helping university leaders develop programs and products that help their institutions build strong links with students and alumni. In business, Jostens' Strategic Recognition™ concept helps clients build recognition and performance programs to build affiliation with employees and motivate them to achieve organizational goals.

"We may be best-known as a ring and yearbook company, but it's really more than that—it's

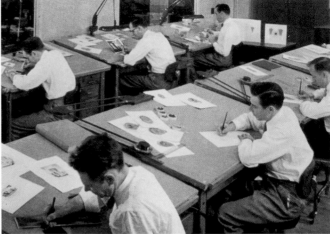

Jostens has a long tradition of original designs for its products. Shown here, in the 1930s, are the company's ring designers hard at work.

about helping people celebrate," says Robert C. Buhrmaster, chairman, president, and chief executive officer of Jostens. "This new direction for the company will enable us to reach out to customers in more ways and in more places."

To support its new, broader direction, Jostens is making major improvements and investments in its infrastructure, from manufacturing to information systems. "As we learn more about our customers, we tailor our products, processes, and programs to become more efficient and to better serve consumer needs," Buhrmaster says.

Jostens has a long-standing commitment to the communities it serves. Since 1976 The Jostens Foundation has contributed more than $25 million primarily to programs related to education and youth. The Jostens employee gift-matching program ensures that the company supports community programs that hold meaning for employees, and hundreds of Jostens employees help improve their communities through volunteerism.

"Our goal is to be the company people choose to help them celebrate the most important moments in their lives, from school days to retirement," Buhrmaster says.

For more than a century Jostens products, including graduation caps, gowns, and diplomas, have helped students celebrate academic achievements.

© Bob Firth/Firth Photobank

THE FUTURE OF ENERGY

CHAPTER EIGHTEEN

MINNESOTANS LOVE TO JOKE THAT THEIR STATE HAS TWO SEASONS: WINTER AND ROAD REPAIR. WHILE FRIGID TEMPERATURES AND CONSTRUCTION DELAYS ARE THE EXCEPTION RATHER THAN THE RULE, BOTH HAVE CONTRIBUTED TO THE STATE'S FOCUS ON THE IMPORTANCE OF EFFICIENT, HIGH-QUALITY SOURCES OF ENERGY AND FUEL.

The state has several types of energy utilities. There are five electric and seven natural-gas investor-owned utilities (IOUs), which own and operate their own generating plants, transmission, and distribution lines. Seven other companies provide generation and transmission services to forty-five distribution cooperatives throughout the state. The cooperatives are owned and operated by members/customers. All but one of these cooperatives operate as unregulated, nonprofit entities. Cities and towns can also be their own providers as municipally owned utilities. One hundred thirty-one such entities, known as "munis," provide gas or electricity to their communities. Most all of the utilities offer energy-conservation programs to their residential and commercial customers.

Minnesota law requires public utilities to invest portions of their revenues in programs designed to reduce consumption as well as improve the overall efficient use of the state's energy resources. The 1991 Energy Omnibus bill clarified the requirements by specifically designating the dollar amount that each type of utility must invest.

The payoffs of the conservation effort were immediate and effective. The electrical savings in the first five years of the program in the IOUs alone was enough to power all residences in the city of Minneapolis for an eighteen-month period, and enough natural gas was conserved by the IOUs in the same period to serve fourteen thousand residences for a full year.

Minnegasco, one of three natural-gas distribution divisions of Nor Am Energy Corporation, the third-largest natural gas distribution company in the United States, is based in Minneapolis. The company, formerly known as Minneapolis Gas Light Company, was founded in 1870 to provide gas for the city's first streetlights. Today, Minnegasco is the state's largest natural-gas utility, serving some 640,000 customers in 225 communities. Northern States Power (NSP) also has deep roots in the state. Originated in 1916, NSP generated seventy megawatts from its sole fossil fuel plant in northeastern Minneapolis, enough power to meet almost the entire electrical demand of the city. NSP currently fulfills its customers' electrical demands via a mix of nuclear, coal, and hydroelectric plants, as well as with a

Opposite: A lineman works up high to keep residents down low warm during Minnesota's notoriously cold winters. © Greg Ryan-Sally Beyer. Above: Corn is used in the production of ethanol, a cleaner-burning fuel than gasoline. Minnesota is the country's fourth-largest producer of corn. © Conrad Bloomquist/Scenic Photo!

HONEYWELL, THE WORLD'S LEADING ENERGY-CONTROL MAKER, MADE THE FIRST ELECTRIC HEAT REGULATOR IN 1885. AL BUTZ PATENTED HIS "DAMPER FLAPPER," WHICH AUTOMATICALLY OPENED FURNACE VENTS.

couple of relatively new methods: wind turbines and "renewable" facilities that burn refuse-derived fuel, oil, wood, and gas.

A 1990 study by the Minnesota Department of Public Service found that an area in the western part of the state, along the Buffalo Ridge near Lake Benton, has enough wind to produce the energy required to power the entire state for over a full year. In 1994, NSP began its first phase of harnessing that wind power. Seventy-three wind turbines began producing twenty-five megawatts of pollution-free electricity. By the end of 1998, another 143 turbines will be in place. NSP's commitment is to install 425 megawatts of wind-generated power by the end of 2002. When complete, the Lake Benton area will be one of the principal wind-power sites in the world.

Using its typical creativity and knack for innovation, Minnesota is uniting its drive to reduce landfills and its goal to find more sources of renewable energy. NSP has developed processing facilities that remove recyclables and noncombustibles from municipal solid waste and then shred the remainder into a product known as refuse-derived fuel, or RDF. RDF is currently used to generate electricity at three NSP power plants.

The synergy between the state's focus on renewable energy and its high level of corn production (it's ranked fourth in the nation) places Minnesota on the cutting edge of the emerging ethanol industry. Minnesota's development of this segment began in 1992 when the state enacted one of the most progressive clean-air fuel programs in the country. By 1997, state law mandated that all gasoline sold in the state contain an oxygenate, an oxygen-containing substance designed to reduce carbon monoxide and other toxic emissions. In Minnesota, the most commonly used oxygenate is ethanol, a noncorrosive

A work crew with Northern States Power (NSP) company places piping in the ground. NSP uses a variety of sources to fulfill its customers' energy needs. © Northern States Power

Above: Managers at NSP's Becker coal-burning facility in Minneapolis help Minnesota use energy efficiently. Coal prices in Minnesota are almost 13 percent lower than the national average of $1.40 per million Btu's. © Jeffrey P. Grosscup. Below: The wind-power generators at Buffalo Ridge will place Minnesota at the forefront of developing sources of renewable energy. © Telegraph Colour Library/FPG International

MINNESOTA'S BUFFALO RIDGE AREA HAS MORE HIGH-GRADE WIND RESOURCES THAN THE ENTIRE STATE OF CALIFORNIA. AS THE ENERGY INDUSTRY IS RESTRUCTURED NATIONWIDE, CONSUMERS WILL BE ABLE TO CHOOSE WIND POWER AS ONE OF THE SOURCES OF THEIR ELECTRICITY, THEREBY INCREASING THE DEMAND FOR RENEWABLE ENERGY.

alcohol made from corn. Today, the state boasts the most significant cooperative ethanol industry in the nation, with eleven plants, whose combined production capacity is 156 million gallons. The state continues to aggressively develop this industry.

Energy continues to come at a bargain for those living and working in Minnesota. Average electricity prices for commercial users are 19 percent lower than the national average, and industrial users pay 7 percent less for their power than do their national counterparts. Residential users reported prices 15 percent below the national average. Natural gas prices for all users are also lower than U.S. average prices. As expected in the state known for its lakes, most of the water used in Minnesota comes from surface water sources. Power generation, which returns most of the water it requires to its source after use, accounts for the primary use of water in the state. Water prices also

Opposite: A worker with Northern States Power company checks the quality of air being emitted from a vent. © Northern States Power. Right: These blue barrels at a highway rest stop are part of the country's best recycling system. Minnesota is No. 1 in recycling solid waste (38 percent). © Conrad Bloomquist/Scenic Photo!

continue to be lower in Minnesota than in most other areas of the country.

To further promote the state as the international center for renewable energy and energy efficiency that it is becoming, the Minnesota Environmental Initiative developed the Energy Alley program, sponsored by major utility providers NSP and Minnegasco, as well as two of the state's largest corporations: Honeywell, a global leader in energy-control devices, and Andersen Corporation, the largest window and door manufacturer in the world. The program encompasses education, marketing, and promotion related to the state's energy industry. Energy Alley has also aligned itself with the city of Elk River, population fifteen thousand, to showcase energy efficiency and renewable technology. Elk River, situated thirty-five miles northwest of the Twin Cities, will promote energy products, services, and practices that benefit the community, the

economy, and the environment. Current joint projects include the establishment of a business incubator program, which provides physical, clerical, equipment, and financial-advisory support to fledgling companies. This program will focus on energy issues and the construction of an energy-efficient home that will incorporate cutting-edge technology, such as state-of-the-art windows and controls, geo-energy, and ventilation and exchange features.

MORE THAN ONE TRILLION MILES HAVE BEEN SAFELY DRIVEN ON ETHANOL NATIONWIDE. ETHANOL, A CORN-DERIVED OXYGENATE, REDUCES TOXIC EMISSIONS WHEN ADDED TO GASOLINE. MINNESOTA'S ETHANOL INDUSTRY PRODUCES 156 MILLION GALLONS ANNUALLY.

PLEASURABLE PURSUITS

CHAPTER NINETEEN

CATALOG SALES. TRADING STAMPS. FREQUENT-FLYER PROGRAMS. SHOPPING MALLS. THESE CONTEMPORARY PHENOMENA ARE AS AMERICAN AS APPLE PIE. BUT THESE ICONS OF RETAIL AND HOSPITALITY HAVE EVEN MORE IN COMMON, THEY'RE ALSO ALL NATIVE TO MINNESOTA.

Richard Sears was a railroad agent in the town of North Branch, Minnesota, in the late 1800s. When a load of quality watches lay unclaimed at his station, Sears bought then sold them, by mail, to fellow agents along the line. Realizing a healthy profit and a demand for this service, the enterprising Sears quit his day job and went on to found catalog and subsequent retail giant Sears and Roebuck in 1893.

Curtis Carlson is a first-generation Minnesotan, the son of Swedish immigrants. Raised in south Minneapolis, Carlson graduated with a degree in economics from the University of Minnesota in 1937 and went to work as a soap salesman for Procter and Gamble. Intrigued by the success retailers were having stimulating their business with the use of redeemable coupons, Carlson devised and marketed a similar concept to the grocers in his territory. Within a year, he was devoting full time to his new company, Gold Bond Stamps. Three decades later, the trading stamp business conquered both national and international markets and revolutionized the marketing of retail goods.

Carlson diversified his business and changed the name to Carlson Companies in 1973. Today, the multibillion-dollar company, now run by Carlson's daughter, Marilyn Carlson Nelson, is one of the largest privately held corporations in the world and an international leader in travel, hospitality, and marketing.

The Carlson Travel Group network, the most extensive travel-agency operation in the world, encompasses more than two thousand agencies and generates in excess of $7 billion in annual revenues. The hospitality group is anchored by the upscale Radisson Hotels and includes the first American-styled and -operated hotel in post-Soviet Russia, the Radisson Slavjanskaya; it opened in 1991 in a joint venture with the city of Moscow.

Country Inns and Country Kitchens are another component of the hospitality group as is T.G.I. Friday's, a restaurant chain boasting the highest average annual sales per

Opposite: The golf green is another favorite place where Minnesotans go to relax. Minnesota, with more than 720,000 golfers, boasts more golf club–swingers per capita than any other state in the country. © Bob Firth/Firth Photobank. Above: Shoppers rest near Gaviidae Common, one of the more upscale shopping areas in Minneapolis. Since the 1992 opening of the Mall of America, retail centers in the Twin Cities have enjoyed boom times. In fact, developers are still working with city planners to refurbish older urban areas to create more attractive retail districts. © John Elk III

THE MALL OF AMERICA IS LARGE ENOUGH TO HOLD SEVEN YANKEE STADIUMS OR THIRTY-TWO 747 JUMBO JETS. A SEVEN-ACRE AMUSEMENT PARK, COMPLETE WITH A ROLLER COASTER, IS HOUSED IN THE CENTER OF THE MALL OF AMERICA.

OF MALLS AND FUN

"If you build it, they will come," refers to an Iowa base-ball field in the 1989 movie *Field of Dreams,* but it just as aptly describes architect Victor Gruen's 1956 vision for an innovative shopping complex in Edina, Minnesota. Known as Southdale, the nation's first indoor shopping mall has spawned thousands of imitators from coast to coast and is still going strong nearly half a century later. With continual upgrades and innovations, the 1.6 mil-lion-square-foot complex continues to be a national leader in the shopping center industry.

Not even the innovative Gruen could have foreseen the success of the Mall of America, which after only five years in business, surpassed the combined draw of Disney World, the Grand Canyon, and the Statue of Liberty to become the nation's premier tourist destination. The 4.2 million-square-foot complex boasts more than four hundred stores and twelve thousand employees. It receives thirty-five million to forty million annual visits, each lasting an average of three hours, three times the average visit length to any other mall. Once concerned of the negative impact the huge competitor would have on

unit of any national chain in the industry. The Carlson Marketing Group is the largest marketing services organi-zation of its kind in the world. True to its roots, the marketing group aids clients by developing programs to stimulate sales and build customer loyalty. Today's frequent-flyer and other frequency-recognition and reward programs, many developed and managed by the marketing group, are extensions of the trading-stamp philosophy.

Horses race at Canterbury Park Racetrack in Shakopee, south-west of Minneapolis. Among Shakopee's attractions are the Valleyfair Amusement Park, Minnesota Renaissance Festival, and NASCAR racing. © Conrad Bloomquist/Scenic Photo!

Children run along part of the six miles of trails at the Minnesota Landscape Aboretum in Chanhassen. Its 900 acres include a rose garden and a Japanese waterfall garden. © John Elk III

their businesses, Minnesota merchants are now enjoying the benefits of their mega-neighbor. Tourism accounts for nearly 40 percent of the Mall of America's business, and economists estimate that for every dollar spent at the Mall, another $2 or $3 is spent elsewhere in the area.

Other nationally prominent retailers also have a base in Minnesota. The Dayton family opened a department store in downtown Minneapolis in 1902, which today has become a Fortune 500 company and the fourth-largest general merchandise retailer in the nation. Dayton Hudson Corporation's family of stores now includes Hudson's and Marshall Field's as well as midpriced merchandiser Mervyn's and the discount Target stores. Despite its growth, Dayton Hudson Corporation has remained true to its family roots and is ranked highly by *Working Mother* magazine for its family-friendly policies and working environments at its numerous stores.

Other landmark stores in the state include Minneapolis-based Musicland, the largest specialty retailer of home-entertainment products in the country, and Fingerhut, based in St. Cloud, a database marketing company with a broad range of products and services and the second-largest catalog company in the nation.

ONE VISIT, AND YOU'RE HOOKED

Of course, residents and visitors alike know there's more to Minnesota than malls and shopping bags. Tourism is a multibillion-dollar industry, with attractions in every part of the state. Many visitors head to outside locations to enjoy the parklands, lakes, and rivers, others come for professional or collegiate sporting events, or an offering in the arts.

Home to the Minnesota Vikings professional football team and the Minnesota Twins professional baseball team, the state has also hosted more than its share of athletic events, among them the 1998 World Figure Skating Championships, the 1991 Superbowl, the 1987 and 1991 World Series, and all thirteen U.S. Golf Association championships. Second only to New York in the number

THE SEVENTEEN CASINOS ON MINNESOTA'S INDIAN RESERVATIONS TOGETHER MAKE GAMING THE STATE'S SEVENTH-LARGEST EMPLOYER, WITH 1992 REVENUES OF $390 MILLION.

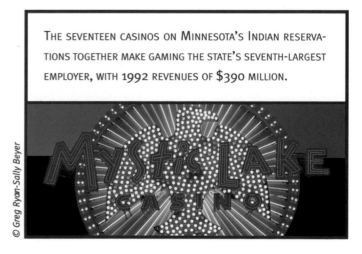

© Greg Ryan-Sally Beyer

THE SCHOOL OF BUSINESS AT THE UNIVERSITY OF MINNESOTA, THE CARLSON SCHOOL OF MANAGEMENT, IS NAMED IN HONOR OF CURTIS CARLSON, A MAJOR BENEFACTOR. IT IS RANKED AS ONE OF THE MOST HIGHLY REGARDED IN THE COUNTRY.

of offerings in the area of arts, the Twin Cities area alone has ten dance companies, twenty classical musical groups, two dozen small theaters, more than one hun-

Opposite: The Naniboujou Lodge, outside of Grand Marais, is a 1920s gem of a building on the National Register of Historic Places. Bright Cree designs bring the interior to life. © Bob Firth/Firth Photobank. Below: In southeastern Minnesota, a man enjoys a serene day of fly-fishing. © Greg Ryan-Sally Beyer

dred art galleries and enough small museums for a different weekly visit for an entire year. National touring companies include the area on their schedules, while several have chosen to stage and open productions here. Those who prefer more risk in their entertainment may opt to visit one of the state's seventeen casinos or the race track at Canterbury Park.

Business travelers are arriving in increasing numbers as cities like Duluth, St. Cloud, Minneapolis, St. Paul, Rochester, and Mankato continue to host conventions and draw delegates to Minnesota. Duluth built a convention center in 1990 specifically to keep up with the demand, only to have it ranked as the eleventh busiest in the country six years later with an occupancy rate of 74.4 percent. Thirty percent of its draw comes from national and international groups. In St. Cloud, a stepped-up promotional effort is the driving force behind a 36 percent growth in conferees over a four-year period from 1992 to 1996. Nearly one-third of the events booked in the city in 1996 were first-time users of

the facility. The St. Paul Civic Center, as well as the Mayo Civic Center in Rochester, are also currently undergoing expansions.

With so many of these Minnesota success stories reading like a Hollywood script, it's no wonder that the motion-picture industry came to investigate the state. Obviously, they liked what they found. To date, more than forty major films have been produced in Minnesota, among them *Grumpier Old Men, Little Big League, The Mighty Ducks,* and *Fargo.* As the century draws to a close, the motion-picture industry continues to showcase life in Minnesota. In fact, it currently tops the state's charts of rapidly growing industries and shows no signs of slowing down.

Left: The Radisson Hotel in Duluth is one of the many locations where the Carlson Companies make visitors feel welcome. © Bob Firth/Firth Photobank. Below: The Minneapolis Convention Center plays host to numerous important national and international gatherings every year. © Minneapolis Convention Center. Opposite: On a workday, sailboats rock idly at the dock before weekenders arrive to enjoy them. © Bob Firth/Firth Photobank

© Bob Firth/Firth Photobank

RETAIL AND WHOLESALE

GOODIN COMPANY

GUARANTEEING

TOTAL SATISFACTION,

SIXTY-YEAR-OLD

GOODIN COMPANY

BRINGS THE REGION

A VAST INVENTORY

OF PLUMBING,

INDUSTRIAL, PUMPING

AND WATER WELL,

AND HVAC SUPPLIES

GOODIN COMPANY

When the people at Goodin Company promise "total satisfaction" with their services and products, they truly are committing the reputation of their sixty-year-old company. Employees of the wholesale distributor of pipe, valves, fittings, plumbing, heating, air conditioning, and waterworks and water well supplies take the promise very seriously.

The Twin Cities skyline is punctuated by gorgeous monuments whose mechanical contractors turned first to Goodin Company to purchase material for these projects. The Norwest Tower, Federal Reserve Bank, Target Center, Galtier Plaza, and Minneapolis–St. Paul International Airport are a few of the symbols of modern Minnesota in which Goodin Company has had a hand. Key to them all is trust built over decades—trust in knowledgeable people who could be depended upon to deliver the right products on time.

Goodin Company was begun in 1937 by four men who became acquainted while working in the wholesale distribution business. Al Goodin, Les Reisberg, Irv Larson, and Howard Nelson wanted to test their belief that they could build a successful company. They set up their business in a small rented building close to downtown Minneapolis, and quickly discovered that their belief was correct. Goodin Company expanded to meet increasing demand, moving into and then outgrowing several downtown sites. Its present headquarters and central warehouse is a modern, 100,000-square-foot facility in an industrial area located minutes from downtown Minnesota.

Goodin has six other Minnesota locations. The St. Paul branch was opened in 1970. The Duluth branch warehouse opened six years later. Goodin Company appeared in Detroit Lakes in

This vignette is a sample of plumbing products on display in the Goodin Company showrooms.

1984, in St. Cloud (Waite Park) in 1990, in Brainerd in 1991, and in Medina—a smaller branch with a residential product-oriented showroom—in 1995. Two additional locations are on the drawing boards.

Regardless of size, all of the branches are "full line," and each is a convenient place for contractors to obtain material and consult with trained customer service representatives. In addition to the 195 employees in those locations, sales representatives are available in towns from Rochester and New Ulm to Faribault and Fargo. Being near its customers helps Goodin anticipate product needs and stock inventory accordingly.

Goodin Company sees its role in the economy as bringing together substantial quantities of material from diverse manufacturers. It is important to customers that goods be available nearby when they are needed.

To efficiently manage its more than 15,000 items of stock from 700 manufacturers, Goodin Company is organized into four divisions: pump and water well; plumbing; industrial; and HVAC (heating, ventilation, and air-conditioning), a group that encompasses both hydronic heating equipment and warm-air heating for residential and commercial customers.

How a vast inventory is managed for the benefit of Goodin Company's customers is a story of understanding and experience. Because they understand their customers' changing needs, Goodin Company's managers have been quick to take advantage of technological developments. Fully computerized sales transactions provide the staff instant access to all inventory and all ordering and reordering information. Current pricing, available stock, and product specifications are available in a single keystroke. All seven locations are on-line twenty-four hours a day.

Not only can customers peruse catalogs on-line, on floppy disk, and on CD, but they also can access their own accounts and inventories and enter orders at any time. Clerical errors are virtually eliminated through full Electronic Data Interchange (EDI), which standardizes transaction formats for purchase orders, shipping documents, invoices, and acknowledgments. This use of EDI ensures faster delivery and guarantees that the

product will be available at the quoted price when customers need it, saving valuable time in receiving, picking, shipping, and billing orders.

Principally, products are marketed to contractors, manufacturers, utilities, governmental agencies, and industrial end-users in Minnesota, western Wisconsin, North Dakota, and South Dakota. Goodin Company occasionally makes shipments elsewhere in the country and sometimes outside the continental United States.

Family members who are presently directors of the closely held, family-owned corporation include founder Les Reisberg's son Bernard D. Reisberg, president and chief executive officer; founder Al Goodin's son-in-law John Skagerberg, and his grandson Gregory D. Skagerberg, secretary and credit manager. Brian J. Sand is company treasurer. Other members of the board are Clarence L. Knudson, vice president; Ernest Lindstrom; Roy Otto; and Donald Vandergon.

Goodin Company officers are active in the American Supply Association, Mid-America Supply Association, United States and Minnesota Chambers of Commerce, and the chambers of cities where Goodin is located.

Using experience as its benchmark and customers' good will as its goal, the employees of Goodin Company intend to continue setting the standards by which the industry is judged.

This well-drilling equipment is in search of potable water. Goodin Company supplies a wide variety of pump and water well equipment used by contractors.

GOODIN COMPANY LOCATIONS

MINNEAPOLIS
2700 Second Street North
Minneapolis, MN 55411-1602
(612) 588-7811 or (800) 328-8433

ST. CLOUD
401 Sundial Drive
Waite Park, MN 56501-3114
(612) 259-6086 or (800) 642-6160

SAINT PAUL
285 Como Avenue
Saint Paul, MN 55103-1862
(612) 489-8831 or (800) 246-6346

BRAINERD
924 Wright Street
Brainerd, MN 56401-4405
(218) 828-4242 or (800) 292-1212

DULUTH
4424 Venture Avenue
Duluth, MN 55811-5706
(218) 727-6670 or (800) 247-0583

MEDINA
4352 Willow Drive
Medina, MN 55340-9794
(612) 478-8994 or (800) 478-8997

DETROIT LAKES
620 Davis Avenue
Detroit Lakes, MN 56501-3114
(218) 847-9211 or (800) 332-7144

BEST BUY CO., INC.

Best Buy Co., Inc., headquartered in Eden Prairie, Minnesota, is the nation's largest volume-specialty retailer in its combined categories. The company offers a wide selection of brand-name consumer electronics, home office products, entertainment software, and home appliances.

In 1966 Richard M. Schulze, the company's founder, chairman, and CEO, started "Sound of Music," a retail audio component systems business. With the advent of the VCR in the early 1980s, Schulze expanded the business to include video products and appliances.

The company adopted its current name in 1983 and became a public corporation in 1985. Four years later, Best Buy introduced Concept II, a new retail format. The company placed all its inventory on the sales floor and, with the help of noncommissioned product specialists, offered consumers great prices without the pressure.

In 1994 Best Buy took its successful format one step further, introducing Concept III. This format brought more product selection, more information, and more fun to the buying experience. The company increased the size of its stores to 45,000 square feet and began using

Best Buy product specialists provide personal service to assist customers in making purchases of the store's more complex digital products.

hands-on displays to aid the customer in understanding various product features.

"Best Buy has developed a solid marketing strategy of offering customers meaningful advantages in every aspect of the consumer shopping experience—from price, selection, and service, to store environment," says chairman and CEO Schulze.

Best Buy also offers a full range of services to better accommodate its customers. Delivery and installation are available for major appliances and large electronic products; most Best Buy stores also will install car stereos and cellular phones. Other services

Best Buy's more than 300 eye-catching stores are located near busy trade areas in major cities across the United States.

include financing, in-home repair, and in-store computer upgrade technicians.

The company's mission statement is: "We improve people's lives by making technology and entertainment products affordable and easy to use." By fulfilling its mission, it aims to create an image of Best Buy as the world's favorite and best-performing entertainment and technology retailer.

Best Buy operates more than 300 retail stores across the country, supported by 45,000 full- and part-time employees. Its corporate headquarters, central distribution warehouse, and central service department are located just outside of Minneapolis. The company also operates distribution centers in Ardmore, Oklahoma; Dinuba, California; Staunton, Virginia; and Findlay, Ohio.

According to Schulze, "We are extremely pleased by consumer response to our initiatives to improve inventory management, advertising effectiveness, and execution of services by employees in our retail stores. These efforts all contribute to our industry-leading sales performance. We created a hassle-free store with most of our products out on the shelf, not in some back room. That way customers can find what they

Richard M. Schulze, founder, chairman, and CEO of Best Buy Co., Inc., started the company in 1966, when he was just twenty-four years old. As "Sound of Music," he carried audio systems, and in the 1980s, expanded as "Best Buy" with video products and appliances.

want, grab it, and go. We replaced pushy salespeople with friendly, knowledgeable product specialists. We made shopping for our products fun. And most of all, we made it easy to get great prices on electronics, appliances, computers, and music."

Over the past six years new-store development and market-share growth have established Best Buy as an industry leader. By testing and conducting market research on its product offerings, the company has been able to create the kind of shopping experience its customers prefer.

Best Buy emphasizes the presentation and sale of digital products, such as cellular communications devices, Personal Digital Assistants (PDAs), and Digital Satellite Systems (DSSs) in a dedicated store space.

New products such as Digital Versatile Disk (DVD)—which customers have received enthusiastically—and High-Definition TV (HDTV) are bringing the future into the present. HDTV, for example, will soon provide digital broadcast television programming at performance levels once only dreamed about.

These new technologies, combined with more powerful personal computers, photo-quality laser printers, and digital cameras, will power Best Buy's business well into the twenty-first century.

"Our vision of the future improves with the opportunities presented by our strategic initiatives and by emerging technologies that are expected to produce enhanced profits. Best Buy will be at the forefront of the industry in the presentation and service of these new products," Schulze says.

Best Buy's leading position in the national launch of Digital Versatile Disc (DVD) hardware and movies is an illustration of the company's success in bringing new technology to consumers.

© Bob Firth/Firth Photobank

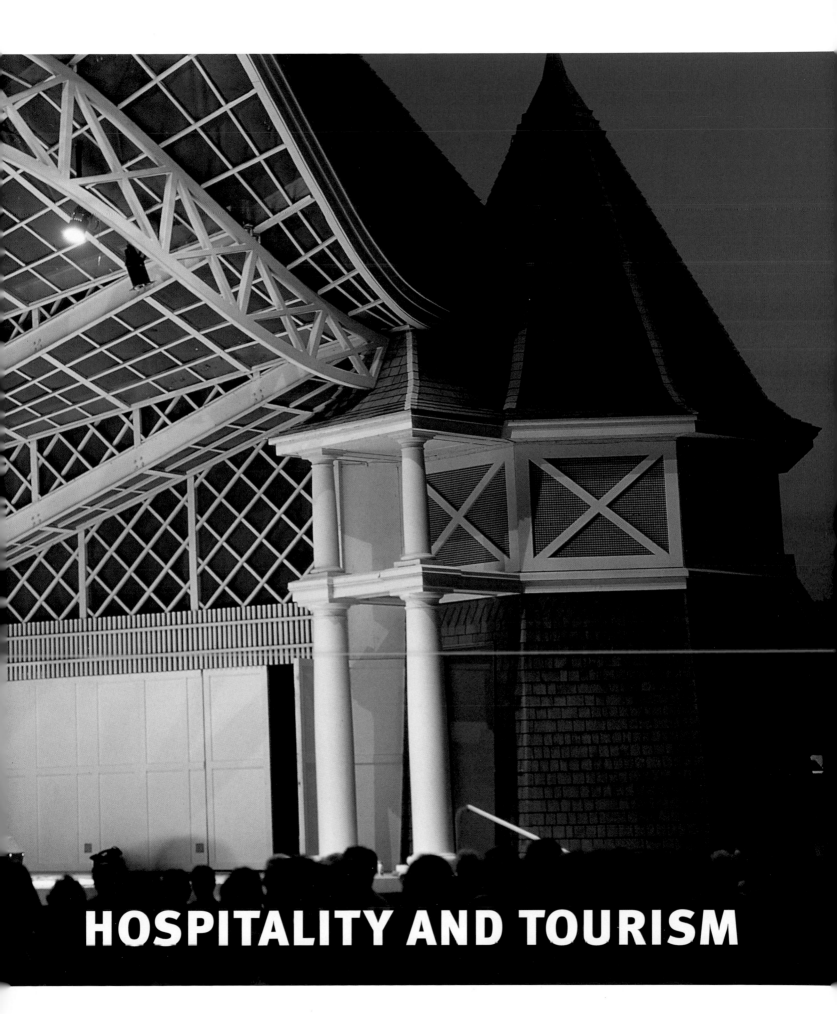

HOSPITALITY AND TOURISM

MILLE LACS BAND OF OJIBWE INDIANS

WITH ITS

WELL-REORGANIZED

GOVERNMENT—A

MODEL OF ITS KIND,

THE MILLE LACS

BAND OF OJIBWE

INDIANS IS

SUCCESSFULLY

REBUILDING ITS

COMMUNITY,

BUSINESSES,

EDUCATION, HOUSING,

HEALTH, AND

NATURAL RESOURCES

By making great strides forward, the Mille Lacs Band of Ojibwe Indians, in Central Minnesota, has established itself as a sound and economically successful community. It has risen through its own efforts, from an earlier period of oppression and poverty, to become recognized as a leader in the region, while keeping sight of its roots and values.

The Mille Lacs Band of Ojibwe is a federally recognized Indian reservation with a long and interesting history. A group of Ojibwe moved into the Mille Lacs Lake area in the 1740s, some thirty years before the existence of the United States. Through a series of agreements and treaties, the Mille Lacs Reservation was established in 1855.

The Mille Lacs Ojibwe have had many triumphs and challenges through the years. By 1901, the tribe was in a perilous economic condition. With overriding courage, it survived for the next thirty-three years. In 1934, when the Indian Reorganization Act was implemented as part of the New Deal, the Mille Lacs Ojibwe began rebuilding their reservation.

Although the effort to rebuild has been a struggle, it has succeeded because the Mille Lacs Ojibwe tribal leaders, such as Shaw Bosh Kung, Stevens, Nayquonabe, Migizi, Misquadace, and many others have worked hard to protect the tribe and to preserve it for future generations.

These leaders have always held that the principles of honesty,

The ceremonial building of the Mille Lacs Band of Ojibwe Indians was the first building constructed with new economic revenue. Ceremonial drums are the focus of spiritual gatherings that take place here throughout the year. The building is designed so the doors face the four directions; the east door, shown here, faces the rising sun. © Erik Risley

kindness, respectfulness, and hard work are the way to endure. Such principles have helped the tribe deal with the tremendous changes it has observed over the last 150 years. The ability to maintain its long-held principles enabled the Band to overcome the obstacles it faced as it sought to renew itself.

The tribal elders have been the stronghold for the tribe's culture, language, and religious beliefs. These cultural and spiritual ties have been the bond that has held the community together. Today the Mille Lacs Band of Ojibwe is considered a model of tribal government, economic prowess, and community development.

Certain changes in the structure of the tribe's government were instrumental in assisting the Mille Lacs Band of Ojibwe in reaching its goals. The tribal government is divided into three

At the Mille Lacs Indian Museum, elder Batiste Sam gives a demonstration of the intricate art of beading. © Duane's Photography

branches: the executive, the legislative, and the judicial, which have become known as the "separations of powers" form of government. The leaders of these branches are elected by the members of the tribe.

With the establishment of a tribal court and a system of laws, the band has enhanced the protection of the tribe's resources and environment. The legislative branch of tribal government, which is led by the secretary-treasurer, enacts the laws. The executive branch, administered by the chief executive, is responsible for implementation of tribal laws. Should issues arise out of the implementation of laws, the judicial branch, headed by the chief justice, has the authority to resolve these issues.

One of the first actions by the reorganized government was to establish a system of written laws and regulations, which are codified and published by West Publishing Company in Eagan, Minnesota. The tribal government operates a number of departments, including health and human services, education, administration, community development, public works, natural resources, finance, and law enforcement. The reorganized government also includes a separate corporate commission that was established to administer, develop, and provide business and economic activities for the Mille Lacs Band.

The corporate commission's first successful venture was the development of Grand Casinos Mille Lacs and Hinckley. These enterprises originated as small bingo operations in the 1980s, and have become successful businesses, employing more than 2,400 people and generating significant revenue for the tribe. The corporate commission also operates Woodlands National Bank, Onamia Bakery, M.L.B. Convenience Store, and Mille Lacs Subway. The profits from these entities help fund the operations of the tribal government, provide economic incentives for new businesses, support the building of the reservation's infrastructure, and assist in the development of much-needed housing on the reservation.

In addition, the income generated by the casino has helped the tribal government to build two ceremonial buildings for spiritual and cultural events, a new health facility, two educational facilities, two community centers, a water tower, new roads, a museum, and a new government center.

The development of the reservation's infrastructure has helped improve the standard of living, not only on the reservation, but also in the surrounding communities. Casino revenues have been used to strengthen tribal programs, to provide low-interest loans for tribal members' housing, and to grant scholarship funds for education.

By continuing perseverance, the Mille Lacs Band of Ojibwe goes forward with promising activities such as these, while at the same time maintaining the rich and important traditions and values of its long heritage.

Casting its rays of golden light across Mille Lacs Lake, the sun sets on one more day of growth and renewal for the Mille Lacs Band of Ojibwe Indians. © Sean Fahrlander

FIRSTS & INNOVATIONS FROM

1882 Minneapolis's forty-nine-foot St. Anthony Falls becomes the site of the first hydroelectric generating plant in the Western Hemisphere.

1889 Dr. William W. Mayo and his physician sons, Charles (right) and William (left), establish a clinic within St. Marys Hospital in Rochester that would soon become the Mayo Clinic—the world's first private, integrated group practice. It set the standard for the group-practice delivery of medicine worldwide.

1893 Former railroad agent Richard Sears founds the catalog sales company Sears and Roebuck.

1901 Professor Alexander Anderson invents the puffing process at the University of Minnesota, paving the way for all the puffed cereals to come.

1904 Minnesota Mining and Manufacturing (3M) develops the first sandpaper.

1911 Minnesota opens the first Better Business Bureau to fight deceptive advertising.

1917 Minnesota passes America's first comprehensive law on adoption and child welfare.

1918 Carl Wickman supervises the building of the first commercial twelve-passenger bus, an innovation that leads to the founding of the Greyhound bus company.

1919 Minnesota unveils the first armored car.

1919 Mesabi Iron Works Company begins the first taconite production.

1925 Richard Drew of 3M develops Scotch masking tape.

1926 Minneapolis's McGraw Electric Company begins selling the first electric toaster.

1926 Northwest Orient introduces the first closed-cabin commercial airplane.

1927 Minnesotan Charles Lindbergh is the first pilot to fly solo across the Atlantic Ocean.

1930 3M releases commercial-quality magnetic recording tape and Scotch transparent tape.

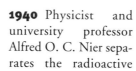

1938 Northwest Airlines tests the first practical high-altitude oxygen mask, which they developed in concert with the Mayo Clinic and Charles Lindbergh.

1940 Physicist and university professor Alfred O. C. Nier separates the radioactive isotopes uranium-238 and uranium-235, a major step into the atomic age.

1941 General Mills develops Cheerioats, the first ready-to-eat oat cereal. The company later shortens the name to Cheerios.

1941 Willis Gille of Honeywell invents the first electronic automatic pilot for aircraft.

1947 General Mills takes the powdered eggs out of its Betty Crocker cake mix, and bakers everywhere start adding fresh eggs—with excellent results.

1948 Postal worker Herb Schaper invents the Cootie game.

1949 Northwest Orient is the first airline to offer beverage service.

1950 KSTP-TV begins telecasting the first regularly scheduled 10 p.m. news program in the nation.

1950 Mayo Clinic doctors Edward C. Kendall and Philip S. Hench receive the Nobel Prize for discovering cortisone.

1952 The world's first successful open-heart surgery is performed at the University of Minnesota Hospitals and Medical School.

1953 Polaris Industries is the first company to mass produce snowmobiles.

1955 The University of Minnesota Hospitals and Medical School unveils the world's first successful heart-lung machine.

1956 Southdale, the first enclosed shopping mall, opens in Edina.

1958 Doctors at the University of Minnesota Hospitals and Medical School perform the world's first successful heart-valve replacement surgery with an artificial valve.

1962 Lyle Stevmermer introduces the first agricultural weighing device to weigh a continuous flow of grain.

THE LAND OF 10,000 LAKES

1962 Sidney Knutson of Minnesota introduces a plastic holder for the one-half-gallon milk carton.

1964 Carl Oja introduces the four-footed "quad cane," which gives users more confidence and stability, especially going up and down stairs.

1966 Doctors at the University of Minnesota Hospitals and Medical School perform the world's first successful pancreas transplant.

1968 Doctors at the University of Minnesota Hospitals and Medical School perform the world's first successful bone-marrow transplant.

1969 Doctors at the Mayo Clinic perform the first hip-replacement surgery.

1973 The Mayo Clinic installs the first CAT scanner in North America.

1973 The Minnesota Educational Computing Consortium (MECC) creates the first instructional computer simulation for classroom use.

1977 The University of Minnesota builds the world's first total-body CAT scanner.

1979 MECC creates and grants the first school-site licenses in the country.

1979 3M begins a major Post-it Notes rollout, resulting in nationwide acceptance of, and thousands of orders for, the new office item by 1980.

1980 Brothers Scott and Brennan Olson create the first Rollerblades in their parents' Minneapolis basement.

1985 Minnesota begins the first state-tax-funded public information and education campaign to deter young people from smoking.

1985 3M releases refastenable diaper tapes.

1986 Musicland Group opens Suncoast Motion Picture Company, the first retail chain to specialize in selling movies on videotape.

1986 Minnesota senator Walter Mondale is the first candidate for the U.S. presidency to choose a woman, Geraldine Ferraro, as his running mate.

1986 St. Paul–born teacher Ann Bancroft spends fifty-six days walking 550 miles to the North Pole.

1988 Northwest Airlines is the first national carrier to ban smoking on domestic flights.

1989 Minnesotan Will Steger leads the first Antarctic crossing by dogsled.

1991 Paul Lindner and Mark P. McCahill from the University of Minnesota release the Gopher, one of the Internet's first search engines.

1992 Mall of America, the largest shopping and entertainment complex in the country, opens in Bloomington.

1992 The state passes the Minnesota-Care law, a milestone in health-care reform that provides subsidized health coverage for the uninsured, particularly preventive care for children.

1992 Minnesota passes one of the most progressive clean-air fuel programs in the country, requiring all gasoline sold in the state to contain an oxygenate by the year 1997.

1993 The University of Minnesota's Crookston campus is the first in the United States to provide every full-time student with a notebook computer.

1993 Ann Bancroft concludes her 1,700-mile trek on skis to the South Pole, becoming the first woman to reach both poles by foot.

1994 Cargill introduces a process for making a biodegradable plastic on a large scale, lowering the cost of production from $300 per pound to $3 per pound.

1994 Colonial Craft in St. Paul becomes the first Minnesota millwork manufacturer to receive "green certification" from the USDA Forest Service.

1994 Honeywell launches the country's first mail-in thermostat recycling plan to protect the environment from mercury in thermostats.

1997 The "Mankato Connection," born through a collaboration of Mankato State University, South Central Technical College, Lucent Technologies, AT&T, and Motorola, is the first program established anywhere to train technical professionals in cellular communications.

HISTORICAL HIGHLIGHTS

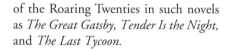

AREA: 86,943 square miles
POPULATION: 4,685,549
STATE CAPITAL: St. Paul, since 1849
STATE MOTTO: *L'Etoile du Nord,* "The Star of the North"
STATEHOOD: Admitted as the thirty-second state on May 11, 1858
STATE BIRD: Common loon
STATE FLOWER: Showy lady's slipper
STATE NICKNAMES: Gopher State, North Star State, Land of Ten Thousand Lakes, Land of Sky-Blue Waters, and Bread and Butter State

© Hilber Nelson

PEOPLE

LA VERNE (1916–1967), **MAXENE** (1918–1995), and **PATTI** (1920–) **ANDREWS,** Minneapolis-born singers who later became the popular Andrews Sisters. They entertained U.S. troops and Americans during World War II. Famous tunes included "Rum and Cola" and "Boogie Woogie Bugle Boy of Company B."

PATTY BERG, born Patricia June Berry in Minneapolis in 1918; champion golfer. She won eighty-three golf tournaments between 1935 and 1981, including the 1938 U.S. Women's Amateur championship and 1946 U.S. Women's Open championship.

WILLIAM ORVILLE DOUGLAS (1898–1980), born in Maine, Minnesota; teacher, lawyer, judge; U.S. Supreme Court associate justice from 1939 to 1975. A staunch defender of the Bill of Rights and the indigent, he led fights for conservation and freedom of speech.

BOB DYLAN, born Robert Zimmerman in 1941 in Duluth. As a folk, rock, and country musician and composer, he influenced a whole generation of people. His well-loved songs include "Blowin' in the Wind" and "Like a Rolling Stone."

FRANCIS SCOTT FITZGERALD (1896–1940), born in St. Paul; writer. He depicted free-living wealthy society of the Roaring Twenties in such novels as *The Great Gatsby, Tender Is the Night,* and *The Last Tycoon.*

JUDY GARLAND (1922–1969), born Frances Gumm in Grand Rapids; singer and actress. Her best-known films are *The Wizard of Oz, Meet Me in St. Louis, A Star Is Born,* and *Easter Parade.*

JEAN PAUL GETTY (1892–1976), born in Minneapolis; businessman. He earned $4 billion in the oil business. Much of his extensive art collection is now housed at The Getty Center in Los Angeles, one of North America's premier art institutions.

JESSICA LANGE, born in Cloquet in 1949; actress. Lange won the 1982 Academy Award for Best Supporting Actress in the film *Tootsie.* Some of her other memorable movie performances include roles in *Frances* and *A Streetcar Named Desire.*

SINCLAIR LEWIS (1885–1951), born in Sauk Centre; writer. He portrayed small-town life in such books as *Main Street, Arrowsmith, Babbitt,* and *Elmer Gantry.* He was the first American to win the Nobel Prize in literature (1930).

PRINCE ROGERS NELSON, born in Minneapolis in 1958; singer, musician. His *Purple Rain* album has sold more than ten million copies. He has a recording studio in the Twin Cities area.

WINONA RYDER, born in Winona, Minnesota, in 1971; actress. Her work includes roles in the films *Edward Scissorhands, Mermaids,* and *Little Women.*

CHARLES SCHULZ, born in Minneapolis in 1922; cartoonist. He created the widely popular "Peanuts" strip in 1950. Today, it appears in 2,300 newspapers in sixty-eight countries.

ELAINE STATELY (1937–1988), born on the White Earth Indian Reservation in the west-central part of the state; activist. An Ojibwa, Stately helped found the American Indian Movement and the Native American Olympics.

DID YOU KNOW...?

! In 1997 and 1998, Minnesota received the Most Livable State Award from Morgan Quitno Press, which compiles and publishes annual statistics on the fifty states. Minnesota's superior quality of life includes a low crime rate, excellent educational opportunities, above-average level of personal income and growth in the same, and the highest rate of home ownership in the nation, 75.4 percent.

! Calling Minnesota the Land of 10,000 Lakes is an understatement. Truth is, the state has 15,291 lakes, or 22,000 when ponds of less than ten acres are counted.

! Minnesota's state art agencies spend more than twice the national average per capita on the arts, ranking the North Star State second, behind Hawaii.

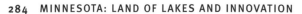

! Eagle Mountain, at 2,301 feet, is the highest point in Minnesota. The lowest elevation is along Lake Superior, at 602 feet.

! Duluth, Minnesota, together with nearby Superior, Wisconsin, is the busiest freshwater port in North America and the farthest inland ocean port in the United States.

! Ninety-five percent of Minnesotans live within five miles of recreational water.

! The country's oldest winter festival is the St. Paul Winter Carnival, begun in 1886. Attracting fun-lovers from miles around, the fête features speed-skating and ice-carving contests and horse-drawn sleighs. When weather permits, an ice castle is built. The 1992 castle, with its 167-foot tower, was the tallest ice structure ever made.

! Minnesota Public Radio has one of the largest bases of membership for public radio in the country, with more than seventy thousand members. With twenty-nine public stations, it is the nation's largest regional public radio system. MPR developed the country's most popular radio program of the last quarter-century, *A Prairie Home Companion*.

! In 1938, entrepreneur Curtis L. Carlson took out a fifty-five dollar loan and established the Gold Bond Stamp Company. Today the business is known as Carlson Companies, one of the largest privately held companies in the world.

! The Greater Twin Cities Youth Symphony, begun in 1972, is the largest youth symphony program in the United States, allowing about one thousand students to participate in several area orchestras throughout the year.

! A surveyor's error in the 1820s resulted in the Northwest Angle's being cut off from the rest of the state—and country. This peninsula, which is home to the Red Lake Indian Reservation, is the northernmost point of the lower forty-eight states and is separated from Minnesota by Canada and Lake of the Woods.

MEMORABLE MOMENTS OF THE 20TH CENTURY

1905 The construction of the present state capitol in St. Paul is completed.

1915 The Mayo Clinic, located in Rochester, opens the first graduate school of medicine.

1926 WCCO Radio broadcasts the first singing radio commercial to cross U.S. airwaves, posing the musical question, "Have you tried Wheaties?"

1928 Minnesota-based Northwest Airlines is the first U.S. airline to operate an international route.

1931 Minnesota establishes a department of conservation, one of the first states to do so.

1948 The National Broadcasting Company (NBC) gets its first affiliate when the Twin Cities' KSTP-TV signs on, also becoming the first television station between Chicago and the West Coast.

1957 Earl Bakken develops the first wearable, external, battery-powered, transistorized pacemaker. His company, Medtronic,

begins production on the first implantable cardiac pacemaker.

1962 Myrtle Allen exhibits the first inflatable life preserver, which also is the first life preserver with a pillow in back to support an unconscious person's head.

1971 Minnesota is the first state to ratify the Twenty-sixth Amendment, which gave eighteen-year-olds the right to vote.

1977 Minnesotan Walter Mondale, a U.S. senator from 1964 to 1977, becomes vice president of the United States under President Jimmy Carter.

1985 Seymour Cray, inventor of the supercomputer, which was unveiled in 1976, develops the Cray-2 supercomputer, ten times faster than the first edition and featuring circuits of gallium arsenide instead of silicon chips.

1987 The Minnesota Twins best the St. Louis Cardinals to win the World Series, the state's first national sports championship in more than thirty years. They do it again, against the Atlanta Braves, in 1991.

1992 Augustine Medical develops the Bair Hugger warming blanket, reducing risks from distress associated with perioperative hypothermia.

1992 The Mall of America, the largest shopping and entertainment complex in the country, opens in Bloomington and becomes a resounding success for itself and the surrounding community. As of 1998, with its more than 40 million annual visitors, many of them tourists, the mall attracts more people than Disney World, the Grand Canyon, and the Statue of Liberty combined.

STATE REFLECTIONS: ESSAYS

PART FOUR

MINNESOTA'S TOP LEADERS, VISIONARIES IN BOTH THE PUBLIC AND PRIVATE SECTORS, ARE PERFECTLY POSITIONED TO REFLECT UPON THE EXPANDING PARAMETERS OF OUR WORLD. LOOKING BACK AT REMARKABLE MOMENTS IN THEIR SECTORS' HISTORY, REPRESENTATIVES FROM AGRICULTURE, ARTS, BANKING, CHARITABLE CONTRIBUTIONS, COMMUNICATIONS, EDUCATION, ENERGY, MANUFACTURING, PROFESSIONALS, TRADE AND ECONOMIC DEVELOPMENT, AND TRANSPORTATION OFFER US A GLIMPSE OF THE FUTURE—BOTH AS THEY SEE IT AND AS THEY WOULD LIKE IT TO BE.

EACH ESSAYIST HAS WITNESSED DEVELOPMENTS IN HIS OR HER FIELD THAT CHANGED OUR LIVES, GAVE HOPE TO THE WORLD. AND EACH LOOKS TO THE PIONEERS OF THE NEXT CENTURY TO CARRY THE DREAM FORWARD. JUST AS YESTERDAY'S IMPOSSIBILITIES BECAME TODAY'S "ORDINARY MIRACLES," IN THE WORDS OF ONE ESSAYIST, SO THE CHALLENGES OF TOMORROW WILL BE MET BY THE INGENUITY OF TODAY. IT IS OUR TASK, THE ESSAYISTS BELIEVE, TO BOTH EMBRACE GLOBALIZATION AND EXPAND THE VALUE WE PLACE ON HUMAN INTERACTION. WHEN WE ALLOW THE IMAGINATION TO SOAR, THEY SAY, NOT ONLY WILL WE TRANSFORM THE SOCIAL AND ECONOMIC LANDSCAPES OF MINNESOTA, BUT ADVANCE EARTH'S CIVILIZATION IN THE NEW MILLENNIUM.

A summer sunset layers the colors of the heavens over central Minnesota's Lake Mille Lacs, where a solitary boat waits to greet the coming dawn. A perfect time for reflection, the closing of today brings new ideas for tomorrow. © Grey Ryan-Sally Beyer

THE LIGHTS OF TOMORROW

ERNEST S. MICEK,
Chairman and Chief Executive Officer, Cargill, Inc.

After graduating from the University of Wisconsin in 1959 with a chemical engineering degree, Ernest S. Micek got his start with Cargill, Incorporated, as a shift supervisor at a soybean processing plant in Virginia. From there, Mr. Micek assumed a series of additional responsibilities, including being named president of the corn milling division in 1981 and of Cargill's food sector in 1992. In 1995 he was named chairman and chief executive officer of the company, which markets, processes, and distributes agricultural, food, financial, and industrial products internationally. Cargill has grown from a single grain warehouse in Conover, Iowa, back in 1865 into a global company with 79,000 employees in more than 1,000 locations in 72 countries.

I grew up on a hilly, 250-acre dairy farm in west central Wisconsin, where my family's main income came from twenty-five dairy cows and a few hogs, sheep and laying hens that were fed from corn, oats, and hay grown on the farm.

It was during this era in the 1940s that hybrid seeds—specially bred to incorporate the best of what a plant species has to offer—came into widespread use. Production skyrocketed over the next fifty years. Nationwide, corn yields per acre today are four times what they were when I was a young boy.

Hybrid seeds—along with the careful use of fertilizers and other crop inputs—revolutionized life on the farm. They brought rising yields and more income for my family as well as for our neighbors. Soon these innovations began to spread around the world. Several years later, the Argentine Ministry of Agriculture called hybrid corn "the most important single development in our agriculture today."

Norman Borlaug, a University of Minnesota graduate who won the Nobel Peace Prize in 1970, carried these improvements to new heights. Borlaug helped develop the high-yield dwarf wheat that literally helped save the lives of millions of people in the developing world—most notably in India and Pakistan in what came to be known as the Green Revolution.

HIGH-YIELD DWARF WHEAT LITERALLY HELPED SAVE THE LIVES OF MILLIONS OF PEOPLE IN THE DEVELOPING WORLD

GROWTH STIMULATES DEMAND

The income of Indian farmers increased by a factor of four, which triggered more investment in farm equipment. Brick houses began to replace those made of earth. And people began investing in a variety of things to improve their lives, including transistor radios, which provided an avenue for the government to broadcast educational programs.

Newfound economic growth in much of the developing world is stimulating the demand for agricultural products produced on farms such as this. © Greg Ryan-Sally Beyer

Throughout history and throughout the world, improvement in the agricultural sector has been the spark that has fueled both economic and intellectual growth, beginning with the scratch plow in ancient Egypt and continuing today with the biotechnology revolution.

The newfound economic growth in much of the developing world is stimulating the demand for agricultural products. And the bold steps taken after World War II to promote trade and economic development through international agreements such as the General Agreement on Tariffs and Trade have helped ensure this demand could be met.

Today's global food system—built upon expanding international trade—should mark this century as the one that ended the threat of famine. Food production is outpacing population growth. And dramatic improvements in the distribution system enable areas of surplus to quickly supply areas of need, creating unprecedented food security. Only where there is civil disorder or decisions by leaders to isolate their people are food supplies still physically insecure. And only where poverty is extreme are food supplies still financially insecure.

NEW TOOLS FOR A NEW WORLD

But there is hope there, too. Cargill's vision is to raise living standards around the world. Everywhere we look, we see people lifting themselves up. Globalization is creating a more open world. Trade barriers are falling. The centrally planned economies of the former Soviet Union are restructuring. The Internet is ushering in rapid change. And the freedoms embodied by market-oriented reforms are spreading.

Electricity didn't come to my family's farm until 1948. The day the lights came on in rural America is very real for me. Today, more lights are coming on everywhere I look.

A supervisor at a forest tree nursery in Willow River checks the progress of red pine seedlings, thus ensuring the continuation of this vital part of the environment. © Greg Ryan-Sally Beyer

THROUGHOUT HISTORY, IMPROVEMENTS IN AGRICULTURE WERE THE SPARK THAT FUELED BOTH ECONOMIC AND INTELLECTUAL GROWTH

Biotechnology is poised to usher in the next revolution in agricultural production. It offers new tools for combating pests and disease, increasing yields, protecting the environment, and developing nutritional and other qualities consumers want. Farmers are using satellites and computers to map their fields, which allows them to deliver nutrients more precisely to crops and reduce the impact on the environment. In the coming century, environmental concerns and finding renewable energy sources will be more important than ever.

I spent the first four years of my formal education attending a one-room schoolhouse. A lot has happened since then, to say the least. But I've learned never to underestimate the power of the human mind and the will of the human spirit to meet the challenges ahead. From my perspective, the future has never looked brighter.

ARTS: THE GATEWAY TO LIFE

ROBERT C. BOOKER,
Executive Director, Minnesota State Arts Board

Robert C. Booker joined the staff of the Minnesota State Arts Board in 1985 and has served as executive director of the organization since 1997. After beginning his career in arts administration with the South Dakota Arts Council, in 1977 he accepted an invitation to join the staff of the Minneapolis Institute of Arts, making Minnesota his home. Among Mr. Booker's many activities, he has served on advisory panels for the National Endowment for the Arts and a number of state, regional, and local funding agencies. He is a member of the Minnesota AIDS Project board of directors as well as the Leadership Committee of the National Assembly of State Arts Agencies.

When I was seven my dad purchased season tickets for us to attend the Virginia Children's Theater. Mom reminded me over and over again that live theater was very different from cartoons. "The people on the stage are real, just like you and me," she said. "It's not like movies or cartoons."

So one Saturday morning, Dad and I headed for our first live theatrical experience. The production began with a flourish, and all of a sudden a fairy godmother flew through the window onto the stage!

At that moment, the reality and the power of theater were clear to me.

Astonished, I jumped out of my seat and ran down the aisle for the back of the theater, with my father close behind. All I could gasp was, "Too real for me, Dad, way too real."

Having overcome the initial shock, I now regularly attend live theater with little or no fear of what I will experience there. Like many of us, I savor the experience.

A number of studies report that attending arts events at a young age increases one's attendance at such activities as an adult. Studies also show that those early childhood experiences in the arts serve us for a lifetime.

As evidence, students of the arts continue to outperform their nonarts peers on the Scholastic Assessment Test, according to the College Entrance Examination Board. Another report from the United States Department of Education shows that 72.5 percent of tenth-grade students who actively participated in the arts scored within the top two quartiles of the Grade 10 Standard Test Composite. Those who had little involvement in the arts measured considerably lower.

Children who participate in the arts develop more advanced problem-solving skills and interpersonal communication tools. Their cognitive development is increased and they gain better critical thinking ability.

CHILDREN EXPOSED TO THE ARTS BECOME 'CHANGE AGENTS' AS ADULTS, DRIVING NEW TRENDS

Federal, state, and local support for the arts, including the Minnesota Orchestra, shown here, will continue to have an impact on the state's economy. © Alvin Upitis

An Upward Spiral

The future of our state is dependent upon children with skills such as these. Young people not only will be our audience members in the years to come, but will have important roles as decision makers and leaders in our communities. Children exposed to the arts become the adults who are called "change agents"—those who create new technologies . . . drive new trends.

Our children's solid background in the arts will ensure the high quality of life we in Minnesota have come to expect, and will maintain a standard of living that will continue into the new millennium.

Looking to the future I see a number of trends. Technology will continue to expand access to the arts in many ways. Locally, Minnesota museums are working to digitize their collections for use in classrooms across the state. Currently a group of Minnesota artists is involved in a project that will allow artists from around the world to work with students in Minnesota classrooms through real-time interactive television. The examples are endless.

SOON ARTISTS AROUND THE WORLD WILL BE WORKING WITH STUDENTS IN MINNESOTA CLASSROOMS THROUGH REAL-TIME INTERACTIVE TELEVISION

We will also see the continued economic impact of the arts. Communities statewide are experiencing revitalization as historic theaters situated on their main streets are renovated, regional arts centers are expanded, and arts festivals become tourist destinations. The economic impact on our communities is visible.

Leading the Way

A recent economic study shows that arts in Minnesota generate 900 million dollars in indirect revenue for the state. Federal, state, and local support for the arts will continue to have an impact on the Minnesota economy as, it is said, one dollar from the National Endowment for the Arts leverages between eleven and twenty dollars from other sources—a hard investment record to match in any sector.

In the future, I believe Minnesota arts will continue to lead the nation in innovative programming that entertains and engages. Our museums, dance companies, theaters, and literary organizations will continue to be recognized for their excellent work. Arts will continue to be an important part of a well-rounded education. Artists will continue to expand partnerships with community groups that address social issues of importance to both rural and urban areas.

Isn't it good to know that some things remain the same?

Artists will continue to inspire us with their voices in our temples and churches. Musicians will continue to march in our towns' Fourth of July parades. Minnesota writers will continue to craft the books that we curl up with at bedtime.

. . . And actors will continue to make our stories so real that our children can fly, too.

A Minnesota Ballet performance is one of many such arts experiences that plant the seed for young people to become decision makers and leaders.
© *Jeff Frey & Associates*

BANKING IN MINNESOTA

WES W. EHRECKE,
Executive Vice President and Chief Executive Officer,
Minnesota Bankers Association

Wes Ehrecke is executive vice president and chief executive officer of the Minnesota Bankers Association, positions he has held since July 1, 1995. Prior to assuming these responsibilities, Mr. Ehrecke was chief executive officer of the Iowa Association of Rural Electric Cooperatives and previously held the position of senior vice president of the Iowa Bankers Association. He is an active member of the American Society of Association Executives and earned his Certified Association Executive (CAE) designation in 1990.

In retrospect, the banking industry in Minnesota experienced significant changes throughout the 1900s. From our state's first private bank, which was established in 1834, to today's readily available banking services industry, the changes are easy to note.

Banks are no longer private, but instead are chartered by either the state of Minnesota or the federal government. Because of the powerful influence banks have had on commerce and the economy, the industry has become one of the most highly regulated in the nation.

These regulations were put in place to protect both the consumer and the financial institutions themselves.

> **TECHNOLOGICAL ADVANCES HAVE INCREASED SEVERALFOLD THE CHOICES AND CONVENIENCE NOW AVAILABLE**

With the enactment of legislation in 1933 that provided for the Federal Deposit Insurance Corporation, consumers are now assured that their personal accounts will be protected up to the amount of 100,000 dollars per account. This congressional action served to allay customer fears and enabled the financial industry to continue growing strongly.

In the last decade of the twentieth century, lawmakers began deregulation of this very regulated industry, with the result that more and more nonbank entities have begun offering banklike services and products. This increased competition has been a boon for the consumer, in that a wide range of financial services with varied fee structures has become available at a great many different types of institutions.

ANYWHERE, ANYTIME

Couple these changes with the technological advances of the last half of this century, and you will find that banking services are now available twenty-four hours a day, 365 days per year, essentially making banking available anywhere, anytime. Innovations such as ATMs (automatic

Like telephone and online banking services, automated teller machines such as this have made banking available anytime—quite a change from just a few decades ago. © PhotoDisc, Inc.

teller machines), telephone banking, and on-line banking have increased severalfold the choices and convenience of opportunities available to every consumer.

Banks are also a linchpin in their communities. They have been and will continue to be a catalyst for helping their communities grow. As an industry, we bankers point with pride to the economic assistance we provide our community and neighbors, which in turn strengthens our hometowns and the nation.

At its essence, commercial banking activity remains today, and into the future, responsible for deposit taking, transactions, lending, and investing. However, the form that each of those activities takes may be very different in the future. From the time of the Industrial Revolution at the turn of the century to the coming Information Age at the turn of the next century, our

'THE IMPOSSIBILITIES OF TODAY HAVE BECOME THE CUSTOMARY THINGS OF THE MORROW. BUT WHAT AMERICAN IS EVER CONTENT?'

industry has made—and will continue to make—the changes necessary to meet our customers' needs.

We are convinced that competition will continue in the financial services marketplace. Knowing and understanding our customers on an individual basis and providing the services they desire necessitate strong sales, marketing, and technology skills. Looking to the future, banking will require a highly trained workforce that is able to provide the diversity of products and services that will be expected by our customers and communities in years to come. At its heart, a balanced combination of high-contact relationships and high-tech services will be essential in order for the industry to continue to grow and prosper.

At the centennial celebration of the Minnesota Bankers Association in 1989, we had the opportunity to remember our industry's past and make predictions to be placed in a time capsule. In reviewing that event, I was particularly struck by the recorded remarks of a speaker at our organization's annual convention in 1901.

LIMITLESS TOMORROWS

"Looking back upon the achievements of the past century, one is struck with the marvelous progress made in the adaptability of material things to the uses of mankind, until one is almost tempted to ask, Is not this the end? The impossibilities of today have become the customary things of the morrow. But what American is ever content? Past successes seem but to stimulate [one] to greater zeal, and the desire to exploit new fields, to attain greater deeds, engages [both] waking hours and dreams at night."

As we move into the coming millennium, Minnesota bankers will continue to be optimistic about the future and to provide our customers and communities with the services that have made this state and nation strong.

The new federal reserve building in downtown Minneapolis stands as a symbol of industry regulation, protecting both the consumer and financial institutions themselves. The deregulation of the nineties, however, has increased competition and enabled nonbank entities to offer banklike services with a variety of fee structures. © Conrad Bloomquist/Scenic Photo!

CHARITABLE CONTRIBUTIONS

THE ROLE OF PHILANTHROPY

REATHA CLARK KING, PH.D.,
President and Executive Director, General Mills Foundation

Dr. Reatha Clark King was named president and executive director of the General Mills Foundation in 1988. The foundation, established in 1954, makes grants to tax-exempt organizations in the areas of education, family life, health and nutrition, and arts and cultural affairs. In addition to being CEO for the foundation, Dr. King is in charge of the company's overall 30 million dollar citizenship and charitable giving program. She joined General Mills after eleven years as president of Metropolitan State University in the Twin Cities. In addition to her many community service activities, Dr. King is well known as a pioneer in social change and for outstanding leadership in the fields of education, business, and philanthropy.

As a community, Minnesota is like a tough, beautiful fabric with several vital threads interwoven to make it so unique and such a star on the national scene. The nonprofit sector, which includes philanthropy, is one of the threads that make Minnesota such a progressive state. While philanthropy technically means making grants to nonprofit organizations and contributions to favorite charities, philanthropy in Minnesota implies a long tradition of leadership in problem solving and services to individuals and communities. Minnesota's heritage of maintaining a strong nonprofit sector is vital for addressing our country's demographic, social, and economic issues of the twenty-first century.

INCREASING THE FULLNESS OF OPPORTUNITY FOR PEOPLE IS OFTEN AN OBJECTIVE OF PHILANTHROPIC PROJECTS

Among the many major social and political changes in this century that have had an impact on the philanthropic community is the structuring of the Internal Revenue Service tax code to allow tax deductions for charitable contributions. This law helped create a favorable climate for philanthropic contributions and greatly increased the donation of charitable dollars by individuals and for-profit organizations, making possible many community services, innovations, and discoveries that would not have been possible without the private funding.

Another important change has been the passage of laws that have made our society fairer, more just, and more equitable in its treatment of people. This includes the passage of civil rights laws that made racial and gender discrimination illegal, increased voter registration, reduced discrimination in housing and employment practices, increased educational opportunities, and improved health services for children and families. Philanthropy was a factor in getting the laws changed because many individuals and foundations provided charitable contributions to support the pioneer civil rights movements in this century. Because increasing the fullness of

The nonprofit sector contributes volunteers, cash, and in-kind resources to the community, helping make possible this Guthrie Theatre performance, Too Clever by Half. © Greg Ryan-Sally Beyer

opportunity for people is so often an objective of philanthropic projects, the field itself is helped by having laws in place that favor the good treatment of people.

ADVANCING SOCIAL CHANGE

Many great minds and discoveries have influenced our sector in this century. Eleanor Roosevelt and Martin Luther King Jr. were courageous leaders; Mary McLeod Bethune was dedicated to educating young minds; John Gardner believed in the power of the nonprofit sector and private initiative; Kenneth Dayton of Minnesota set the example of giving back to the community. These individuals epitomize what servant leadership is about, and they are great models for the next millennium. The polio vaccine, the elimination of apartheid in South Africa, and thousands of educational scholarships to students are examples of the social progress made possible by private philanthropy in this century, and are indicators of the power of philanthropy to advance social change and civilization in the next millennium.

Gazing into my crystal ball, I see progress toward world peace, increased prosperity for people in underdeveloped countries, and a "smaller" and less distant world made possible by instant communication on the Internet.

Because of the effectiveness of its business, government, and nonprofit sectors, the state of Minnesota will continue to be a leader in the next millennium for addressing social, economic, and political issues. The nonprofit sector contributes volunteers, cash, and in-kind resources to the community, along with a bundle of ideas and innovations for solving community problems *while they are small.* In Minnesota, if someone has a good idea for improving the community, it is easy to convene a group to discuss it and develop plans to test whether it is workable.

This kind of community activism is the genesis of Minnesota's vibrant character and quality of life.

Increased educational opportunity, as illustrated by this young social studies student, is typical of the social progress made possible in this century by private philanthropy. © David Stover/Uniphoto, Inc.

THE POLIO VACCINE, MADE POSSIBLE BY PRIVATE PHILANTHROPY, IS AN INDICATOR OF THE POWER TO ADVANCE CIVILIZATION IN THE NEXT MILLENNIUM

Philanthropy in Minnesota is enduring and effective because there are many players and a fine balance of large and small grant-making foundations involved, along with a large number of individual givers. There exists a tradition of giving by all for the common good.

TOWARD A PROGRESSIVE FUTURE

In the twenty-first century, our philanthropic community will benefit tremendously from the intergenerational transfer of wealth, globalization of the marketplace—which will also be the vehicle for increased communications of nonprofit organizations in different countries—the Internet, and other yet-to-be-discovered tools for communication. In the future, effective leaders of our sector must seek to understand and alleviate poverty, support innovations and encourage discoveries that might alleviate human suffering, and be tenacious about pursuing good ideas for social progress that governments and businesses might hesitate to pursue.

COMMUNICATIONS
BEYOND WORDS

WILLIAM J. CADOGAN,
Chairman and Chief Executive Officer, ADC Telecommunications, Inc.

After joining ADC in 1987 as vice president, private network marketing, William J. Cadogan was appointed president and chief operating officer in 1990 and elected president and chief executive officer in 1991. He has been chairman of the board since 1994. Mr. Cadogan joined ADC from the International Telecommunications Satellite Organization (Intelsat) in Washington, D.C.; his extensive background in telecommunications also includes fifteen years with AT&T. He is currently vice chairman of the Telecommunications Industry Association (TIA) and a member of the board of governors of the Electronics Industry Association (EIA), and serves on the boards of several other companies.

As humans, we are unique in our ability to master information and in our innate desire to communicate what we know. Communications technology increases both the quantity and quality of information we can convey, and basically changes the way we relate to one another and understand ourselves.

Spoken language, one of our earliest forms of communication, allowed us to begin developing culture, history, and technology. Eventually writing extended the reach of communication so that face-to-face transfer was no longer required. Those few with access to the written word could learn from people of other places and times. In 1450, Gutenberg's printing press replaced laborious hand copying and gave many more of us access to information, old and new, from around the world.

With the invention of the telephone in 1876, communication could combine the immediacy of the spoken word with writing's geographic reach. Modern telecommunication was born. And as telephony developed, two even newer industries—data processing and broadcasting—emerged and grew. By the late 1970s, each communications field was dominated by a handful of industry giants, each heavily invested in the status quo. Then, less than twenty years ago, everything changed.

> ## THE SPEED WITH WHICH CHANGE OCCURS SUGGESTS THE STRENGTH OF OUR DRIVE TO COMMUNICATE

INFORMATION REVOLUTION

In the 1980s, the dominance of the mighty mainframe was challenged by the personal computer; network television found itself competing with dozens of cable TV companies; and Judge Harold Greene forced telephone giant AT&T to divest itself of seven regional Bell operating companies and opened the door to the industry's first real competition in a century. The changes shook

Still a boon in this age of unlimited access to information, a headset brings the spoken word directly—and quietly—to the user at any time.
© Harry Bartlett/FPG International

all three industries, but also generated unprecedented growth and innovation. What has been called the Information Revolution will likely be seen as a turning point in history rivaling the Industrial Revolution. The 1980s were a decade of chaotic change, but they gave rise to a new order that will affect business and the world well into the next century.

While leadership of the telephone, broadcasting, and data processing industries was fragmenting, the industries themselves began to converge. With the help of communications technology, computing decentralized, first within the office over small local area networks (LANs) and then worldwide. Today most computer users think nothing of accessing data from distant servers (surfing the Net) whose locations they'll never know.

TELEPHONES SPROUT MODEM JACKS, TINY VIDEO CAMERAS PERCH ATOP OUR PCS, AND DATA STREAMS INTO THE GROWING RIVER OF INFORMATION

At the same time, cable and telephony began nibbling at one another's markets. The very concept of broadcasting was challenged as cable and then the Internet began "narrowcasting," creating increasingly specialized data streams focused on areas such as sports, news, finance, and entertainment. Telephones detached themselves from our walls and migrated, first into our cars, then into our pockets.

Fifteen years ago, the modems that allowed computers to communicate over phone lines operated at 300 bits/second. Today the standard has become 56,000 bits/second, with even faster technologies already emerging. The speed with which these changes are occurring can't be attributed solely to technology. Change is being "pulled" by market demand, a suggestion of the strength of our drive to communicate.

Today the dissolution of industry boundaries gallops on. Our children think nothing of plugging Sega or Nintendo computers into our televisions. Web TV is moving data communication from computers to televisions. Telephones have

Millions of tiny data streams flow over increasingly fast modems as the drive to communicate rushes ever forward. © ADC Telecommunications, Inc.

sprouted modem jacks, tiny video cameras perch atop our PCs, and millions of tiny data streams join together in a river of information that grows larger every day.

Over the last fifteen years, the individual user's access to stored data has risen from kilobytes (thousands) to megabytes (millions) to gigabytes (billions) of characters of data. Terabytes (trillions) are just around the corner. Startling as they are, the numbers do not begin to measure the change taking place around us.

Via the Internet, users can access unlimited stores of information. Time frames for knowledge dissemination, once limited by the pace of print-based publishing, have shrunk to days, hours, or even minutes.

LIMITLESS POSSIBILITIES

The change is affecting the way we think. Academics and scientists who once worked in isolation, communicating their findings in quarterly journals and at annual conferences, can now share their ideas from the moment they arise. Communication costs are plummeting as the degree of access grows. This access to knowledge is beyond anything that philosophers ever dreamed of. As we enter the new millennium, we can continue to innovate, but as for the technology itself, we can only guess at its power and possibilities.

KNOWLEDGE DRIVES THE FUTURE

MARK G. YUDOF,
President of the University of Minnesota

Mark Yudof became the fourteenth president of the University of Minnesota in 1997 after serving as executive vice president and provost of the University of Texas at Austin. A constitutional lawyer and former dean of the University of Texas Law School, he has won awards from the American Society of Writers on Legal Subjects and the American Bar Association for his book *When Government Speaks: Politics, Law, and Government Expression in America*. Since taking the office of president, he has visited nearly thirty Minnesota cities to learn more about the state, and has announced major initiatives to improve the university's programs in molecular and cellular biology, digital science, agricultural research, design, and new communications media.

What time is it?" How many times a day do you ask that, or glance at your watch?

For physicists, relativity has rendered the concept of time illusory. But for most of us, it is simple. We live our days in minutes and hours; we mark our lives in decades. History bundles decades into centuries. A millennium is nothing more than mindless arithmetic: decades add up to centuries that add up to a thousand years.

But time is more than mathematics. It stirs aspiration and remembrance. The anticipation of moving into a new decade, a new century, *and* a new millennium elevates the sense of purpose and triggers the imagination. Even the most pessimistic among us seems hopeful.

> **MOVING INTO A NEW DECADE, A NEW CENTURY, *AND* A NEW MILLENNIUM TRIGGERS THE IMAGINATION**

Americans are a very impatient people. We seek clarity, and are surrounded by ambiguity, like travelers trying to see around the next curve. Who knows what our scientists will discover in the years ahead? What will be the winning economic sectors in 2025? What will occur in international markets? What kind of education will be the right kind of education to ensure meaningful careers for our young people?

There are no answers. But in a world of cultural fragmentation and an explosion of knowledge, universities and colleges, both public and private, have embraced values and set priorities. The focus will increasingly be on areas that spur economic growth and employment in the state, prepare students for twenty-first-century jobs, improve the health of our people, facilitate the creation of new technologies, preserve cultural and artistic traditions, and insure that our children—of all races, genders, and family incomes—live as well or better than their parents.

THE STIMULUS FOR GROWTH

I am a practical man, a university president and a lawyer, not a futurist. But if the University of Minnesota's past is a guide, the future will be full of discoveries—new knowledge—that will drive the future of the state.

With concepts learned from her teacher, this student of molecular cellular biology may one day unlock mysteries that lead to undreamed-of therapies. © Uniphoto, Inc.

The state has also benefited greatly in the past from an educated citizenry, and from research that spawned hundreds of Minnesota companies and provided thousands of jobs. I am confident that the new molecular cellular biology facility the university plans to build on the Twin Cities campus will provide the same stimulus for future growth and an improved quality of life. The facility will house world-class faculty whose passion it is to unlock mysteries that lead to undreamed-of therapies for sick plants, animals, or humans. Researchers tell me that today we are saving lives by implanting devices invented at the university. Tomorrow we could be helping patients with artificial organs or arteries or skin grown to an exact genetic match.

TOMORROW WE COULD BE HELPING PATIENTS WITH ARTIFICIAL ORGANS OR ARTERIES OR SKIN GROWN TO AN EXACT GENETIC MATCH

AN AID, NOT A SUBSTITUTE

One cannot talk about the future without talking about technology. All colleges and universities are committed to facing the challenges of the digital age. Technology will change the ways in which we teach and serve our students and the ways we conduct our research.

Technology, as it relates to higher education, also has some people wondering if colleges and universities as we know them—earthbound brick and mortar entities—will even be necessary in the digital age. They predict that the "virtual university"—only a link away—will make going to a university obsolete. Under this scenario, the traditional student, going off to college for a degree, will be a thing of the past. I reject that scenario. A virtual university? Can you imagine being sent to your room for four years? And paying for it! It is true that technology will give us new ways of reaching underserved populations, of providing life-long learning, of increasing the effectiveness of the classroom environment. But in my judgment, commuting and residential settings for students will continue to be the mainstay of higher education.

While digital technology will keep this upcoming scientist on the cutting edge of new developments, nothing can replace her actual experience in the lab. © Michael Krasowitz/FPG International

It is up to all of us in higher education to make sure that what we have to offer continues to be a valuable experience. To that end, we are listening better to what students, parents, business leaders, and lawmakers expect of us. Fortunately for me and my peers at other Minnesota institutions, Minnesotans value education. As humorist Garrison Keillor so wisely put it a few years ago, "If you don't value education, you're not from Minnesota—no matter where you were born!" Today, and I believe for the foreseeable future, a college education will be regarded as a necessity if a person is to have a reasonably comfortable life. Our responsibility is to continue to press for quality education that is available and affordable for all our citizens.

What time is it for our colleges and universities? It is time to celebrate the past but focus on tomorrow.

THE ELECTRIC ERA IN MINNESOTA

EDWIN L. RUSSELL,
Chairman, President, and Chief Executive Officer, Minnesota Power

Ed Russell became president of Minnesota Power in 1995, was named CEO in early 1996, and was elected board chairman in May of that year. He brought to the company a twenty-five-year record of diversified business experience that included responsibility in general management, strategy, manufacturing, sales and marketing, product development, human resources, and acquisitions. Mr. Russell is a graduate of Bowdoin College and Harvard Business School. He serves on the board of directors of Minnesota Power, Advantage Minnesota, Capital Re Corporation, Edison Electric Institute, Tennant Company, Duluth's Great Lakes Aquarium, and United Way. Ed, his wife, Lisa, and their two children live on the shore of Lake Superior.

Future historians may well look back at the twentieth century and dub it the era of electric power.

In 1900, electricity was bright with promise. Thomas Edison's invention of a workable incandescent lighting system was already two decades old, and the streets of cities such as Duluth, Minneapolis–St. Paul, and St. Cloud were lighted by arc lamps powered by electric generators. But only the wealthiest residents had electric lights in their homes. Electric ranges and washing machines and refrigerators were still more than a decade away for most Minnesotans.

In the farmland, mines, and forests of Minnesota, electricity was still an unattainable dream. A farmer in the Red River Valley plowed his fields and threshed his hard red spring wheat with teams of horses. Miners scooped the rich red hematite iron ore from the Mesabi Range with steam shovels. Lumberjacks cut the red and white pine of the boreal forests with two-man band saws.

In the 1920s and 1930s, visionaries such as M. L. Hibbard of Minnesota Power & Light Company, Henry Marison Byllesby of the Northern States Power Company, and the Wrights of Ottertail Power Company in Fergus Falls created the electric power infrastructure that helped transform Minnesota's society and economy.

> **MINNESOTA'S ABUNDANT, LOW-COST ELECTRIC POWER BROUGHT ABOUT A SECOND INDUSTRIAL REVOLUTION**

AHEAD OF THEIR TIME

They harnessed the state's streams with reliable, clean hydroelectric stations. They built steam electric generating plants, then tied together the electric grid with a network of high-voltage transmission lines. They proved to be good corporate citizens, contributing to worthy causes and funding the economic development efforts to bring jobs and prosperity to Minnesota.

The electric power industry made it its goal to be an excellent steward of the environment.

Visionaries of the 1920s and 1930s tied together Minnesota's electric grid with power plants similar to this one, transforming the state's society and economy. © Bob Firth/ Firth Photobank

Minnesota Power not only constructed the state's largest hydro facility to provide renewable and clean electric energy, but also pioneered the movement of low-sulfur western coal to Minnesota plants before we were all concerned about clean air. In addition, both Minnesota Power and Northern States Power contributed thousands of acres of riparian land throughout the state for use as recreation lands for all.

Abundant and low-cost electric power brought about the second industrial revolution in Minnesota. It contributed to a standard of living that today places Minnesota among the nation's leaders in quality of life. Such power makes the state a nationally ranked producer of wheat, corn, and soybeans and keeps the Seaway Port Authority of Duluth busy exporting products around the world. It electrified the mines of the Mesabi Range and made it possible for the United States to help win two world wars using Minnesota iron ore. Abundant, low-cost power helped accomplish the equally difficult task of converting the natural iron ore industry to a complex taconite processing industry that is still the basic feedstock of the nation's integrated steel industry. It also made possible the pumping stations that brought natural gas to Minnesota from the fields of Texas and Oklahoma in the postwar years.

A NEW ERA OF REVOLUTION

Minnesota has witnessed two industrial revolutions since it became a state nearly 150 years ago. The first was the age of steam, which proceeded inexorably toward powering the era of electricity. A third industrial revolution is at hand, and it will govern the way we live and work and play in the next century. This high-tech revolution, driven by the ever more complex and powerful microchip, is already well under way. And all those silicon chips on the motherboards that run the hardware are powered by electricity.

Minnesota companies such as Honeywell, Medtronic, General Mills, 3M, and Tennant—to name a few—are in

> **THE WEDDING OF HIGH-TECH EQUIPMENT AND ELECTRIC POWER WILL TRANSFORM THE ECONOMIC AND SOCIAL LANDSCAPES OF MINNESOTA**

the forefront of innovations that will continue to revolutionize our lives in the decades ahead. A number of smaller but progressive companies will move forward in the next century. We will see quantum leaps in productivity on our farms, mills, and factories with reliable, low-cost electricity to power the computers controlling industrial processes and machines.

Coincident with this are substantive changes within the electric industry itself. Moving from the highly regulated environment in which we have historically operated into a deregulated environment brings real uncertainty and shifting landscapes.

The wedding of high-tech equipment and electric power will continue to transform the economic and social landscapes of Minnesota in the twenty-first century. Electricity is the underpinning of this transformation—no one goes anywhere without it. It has enriched all facets of our lives in the twentieth century, and it will continue to do so in ways we cannot yet envision—ways not unlike its revolutionary impacts earlier in this century.

The electrical lines being installed will provide reliable, low-cost electricity to power the computers controlling industrial processes, eventually sparking a quantum leap in productivity. © Greg Ryan-Sally Beyer

MANUFACTURING

ORDINARY MIRACLES

L. D. DeSimone,
Chairman and Chief Executive Officer, 3M

In his forty-one years at 3M, L. D. DeSimone has managed most of the company's major businesses as well as some of its overseas operations. After serving as executive vice president for each of 3M's business sectors, he became chairman of the board and CEO in 1991. He is the past chairman of the World Business Council for Sustainable Development and a current director of Cargill, Inc.; Dayton Hudson Corporation; General Mills, Inc.; Vulcan Materials Company; and the 3M Foundation. Mr. DeSimone is a trustee of the University of Minnesota, the Conference Board, and a member of the National Board of Directors for Junior Achievement Inc. He participates in numerous other business, education, and philanthropic organizations.

The twentieth century has many measures. Some of the gains can be registered on only the grandest scale: we began the century with the earliest automobiles and we're ending it with space stations and interstellar explorers. In medicine, we've moved from the rudiments of infection control to the first, partial maps of the human genome.

Other transitions are perhaps less epic but equally remarkable, and they touch our lives a thousand times a day. We can communicate faster with people farther away; our homes are more comfortable and more energy efficient; sophisticated farming techniques and equipment have made the food supply in much of the world safer and more varied. As much as I'm impressed with space travel, I think the most striking measure of the century is that extraordinary technology has become such a large part of what appear to be common, everyday products.

In my career, I've been privileged to meet many of the men and women who are responsible for these ordinary miracles. I've talked with the man who created the first copy machine, the woman who codeveloped the first fabric protectors. I know a scientist who recently developed a drug that stimulates the body's immune system. And I know Phil Palmquist, the scientist who figured out how to make stop signs appear red at night, guaranteeing that they stand out as well then as they do in daylight. Think of that: every day, this type of creativity and scientific discipline are woven into the lives, commerce, and safety of billions of people around the globe.

> **EVERY DAY, CREATIVITY AND SCIENTIFIC DISCIPLINE ARE WOVEN INTO THE LIVES OF BILLIONS**

MULTIPLE SOLUTIONS

All of the men and women I've mentioned worked at 3M in Minnesota. I'm confident

Paper machines utilizing the latest technology touch us in small ways, but are remarkable in their capacity to make life more efficient. © Telegraph Colour Library

that people here—and their colleagues around the world—will continue to create ordinary miracles for the next century. And just as important, they will develop new ways to commercialize those miracles and make them available to even more people. The importance of commercializing technology has never been greater. As science and technology advance, we find that we can create multiple solutions for many problems. During most of the past century, for example, the only practical option for powering a car was the gasoline-powered internal combustion engine. In the next decade or so, that will change: consumers will be able to pick among gas engines, electric motors, fuel cells, hybrids—choices that are also increasingly responsive to sustainable development. Given the pace of change in this area, we'll surely have other options, too.

INCREASED ACCESS

Thanks to changes in politics, economics, and communications technology, customers around the world will also have more access to these multiple solutions. We don't know where the best power sources of the future will come from—they may be made in Minnesota or Brazil or India—this will matter less and less as the flow of products across borders becomes more common. This of course means that competition will be constant and fierce.

Because of the greater access to products from around the world—and greater information about the price, performance, and characteristics of those products—customers will be able to make intelligent choices among options. Often, we think of successful "information age" companies as those that provide the information; the real winners will be companies that respond to changes in customer demand based on that swift flow and use of information.

As science and technology advance, this aircraft refurbisher will have at his disposal options far beyond the abrasives, sealants, and respirators he uses today.
© Steve Niedorf/3M

> **THE REAL WINNERS WILL BE COMPANIES THAT RESPOND TO CHANGES IN CUSTOMER DEMAND BASED ON THE SWIFT FLOW AND USE OF INFORMATION**

Combine the likelihood of multiple solutions with a free flow of those solutions and customer information and you get a rough sketch of how competitive battles will be waged in the coming century. Successful manufacturers (as well as successful companies in other segments of the economy) will be responsive to technological advances—and changing customer needs. They will be close to the cutting edge of science—and they will be close enough to their customers to understand and anticipate their requirements. The next century will have its advances, and some of them will be awe-inspiring. Many of the most important changes will be ones that affect us where we live—the advances that will touch us in small ways, every day. And the companies that will provide those ordinary miracles will be the ones that understand not only what nature and human ingenuity can provide, but also what human nature genuinely wants.

TOOLS FOR PROSPERITY

CORNELL L. MOORE,
Partner, Dorsey & Whitney LLP

Cornell L. Moore has been a partner in the Minneapolis law office of Dorsey & Whitney since 1995, when he came to the firm after eight years at Miller & Schroeder Financial, Inc. His extensive experience in law and finance also includes nine years managing family-owned real estate investments and equipment leasing and financial services companies. Mr. Moore is a board member of numerous organizations such as the Greater Minneapolis Metropolitan Housing Corporation and the Greater Minneapolis Convention and Visitors Association, among others. Recognizable throughout the state, he serves as the commodore of the Minneapolis Aquatennial Summer Festival.

Minnesota is attractive for diverse reasons, among them livability, educational opportunity, business enterprise, a caring and concerned population, and the refreshing change of pace the state offers when compared to other similar areas.

The practice of law and the transaction of business in our marketplace have been enhanced by the type and quality of the people here, a group not necessarily born in or identified

MINNESOTA HAS A GOOD REPUTATION FOR TACKLING PROBLEMS HEAD-ON IN ALL ASPECTS OF SOCIAL JUSTICE

with this part of the country. The common perception of observers and commentators in this region of the Midwest assumes a homogenous population; homogeneity, however, is not as easy to paint as it was thirty or more years ago.

The mix of the population has resulted in a diversified workforce and, therefore, a diversified potential client base. A diversified potential client base, in turn, demands sensitivity to its various cultures, mores, and feelings. It is quite amazing to me that some practitioners of law blanch upon realizing that people they perceive to be different still demand the normal attention and courtesies. This realization is the beguiling cause for the multiplicity of programs to teach and reinforce the notion of gender and racial equity.

Minnesota has a good reputation for tackling problems head-on in all aspects of social justice, including matters that

During a strategy-planning session, a legal team considers its client's culture and mores.
© Adam Smith/FPG International

allow the practice of law and the diversity and integration of the members of the bar and judiciary as indicators for inclusiveness now and in the future.

A COHESIVE COMMUNITY

Part of this area's appeal is its easy availability of modern tools of communication—telecommunications, videoconferencing, wireless communications, optical transmission facilities—that create an opportunity for all of us to come together on a rapid and timely basis in the advancement of the profession. Rapid communication capabilities cause some trepidation, however, when it comes to taking the quality time necessary to ponder, contemplate, pontificate, and respond with educated wisdom to inquiries and comments from colleagues and the public.

The greatest challenge in the very near future will be the integration of the diverse population with the usage of high-speed communication in a way that ties the total community together, a cohesiveness that allows a better place to live, work, and prosper together. That would be an attraction of real substance and meaning.

The level of sophistication inherent in the state's metropolitan areas results in numerous opportunities for the practice of law and the creation of business. The only limit to growth might be a lack of bright, ambitious, energetic associates. Minnesota has always been a place of innovation and inventiveness; a thriving practice, therefore, is easily attained and maintained.

UTILIZE THE DIVERSITY

The shortage of trainable associates in the fields required to advance the practice of law and business can best be remedied by better utilization of the diverse population that exists in the marketplace. Adequate educational facilities are necessary for proper training; that these facilities are available should be clearly communicated to the population. The area provides a

number of degree-granting institutions committed to excellence in education that strive to balance general and specialized education, both of which enhance success and facilitate lifelong learning.

In the long run, the fair and equitable use of technology by the total diverse population will cause greater efficiency and intelligence in legal practice, as well as better understanding throughout the community of the real meaning of law and order.

The legal community has changed its focus and outreach over the last thirty-plus years. While the numbers of lawyers have increased, the practitioners seem to be better informed and more motivated to assist in community events and offer support through pro bono activities and outreach.

In summary, the profession is a kinder, gentler one, aided by technology and motivated by a diverse, changing clientele and new lawyers.

INTEGRATING THE DIVERSE POPULATION WITH THE USE OF HIGH-SPEED COMMUNICATION COULD TIE THE TOTAL COMMUNITY TOGETHER

Advertising agency partners confer on the way to their first presentation. The level of sophistication in the state's metro areas results in numerous opportunities to create thriving businesses. © Image Club Graphics

A DECADE OF PROSPERITY

JAY NOVAK,
Commissioner, Department of Trade and Economic Development

Jay Novak was appointed commissioner by Governor Arne Carlson in July 1995. The 240-employee department operates the Minnesota Trade Office, which facilitates exportation of Minnesota products; the Minnesota Office of Tourism, which encourages travel to and within Minnesota; and a Business and Community Development division, which includes programs that finance business expansions, fund community development projects, provide custom job-training opportunities, provide advice to managers of small businesses, and promote Minnesota as a state in which to start or expand a business.

As you page through this book, you will reach an inescapable conclusion: Minnesota has long been a state of enterprise. It is a place in which the development of technologically advanced products has become commonplace, where invention and innovation have come almost to be taken for granted.

In the 1990s, Minnesota became a state where business prospered. From 1991 through 1997, building upon previous successes and preparing to seize new opportunities, Minnesota businesses created 358,000 new jobs. Although Minnesota's population is less than 2 percent of the U.S. population, it accounted during that period for nearly 3 percent of all new jobs in the nation.

> **IN EVERY MAJOR INDUSTRIAL SECTOR AND IN EVERY COUNTY, THERE WERE MORE JOBS CREATED THAN LOST**

But were they good jobs? A great many were. Minnesota's manufacturing employment expanded by 8.3 percent. The state's software industry grew to more than 650 firms, and its medical technology industry burgeoned. Employment in professional services—especially finance, insurance, and health care—grew faster than in nonprofessional services. Personal income in Minnesota grew by 5.5 percent from 1991 to 1997, almost twice the inflation rate—indicating that new jobs were paying above-average wages.

Moreover, the expansion was widespread. In every major industrial sector and in every one of Minnesota's eighty-seven counties, there were more jobs created than lost. Study after study gave Minnesota high marks for its attractiveness to business, and Moody's became the first of three investment rating services to elevate Minnesota's general obligation bond rating to AAA, citing careful management of the state's finances and the strength of the state's economy.

What accounts for its strength?

ACCESSIBLE ASSETS

Access to expansion capital is a key factor. Minnesota has more than 500 commercial banks and competitive banking in every one of its 830

Health care practitioners treating a critical care patient have access to some of the country's most sophisticated technology. Employment in this sector burgeoned between 1991 and 1998.

communities. Minnesota's banks have always been aggressive lenders, but they became increasingly aggressive in the past decade. They recently reported more collective assets (loans and other investments) than banks in all but eleven other states.

Equity capital is also plentiful. In one forty-eight-month period in the mid-1990s, the number of publicly traded Minnesota companies tripled as Minnesota investment banks assisted 106 Minnesota companies with initial public stock offerings. Meanwhile, an active cluster of venture capital companies helped Minnesota complete its tenth consecutive year among the top ten states both in venture capital pools and disbursements.

Access to markets helped companies grow. Minnesota's central location provides easy access to markets throughout North America, and its 13,000 miles of arterial roads make its highway system the fifth largest in the nation. With 4,765 miles of rail line, Minnesota is one of the nation's railroad hubs. Perhaps most important, access to overseas markets expanded in the 1990s. Since 1995, international flights into Minneapolis–St. Paul International Airport have quadrupled to 255 per week, and the export of Minnesota products has grown much faster than exports from the rest of the United States.

A BOOST FROM THE STATE

Years of having been a leader in education and training paid off for Minnesota in the 1990s. In the 1970s, the state expanded its system of community colleges to provide at least two years of college education within a half-hour's drive of 90 percent of the state's residents—and in doing so, helped create a workforce ready to meet present-day career challenges. Our

Medical device manufacturing in the state employs more than 20,000 people at 200-plus firms, making Minnesota second in the nation in this endeavor. Photos both pages, courtesy Minnesota Department of Trade and Economic Development

thirty technical colleges provide 50,000 Minnesotans per year with training for more than 200 skilled occupations.

Business growth in Minnesota was boosted by a surprising source in the late 1990s: state government. In 1995, our legislature enacted reforms, long sought by Governor Arne Carlson, reducing workers' compensation premiums for manufacturers by 35 percent. The governor won permanent reductions in business property taxes. A tax on capital equipment was repealed. Unemployment compensation premiums were cut. Funds for custom training—training specific to the immediate needs of employers—were tripled.

Meanwhile, state agencies instituted administrative reforms designed to improve Minnesota's economic vitality. Our Pollution Control Agency implemented efforts to encourage businesses to conduct environmental self-audits and reduce environmental management costs without compromising environmental protection. The Department of Trade and Economic Development created the nation's premier site-selection tool in the form of a detailed database of the attributes of each Minnesota city. Our new Office of Technology initiated work on a one-stop licensing program. As Minnesota was about to enter the final year of its most prosperous decade, it had become more business-friendly than anyone active in business could remember—preparing the way for growth in the decade to come.

> **THE STATE HAS BECOME MORE BUSINESS-FRIENDLY THAN MANY CAN REMEMBER, PREPARING THE WAY FOR GROWTH IN THE DECADE TO COME**

TRANSPORTATION IN MINNESOTA

J. Robert Stassen,
Former Vice Chairman, Metropolitan Airports Commission (MAC)

J. Robert Stassen, president of Stassen & Stern International, Inc., retired from the Metropolitan Airports Commission at year-end 1997 after five years as commissioner and eleven years as deputy executive director. Previously, he was vice president of Dain Bosworth, Minneapolis; president of the West St. Paul State Bank; president of North Central Life Insurance Company, St. Paul; and a Minnesota state senator. He holds a B.A. degree from the University of Minnesota and studied law at the William Mitchell College of Law, management at the University of St. Thomas, and finance at the Minnesota School of Banking. He received International Executive Certification from the Minnesota World Trade Center.

Throughout world history, commerce has developed wherever trade routes crossed. With 6,300 square miles of water, nearly 20,000 lakes, and thousands of miles of inland waterways, Minnesota was no exception. In 1823, the steamboat *Virginia* docked at Fort Snelling, at the confluence of the Mississippi and Minnesota Rivers, heralding the territory's connection to the outside world. Across the river, Mendota (meaning "meeting of the waters" in the Sioux language) had been a Native American crossroads of commerce for centuries.

Commerce near Fort Snelling led to the establishment of Pig's Eye (later renamed St. Paul). Oxcarts rumbled and screeched to the Jackson Street landing, where oxcart met riverboat. St. Paul became a thriving center for transshipment for the rapidly developing Northwest.

TURNING POINTS IN HISTORY

Four major developments mark the history of transportation in Minnesota: the advent of the railroad, the opening of the St. Lawrence Seaway, the building of the U.S. Interstate Highway System, and the development of the Minneapolis–St. Paul International Airport into a major hub and international gateway.

Railroads reached Minnesota in the early 1860s, a decade of false starts, controversial land grants to railroad owners, defaults on bond payments, and a major bankruptcy of an empire. A consolidation of the railroad holdings of "Empire Builder" James J. Hill resulted in three great railroads: the Great Northern, the Northern Pacific, and the Chicago, Burlington and Quincy (CB&Q). These three dominated rail traffic between Chicago and the Pacific coast, and were a vital part of the growing transportation system developing in Minnesota.

The second major development in the state's transportation network, the opening of the St. Lawrence Seaway, came in 1959 after

> **FROM DULUTH TO THE ATLANTIC, COMMERCE WAS AT LAST OPENED — FROM THE LAKEHEAD TO THE WORLD**

Northwest planes are among the many operating out of Minneapolis–St. Paul International Airport, a key U.S. hub airport. © Richard H. Smith/FPG International

years of planning and negotiating between the U.S. and Canadian governments. From Duluth to the Atlantic Ocean, a distance of 2,342 miles, commerce was at last opened—from the lakehead to the world.

The third development began in the same decade. Construction of the U.S. Interstate Highway System was the largest, most costly and long-lasting construction project in the modern world; many links of the system have just been completed in the past decade. The interstate system ties together the state highway and state-aid road systems and reduces congestion on these less sophisticated byways. The interstate system and state trunk highways constitute 9 percent of the roadways, but handle 61 percent of the vehicle miles traveled. During rush hour in the seven-county metropolitan area, the interstates are congested and in danger of gridlock. In an attempt to provide an alternative, light rail is seriously being considered between the downtowns of Minneapolis and St. Paul and from each city to the airport and the Mall of America. Difficult and costly decisions must be made in the immediate future.

The growth of the Minneapolis–St. Paul International Airport (MSP) as a key hub airport in the United States was the fourth major development. One of the world's pioneer airports, MSP was an early departure point for air routes serving America's West Coast and the Orient. Following the Lindberghs' 1931 "North to the Orient" exploration flight, Northwest Airlines initiated the Great Circle Route in 1947 from MSP via Anchorage, over the Arctic to Japan, China, Korea, and the Philippines. This route brought cities along the northern boundaries of the United States 2,000 miles closer to Asia than the traditional routes through Hawaii. In 1976, hundreds of miles were shaved off travel to Europe as well by flying across the top of the world from MSP to London and northern Europe.

Today, MSP is the twelfth busiest airport in the United States and the seventeenth busiest in the world, handling more than 30 million ticketed passengers annually. Ironically, the airport is situated adjacent to Fort Snelling at the junction of the Minnesota and Mississippi Rivers, "where the waters meet." This centuries-old crossroads of commerce now is the location of worldwide air service.

A FRAMEWORK FOR THE FUTURE

The Minnesota Department of Transportation has developed the "Minnesota Statewide Transportation Plan—A Work in Progress." The plan is a working document to study goals and future transportation directions. Minnesota has come a long way since canoes and oxcarts were a way of life. Minnesotans tend to look ahead and are very sensitive to balancing progress with fiscal and environmental prudence. The plan provides a framework for making strategic decisions for the future. But it remains a dynamic plan—a working document.

MINNESOTANS TEND TO LOOK AHEAD AND ARE VERY SENSITIVE TO BALANCING PROGRESS WITH FISCAL AND ENVIRONMENTAL PRUDENCE

A tugboat pushes these barges down the Mississippi River, an important leg of Minnesota's transportation network, as is the St. Lawrence Seaway, opened in 1959. © Greg Ryan-Sally Beyer

© Bob Firth/Firth Photobank

BIBLIOGRAPHY

Cerney, Carol, interviewed by the author. Southeastern Minnesota Initiative Fund, 2 May 1997.

Cothran, Tom, and Margaret Kaeter. *Twin Cities Metro Report: 1996–97*. Encino, Calif.: Cherbo Publishing Group, 1996.

Davies, Phil. *Scenic Driving Minnesota*. Minnesota: Falcon Press, 1997.

Encyclopedia Americana, s.v. "Minnesota," 1997.

Fastenal Company. *1996 Annual Report*.

Federal Cartridge Company. *Federal—75th Anniversary*. 1996.

Fodor's Travel Publications. *Mobil 1998 Travel Guide—Minnesota*. New York: Fodor's Travel Publications, 1998.

Fradin, Dennis B., and Judith B. Fradin. *From Sea to Shining Sea: Minnesota*. Chicago: Childrens Press, 1994.

Gaw, Jonathan. "Municipal Utilities Plug into Future." *Star Tribune*, 7 September 1997.

———. "Out of Service." *Star Tribune*, 9 March 1997.

Hintz, Martin. "Touring the Twins." Home and Away, September–October, 1997, 15–23A.

Hadley Companies. *The Hadley Companies*. 1997.

Hoffman, Nancy, east-central regional development planner, interview by the author, 18 November 1997.

Hormel. *100—The Hormel Legacy*. 1991.

Kane, Joseph Nathan. *Famous First Facts*. New York: H. W. Wilson Company, 1981.

Karrmann, Jan, interview by the author. Hubbard Broadcasting, 1 July 1997.

Kauphusman, Tricia. "Family-owned Red Wing Company Puts World on Skates." *Rochester Post Bulletin*, 26 March 1997.

Larson, Lowell, executive director west-central initiative, interview by the author, 12 November 1997.

Madison, Cathy. "Minnesota Firsts." *Minnesota Monthly*, March 1995, 44–72.

Maas, Carol, interview by the author. Voyageurs National Park, 11 February 1998.

Mayo Foundation. *Mayo Clinic*, 1994.

Metropolitan Airports Commission. *Minneapolis/St. Paul International Airport*. 1997.

Minnesota Department of Economic Security. *Minnesota Job Outlook*. 1998.

———. *Regional Spotlights*. 1997.

Minnesota Department of Trade and Economic Development. *Compare Minnesota—1996/1997*. 1997.

———. *Minnesota Living*. 1990.

———. *Minnesota Success Stories*. 1997.

———. *Positively Minnesota*. 1997.

Morgan Quitno Press. *Most Livable State Report*. Lawrence, Kan.: Morgan Quitno Press, 1998.

Moses, George. *Minnesota in Focus*. Minneapolis, Minn.: University of Minnesota Press, 1974.

Multifoods. *Multifoods Today*. June/July, 1992.

O'Leary Morgan, Kathleen, Scott Morgan, and Mark A. Uhlig, eds. *State Rankings 1998: A Statistical View of the Fifty United States*. Lawrence, Kan.: Morgan Quitno Press, 1998.

Olsenius, Richard. *Minnesota Travel Companion*. Minnesota: Bluestem Productions, 1982.

Pickney, Roger. "Duluth." *Star Tribune*, 30 November 1997.

Polaris Industries. *Polaris Pioneers*. 1989.

Sanders, Dennis. *The First of Everything*. New York: Delacorte Press, 1981.

Sears Merchandise Group. *SEARS—Yesterday and Today*, 1994.

Smead. *A History of Continued Growth*, 1996.

Stein, R. Conrad, *America the Beautiful: Minnesota*. Chicago: Childrens Press, 1991.

SPONSORS

Minnesota World Trade Center Corporation
400 Minnesota World Trade Center
30 East Seventh Street
St. Paul, MN 55101-4902
Telephone: (651) 297-1580
Fax: (651) 297-4812

Minnesota Department of Trade and
  Economic Development
500 Metro Square
121 Seventh Place East
St. Paul, MN 55101-2146
Telephone: (800) 657-3858 or (651) 297-1291
Fax: (651) 296-4772
Web site: www.dted.state.mn.us

PATRONS

Buffalo Veneer & Plywood Co.
Contact: Kevin Erickson
7301 Walker Street
St. Louis Park, MN 55426
Telephone: (612) 938-2729
Fax: (612) 938-7269

Dart Transit Company
Contact: Kris Kohls
800 Lone Oak Road
Eagan, MN 55121
Telephone: (612) 688-2000
Fax: (612) 688-2015
Web site: www.dartadvantage.com

Herc-U-Lift, Inc.
Contact: Les Nielsen
5655 Highway 12 West
Maple Plain, MN 55359
Telephone: (612) 479-2501
Fax: (612) 479-2296
Web site: www.HUL@SKYPOINT.com

Park Manufacturing Co., Inc.
Contact: Dennis Kleven
18529 Highway 65 Northeast
Cedar, MN 55011
Telephone: (612) 434-3320
Fax: (612) 434-9077
Web site: www.parkmfg.com

Satellite Industries, Inc.
Contact: Todd Hilde, President
2530 Xenium Lane North
Minneapolis, MN 55001
Telephone: (612) 553-1900
Fax: (612) 559-6525
Web site: www. satelliteindustries.com

Wright-Hennepin Co-op Electric Association
Contact: Sonja Bogart
P.O. Box 330, 6800 Electric Drive
Rockford, MN 55373
Telephone: (612) 477-3000
Fax: (612) 477-3054
Web site: www. whe.org

INDEX OF CORPORATE AND ORGANIZATIONAL PROFILES

THE FOLLOWING COMPANIES AND ORGANIZATIONS HAVE MADE A VALUABLE COMMITMENT TO THE QUALITY OF THIS PUBLICATION. CHERBO PUBLISHING GROUP, THE MINNESOTA WORLD TRADE CENTER CORPORATION, AND THE TRADE OFFICE OF THE MINNESOTA DEPARTMENT OF TRADE AND ECONOMIC DEVELOPMENT GRATEFULLY ACKNOWLEDGE THEIR PARTICIPATION IN *MINNESOTA: LAND OF LAKES AND INNOVATION*.

INDEX

© Bob Firth/Firth Photobank